SOCIAL CONSTRUCTION
of Race, Ethnicity and Diversity

Northeast Wisconsin Technical College
Race Ethnic Diversity Course

Custom Publishing

New York   Boston   San Francisco
London   Toronto   Sydney   Tokyo   Singapore   Madrid
Mexico City   Munich   Paris   Cape Town   Hong Kong   Montreal

**Pearson
Custom Publishing**
is a division of

www.pearsonhighered.com

ISBN 10: 0-558-11780-5
ISBN 13: 978-0-558-11780-1

Copyright Acknowledgments

Contents

THE SOCIAL CONSTRUCTION OF DIFFERENCE

1

RACIAL FORMATIONS

■ ■ ■

Michael Omi and Howard Winant

In 1982–83, Susie Guillory Phipps unsuccessfully sued the Louisiana Bureau of Vital Records to change her racial classification from black to white. The descendant of an eighteenth-century white planter and a black slave, Phipps was designated "black" in her birth certificate in accordance with a 1970 state law which declared anyone with at least one-thirty-second "Negro blood" to be black. The legal battle raised intriguing questions about the concept of race, its meaning in contemporary society, and its use (and abuse) in public policy. Assistant Attorney General Ron Davis defended the law by pointing out that some type of racial classification was necessary to comply with federal record-keeping requirements and to facilitate programs for the prevention of genetic diseases. Phipps's attorney, Brian Begue, argued that the assignment of racial categories on birth certificates was unconstitutional and that the one-thirty-second designation was inaccurate. He called on a retired Tulane University professor who cited research indicating that most whites have one-twentieth "Negro" ancestry. In the end, Phipps lost. The court upheld a state law which quantified racial identity, and in so doing affirmed the legality of assigning individuals to specific racial groupings.[1]

The Phipps case illustrates the continuing dilemma of defining race and establishing its meaning in institutional life. Today, to assert that variations in human physiognomy are racially based is to enter a constant and intense debate. *Scientific* interpretations of race have not been alone in sparking heated controversy; *religious* perspectives have done so as well.[2] Most centrally, of course, race has been a matter of *political* contention. This has been particularly true in the United States, where the concept of race has varied enormously over time without ever leaving the center stage of US history.

WHAT IS RACE?

Race consciousness, and its articulation in theories of race, is largely a modern phenomenon. When European explorers in the New World "discovered" people who looked different than themselves, these "natives" challenged then existing conceptions of the origins of the human species, and raised disturbing questions as to whether *all* could be considered in the same "family of man."[3] Religious debates flared over the attempt to reconcile the Bible with the existence of "racially distinct" people. Arguments took place over creation itself, as theories of polygenesis questioned whether God had made only one species of humanity ("monogenesis"). Europeans wondered if the natives of the New World were indeed human beings with redeemable souls. At stake were not only the prospects for conversion, but the types of treatment to be accorded them. The expropriation of property, the denial of political rights, the introduction of slavery and other forms of coercive labor, as well as outright extermination, all presupposed a worldview which distinguished Europeans—children of God, human beings, etc.—from "others." Such a worldview was needed to explain why some should be "free" and others enslaved, why some had rights to land and property while others did not. Race, and the interpretation of racial differences, was a central factor in that worldview.

In the colonial epoch science was no less a field of controversy than religion in attempts to comprehend the concept of race and its meaning. Spurred on by the classificatory scheme of living organisms devised by Linnaeus in *Systema Naturae*, many scholars in the eighteenth and nineteenth centuries dedicated themselves to the identification and ranking of variations in humankind. Race was thought of as a *biological* concept, yet its precise definition was the subject of debates which, as we have noted, continue to rage today. Despite efforts ranging from Dr. Samuel Morton's studies of cranial capacity[4] to contemporary attempts to base racial classification on shared gene pools,[5] the concept of race has defied biological definition. . . .

Attempts to discern the *scientific meaning* of race continue to the present day. Although most physical anthropologists and biologists have abandoned the quest for a scientific basis to determine racial categories, controversies have recently flared in the area of genetics and educational psychology. For instance, an essay by Arthur Jensen which argued that hereditary factors shape intelligence not only revived the "nature or nurture" controversy, but raised highly volatile questions about racial equality itself.[6] Clearly the attempt to establish a *biological* basis of race has not been swept into the dustbin of history, but is being resurrected in various scientific arenas. All such attempts seek to remove the concept of race from fundamental social, political, or economic determination. They suggest instead that the truth of race lies in the terrain of innate characteristics, of which skin color and other physical attributes provide only the most obvious, and in some respects most superficial, indicators.

RACE AS A SOCIAL CONCEPT

The social sciences have come to reject biologistic notions of race in favor of an approach which regards race as a *social* concept. Beginning in the eighteenth century, this trend has been slow and uneven, but its direction clear. In the nineteenth century Max Weber discounted biological explanations for racial conflict and instead highlighted the social and political factors which engendered such conflict.[7] The work of pioneering cultural anthropologist Franz Boas was crucial in refuting the scientific racism of the early twentieth century by rejecting the connection between race and culture, and the assumption of a continuum of "higher" and "lower" cultural groups. Within the contemporary social science literature, race is assumed to be a variable which is shaped by broader societal forces.

Race is indeed a pre-eminently *sociohistorical* concept. Racial categories and the meaning of race are given concrete expression by the specific social relations and historical context in which they are embedded. Racial meanings have varied tremendously over time and between different societies.

In the United States, the black/white color line has historically been rigidly defined and enforced. White is seen as a "pure" category. Any racial intermixture makes one "nonwhite." In the movie *Raintree County*, Elizabeth Taylor describes the worst of fates to befall whites as "havin' a little Negra blood in ya'—just one little teeny drop and a person's all Negra."[8] This thinking flows from what Marvin Harris has characterized as the principle of *hypo-descent:*

> By what ingenious computation is the genetic tracery of a million years of evolution unraveled and each man [sic] assigned his proper social box? In the United States, the mechanism employed is the rule of hypo-descent. This descent rule requires Americans to believe that anyone who

is known to have had a Negro ancestor is a Negro. We admit nothing in between. . . . "Hypo-descent" means affiliation with the subordinate rather than the superordinate group in order to avoid the ambiguity of intermediate identity. . . . The rule of hypo-descent is, therefore, an invention, which we in the United States have made in order to keep biological facts from intruding into our collective racist fantasies.[9]

The Susie Guillory Phipps case merely represents the contemporary expression of this racial logic.

By contrast, a striking feature of race relations in the lowland areas of Latin America since the abolition of slavery has been the relative absence of sharply defined racial groupings. No such rigid descent rule characterizes racial identity in many Latin American societies. Brazil, for example, has historically had less rigid conceptions of race, and thus a variety of "intermediate" racial categories exist. Indeed, as Harris notes, "One of the most striking consequences of the Brazilian system of racial identification is that parents and children and even brothers and sisters are frequently accepted as representatives of quite opposite racial types."[10] Such a possibility is incomprehensible within the logic of racial categories in the US.

To suggest another example: the notion of "passing" takes on new meaning if we compare various American cultures' means of assigning racial identity. In the United States, individuals who are actually "black" by the logic of hypo-descent have attempted to skirt the discriminatory barriers imposed by law and custom by attempting to "pass" for white.[11] Ironically, these same individuals would not be able to pass for "black" in many Latin American societies.

Consideration of the term "black" illustrates the diversity of racial meanings which can be found among different societies and historically within a given society. In contemporary British politics the term "black" is used to refer to all non-whites. Interestingly this designation has not arisen through the racist discourse of groups such as the National Front. Rather, in political and cultural movements, Asian as well as Afro-Caribbean youth are adopting the term as an expression of self-identity.[12] The wide-ranging meanings of "black" illustrate the manner in which racial categories are shaped politically.[13]

The meaning of race is defined and contested throughout society, in both collective action and personal practice. In the process, racial categories themselves are formed, transformed, destroyed and re-formed. We use the term *racial formation* to refer to the process by which social, economic and political forces determine the content and importance of racial categories, and by which they are in turn shaped by racial meanings. Crucial to this formulation is the treatment of race as a *central axis* of social relations which cannot be subsumed under or reduced to some broader category or conception.

RACIAL IDEOLOGY AND RACIAL IDENTITY

The seemingly obvious, "natural" and "common sense" qualities which the existing racial order exhibits themselves testify to the effectiveness of the racial formation process in constructing racial meanings and racial identities.

One of the first things we notice about people when we meet them (along with their sex) is their race. We utilize race to provide clues about *who* a person is. This fact is made painfully obvious when we encounter someone whom we cannot conveniently racially categorize—someone who is, for example, racially "mixed" or of an ethnic/racial group with which we are not familiar. Such an encounter becomes a source of discomfort and momentarily a crisis of racial meaning. Without a racial identity, one is in danger of having no identity.

Our compass for navigating race relations depends on preconceived notions of what each specific racial group looks like. Comments such as, "Funny, you don't look black," betray an underlying image of what black should be. We also become disoriented when people do not act "black," "Latino," or indeed "white." The content of such stereotypes reveals a series of unsubstantiated beliefs about who these groups are and what "they" are like.[14]

In US society, then, a kind of "racial etiquette" exists, a set of interpretative codes and racial meanings which operate in the interactions of daily life. Rules shaped by our perception of race in a comprehensively racial society determine the "presentation of self,"[15] distinctions of status, and appropriate modes of conduct. "Etiquette" is not mere universal adherence to the dominant group's rules, but a more dynamic combination of these rules with the values and beliefs of subordinated groupings. This racial "subjection" is quintessentially ideological. Everybody learns some combination, some version, of the rules of racial classification, and of their own racial identity, often without obvious teaching or conscious inculcation. Race becomes "common sense"—a way of comprehending, explaining and acting in the world.

Racial beliefs operate as an "amateur biology," a way of explaining the variations in "human nature."[16] Differences in skin color and other obvious physical characteristics supposedly provide visible clues to differences lurking underneath. Temperament, sexuality, intelligence, athletic ability, aesthetic preferences and so on are presumed to be fixed and discernible from the palpable mark of race. Such diverse questions as our confidence and trust in others (for example, clerks or sales-people, media figures, neighbors), our sexual preferences and romantic images, our tastes in music, films, dance, or sports, and our very ways of talking, walking, eating and dreaming are ineluctably shaped by notions of race. Skin color "differences" are thought to explain perceived differences in intellectual, physical and artistic temperaments, and to justify distinct treatment of racially identified individuals and groups.

The continuing persistence of racial ideology suggests that these racial myths and stereotypes cannot be exposed as such in the popular imagination. They are, we think, too essential, too integral, to the maintenance of the US social order. Of course, particular meanings, stereotypes and myths can change, but the presence of a *system* of racial meanings and stereotypes, of racial ideology, seems to be a permanent feature of US culture.

Film and television, for example, have been notorious in disseminating images of racial minorities which establish for audiences what people from these groups look like, how they behave, and "who they are."[17] The power of the media lies not only in their ability to reflect the dominant racial ideology, but in their capacity to shape that ideology in the first place. D. W. Griffith's epic *Birth of a Nation*, a sympathetic treatment of the rise of the Ku Klux Klan during Reconstruction, helped to generate, consolidate and "nationalize" images of blacks which had been more disparate (more regionally specific, for example) prior to the film's appearance.[18] In US television, the necessity to define characters in the briefest and most condensed manner has led to the perpetuation of racial caricatures, as racial stereotypes serve as shorthand for scriptwriters, directors and actors, in commercials, etc. Television's tendency to address the "lowest common denominator" in order to render programs "familiar" to an enormous and diverse audience leads it regularly to assign and reassign racial characteristics to particular groups, both minority and majority.

These and innumerable other examples show that we tend to view race as something fixed and immutable—something rooted in "nature." Thus we mask the historical construction of racial categories, the shifting meaning of race, and the crucial role of politics and ideology in shaping race relations. Races do not emerge full-blown. They are the results of diverse historical practices and are continually subject to challenge over their definition and meaning.

RACIALIZATION: THE HISTORICAL DEVELOPMENT OF RACE

In the United States, the racial category of "black" evolved with the consolidation of racial slavery. By the end of the seventeenth century, Africans whose specific identity was Ibo, Yoruba, Fulani, etc. were rendered "black" by an ideology of exploitation based on racial logic—the establishment and maintenance of a "color line." This of course did not occur overnight. A period of indentured servitude which was not rooted in racial logic preceded the consolidation of racial slavery. With slavery, however, a racially based understanding of society was set in motion which resulted in the shaping of a specific *racial* identity not only for the slaves but for the European settlers as well. Winthrop Jordan has observed: "From the initially common term *Christian*, at mid-century there was a marked shift toward the terms *English* and *free*. After about 1680, taking the colonies as a whole, a new term of self-identification appeared—*white*."[19]

We employ the term *racialization* to signify the extension of racial meaning to a previously racially unclassified relationship, social practice or group. Racialization is an ideological process, an historically specific one. Racial ideology is constructed from pre-existing conceptual (or, if one prefers, "discursive") elements and emerges from the struggles of competing political projects and ideas seeking to articulate similar elements differently. An account of racialization processes that avoids the pitfalls of US ethnic history[20] remains to be written.

Particularly during the nineteenth century, the category of "white" was subject to challenges brought about by the influx of diverse groups who were not of the same Anglo-Saxon stock as the founding immigrants. In the nineteenth century, political and ideological struggles emerged over the classification of Southern Europeans, the Irish and Jews, among other "non-white" categories.[21] Nativism was only effectively curbed by the institutionalization of a racial order that drew the color line *around*, rather than *within*, Europe.

By stopping short of racializing immigrants from Europe after the Civil War, and by subsequently allowing their assimilation, the American racial order was reconsolidated in the wake of the tremendous challenge placed before it by the abolition of racial slavery.[22] With the end of Reconstruction in 1877, an effective program for limiting the emergent class struggles of the later nineteenth century was forged: the definition of the working class in *racial terms*—as "white." This was not accomplished by any legislative decree or capitalist maneuvering to divide the working class, but rather by white workers themselves. Many of them were recent immigrants, who organized on racial lines as much as on traditionally defined class lines.[23] The Irish on the West Coast, for example, engaged in vicious anti-Chinese race-baiting and committed many pogrom-type assaults on Chinese in the course of consolidating the trade union movement in California.

Thus the very political organization of the working class was in important ways a racial project. The legacy of racial conflicts and arrangements shaped the definition of interests and in turn led to the consolidation of institutional patterns (e.g., segregated unions, dual labor markets, exclusionary legislation) which perpetuated the color line *within* the working class. Selig Perlman, whose study of the development of the labor movement is fairly sympathetic to this process, notes that:

> The political issue after 1877 was racial, not financial, and the weapon was not merely the ballot, but also "direct action"— violence. The anti-Chinese agitation in California, culminating as it did in the Exclusion Law passed by Congress in 1882, was doubtless

the most important single factor in the history of American labor, for without it the entire country might have been overrun by Mongolian [sic] labor and *the labor movement might have become a conflict of races instead of one of classes.*[24]

More recent economic transformations in the US have also altered interpretations of racial identities and meanings. The automation of southern agriculture and the augmented labor demand of the postwar boom transformed blacks from a largely rural, impoverished labor force to a largely urban, working-class group by 1970.[25] When boom became bust and liberal welfare statism moved right-wards, the majority of blacks came to be seen, increasingly, as part of the "underclass," as state "dependents." Thus the particularly deleterious effects on blacks of global and national economic shifts (generally rising unemployment rates, changes in the employment structure away from reliance on labor intensive work, etc.) were explained once again in the late 1970s and 1980s (as they had been in the 1940s and mid-1960s) as the result of defective black cultural norms, of familial disorganization, etc.[26] In this way new racial attributions, new racial myths, are affixed to "blacks."[27] Similar changes in racial identity are presently affecting Asians and Latinos, as such economic forces as increasing Third World impoverishment and indebtedness fuel immigration and high interest rates, Japanese competition spurs resentments, and US jobs seem to fly away to Korea and Singapore.[28] . . .

Once we understand that race overflows the boundaries of skin color, super-exploitation, social stratification, discrimination and prejudice, cultural domination and cultural resistance, state policy (or of any other particular social relationship we list), once we recognize the racial dimension present to some degree in *every* identity, institution and social practice in the United States—once we have done this, it becomes possible to speak of *racial formation*. This recognition is hard-won; there is a continuous temptation to think of race as an *essence*, as something fixed, concrete and objective, as (for example) one of the categories just enumerated. And there is also an opposite temptation: to see it as a mere illusion, which an ideal social order would eliminate.

In our view it is crucial to break with these habits of thought. The effort must be made to understand race as *an unstable and "decentered" complex of social meanings constantly being transformed by political struggle.* . . .

NOTES

1. *San Francisco Chronicle*, 14 September 1982, 19 May 1983. Ironically, the 1970 Louisiana law was enacted to supersede an old Jim Crow statute which relied on the idea of "common report" in determining an infant's race. Following Phipps's unsuccessful attempt to change her classification and have the law declared

unconstitutional, a legislative effort arose which culminated in the repeal of the law. See *San Francisco Chronicle*, 23 June 1983.

2. The Mormon church, for example, has been heavily criticized for its doctrine of black inferiority.

3. Thomas F. Gossett notes:

Race theory . . . had up until fairly modern times no firm hold on European thought. On the other hand, race theory and race prejudice were by no means unknown at the time when the English colonists came to North America. Undoubtedly, the age of exploration led many to speculate on race differences at a period when neither Europeans nor Englishmen were prepared to make allowances for vast cultural diversities. Even though race theories had not then secured wide acceptance or even sophisticated formulation, the first contacts of the Spanish with the Indians in the Americas can now be recognized as the beginning of a struggle between conceptions of the nature of primitive peoples which has not yet been wholly settled. (Thomas F. Gossett, *Race: The History of an Idea in America* [New York: Schocken Books, 1965], p. 16).

Winthrop Jordan provides a detailed account of early European colonialists' attitudes about color and race in *White Over Black: American Attitudes Toward the Negro, 1550–1812* (New York: Norton, 1977 [1968]), pp. 3–43.

4. Pro-slavery physician Samuel George Morton (1799–1851) compiled a collection of 800 crania from all parts of the world which formed the sample for his studies of race. Assuming that the larger the size of the cranium translated into greater intelligence, Morton established a relationship between race and skull capacity. Gossett reports that:

In 1849, one of his studies included the following results: The English skulls in his collection proved to be the largest, with an average cranial capacity of 96 cubic inches. The Americans and Germans were rather poor seconds, both with cranial capacities of 90 cubic inches. At the bottom of the list were the Negroes with 83 cubic inches, the Chinese with 82, and the Indians with 79. (Ibid., p. 74).

On Morton's methods, see Stephen J. Gould, "The Finagle Factor," *Human Nature* (July 1978).

5. Definitions of race founded upon a common pool of genes have not held up when confronted by scientific research which suggests that the differences *within* a given human population are greater than those *between* populations. See L. L. Cavalli-Sforza, "The Genetics of Human Populations," *Scientific American* (September 1974), pp. 81–9.

6. Arthur Jensen, "How Much Can We Boost IQ and Scholastic Achievement?" *Harvard Educational Review*, vol. 39 (1969), pp. 1–123.

7. Ernst Moritz Manasse, "Max Weber on Race," *Social Research*, vol. 14 (1947), pp. 191–221.

8. Quoted in Edward D. C. Campbell, Jr., *The Celluloid South: Hollywood and the Southern Myth* (Knoxville: University of Tennessee Press, 1981), pp. 168–70.

9. Marvin Harris, *Patterns of Race in the Americas* (New York: Norton, 1964), p. 56.

10. Ibid., p. 57.

11. After James Meredith had been admitted as the first black student at the University of Mississippi, Harry S. Murphy announced that he, and not Meredith, was the first black student to attend "Ole Miss." Murphy described himself as black but was able to pass for white and spent nine months at the institution without attracting any notice (ibid., p. 56).

12. A. Sivanandan, "From Resistance to Rebellion: Asian and Afro-Caribbean Struggles in Britain," *Race and Class*, vol. 23, nos. 2–3 (Autumn–Winter 1981).
13. Consider the contradictions in racial status which abound in the country with the most rigidly defined racial categories—South Africa. There a race classification agency is employed to adjudicate claims for upgrading of official racial identity. This is particularly necessary for the "coloured" category. The apartheid system considers Chinese as "Asians" while the Japanese are accorded the status of "honorary whites." This logic nearly detaches race from any grounding in skin color and other physical attributes and nakedly exposes race as a juridical category subject to economic, social and political influences. (We are indebted to Steve Talbot for clarification of some of these points.)
14. Gordon W. Allport, *The Nature of Prejudice* (Garden City, New York: Doubleday, 1958), pp. 184–200.
15. We wish to use this phrase loosely, without committing ourselves to a particular position on such social psychological approaches as symbolic interactionism, which are outside the scope of this study. An interesting study on this subject is S. M. Lyman and W. A. Douglass, "Ethnicity: Strategies of Individual and Collective Impression Management," *Social Research*, vol. 40, no. 2 (1973).
16. Michael Billig, "Patterns of Racism: Interviews with National Front Members," *Race and Class*, vol. 20, no. 2 (Autumn 1978), pp. 161–79.
17. "Miss San Antonio USA Lisa Fernandez and other Hispanics auditioning for a role in a television soap opera did not fit the Hollywood image of real Mexicans and had to darken their faces before filming." Model Aurora Garza said that their faces were bronzed with powder because they looked too white. "'I'm a real Mexican [Garza said] and very dark anyway. I'm even darker right now because I have a tan. But they kept wanting me to make my face darker and darker'" (*San Francisco Chronicle*, 21 September 1984). A similar dilemma faces Asian American actors who feel that Asian character lead roles inevitably go to white actors who make themselves up to be Asian. Scores of Charlie Chan films, for example, have been made with white leads (the last one was the 1981 *Charlie Chan and the Curse of the Dragon Queen*). Roland Winters, who played in six Chan features, was asked by playwright Frank Chin to explain the logic of casting a white man in the role of Charlie Chan: "'The only thing I can think of is, if you want to cast a homosexual in a show, and you get a homosexual, it'll be awful. It won't be funny . . . and maybe there's something there . . .'" (Frank Chin, "Confessions of the Chinatown Cowboy," *Bulletin of Concerned Asian Scholars*, vol. 4, no. 3 [Fall 1972]).
18. Melanie Martindale-Sikes, "Nationalizing 'Nigger' Imagery Through 'Birth of a Nation'," paper prepared for the 73rd Annual Meeting of the American Sociological Association, 4–8 September 1978, in San Francisco.
19. Winthrop D. Jordan, op. cit., p. 95; emphasis added.
20. Historical focus has been placed either on particular racially defined groups or on immigration and the "incorporation" of ethnic groups. In the former case the characteristic ethnicity theory pitfalls and apologetics such as functionalism and cultural pluralism may be avoided, but only by sacrificing much of the focus on race. In the latter case, race is considered a manifestation of ethnicity.
21. The degree of antipathy for these groups should not be minimized. A northern commentator observed in the 1850s: "An Irish Catholic seldom attempts to rise to a higher condition than that in which he is placed, while the Negro often makes the attempt with success." Quoted in Gossett, op. cit., p. 288.

22. This analysis, as will perhaps be obvious, is essentially DuBoisian. Its main source will be found in the monumental (and still largely unappreciated) *Black Reconstruction in the United States 1860–1880* (New York: Atheneum, 1977 [1935]).

23. Alexander Saxton argues that:

North Americans of European background have experienced three great racial confrontations: with the Indian, with the African, and with the Oriental. Central to each transaction has been a totally one-sided preponderance of power, exerted for the exploitation of nonwhites by the dominant white society. In each case (but especially in the two that began with systems of enforced labor), white working-men have played a crucial, yet ambivalent, role. They have been both exploited and exploiters. On the one hand, thrown into competition with nonwhites as enslaved or "cheap" labor, they suffered economically; on the other hand, being white, they benefited by that very exploitation which was compelling the non-whites to work for low wages or for nothing. Ideologically they were drawn in opposite directions. *Racial identification cut at right angles to class consciousness.* (Alexander Saxton, *The Indispensable Enemy: Labor and the Anti-Chinese Movement in California* (Berkeley and Los Angeles: University of California Press, 1971), p. 1; emphasis added.)

24. Selig Perlman, *The History of Trade Unionism in the United States* (New York: Augustus Kelley, 1950), p. 52; emphasis added.

25. Whether southern blacks were "peasants" or rural workers is unimportant in this context. Sometime during the 1960s blacks attained a higher degree of urbanization than whites. Before World War II most blacks had been rural dwellers and nearly 80 percent lived in the South.

26. See George Gilder, *Wealth and Poverty* (New York: Basic Books, 1981); Charles Murray, *Losing Ground* (New York: Basic Books, 1984).

27. A brilliant study of the racialization process in Britain, focused on the rise of "mugging" as a popular fear in the 1970s, is Stuart Hall *et al., Policing the Crisis* (London: Macmillan, 1978).

28. The case of Vincent Chin, a Chinese American man beaten to death in 1982 by a laid-off Detroit auto worker and his stepson who mistook him for Japanese and blamed him for the loss of their jobs, has been widely publicized in Asian American communities. On immigration conflicts and pressures, see Michael Omi, "New Wave Dread: Immigration and Intra–Third World Conflict," *Socialist Review*, no. 60 (November–December 1981).

2

DEFINING RACISM

"Can We Talk?"

■ ■ ■

Beverly Daniel Tatum

Early in my teaching career, a White student I knew asked me what I would be teaching the following semester. I mentioned that I would be teaching a course on racism. She replied, with some surprise in her voice, "Oh, is there still racism?" I assured her that indeed there was and suggested that she sign up for my course. Fifteen years later, after exhaustive media coverage of events such as the Rodney King beating, the Charles Stuart and Susan Smith cases, the O. J. Simpson trial, the appeal to racial prejudices in electoral politics, and the bitter debates about affirmative action and welfare reform, it seems hard to imagine that anyone would still be unaware of the reality of racism in our society. But in fact, in almost every audience I address, there is someone who will suggest that racism is a thing of the past. There is always someone who hasn't noticed the stereotypical images of people of color in the media, who hasn't observed the housing discrimination in their community, who hasn't read the newspaper articles about documented racial bias in lending practices among well-known banks, who isn't aware of the racial tracking pattern at the local school, who hasn't seen the reports of rising incidents of racially motivated hate crimes in America—in short, someone who hasn't been paying attention to issues of race. But if you are paying attention, the legacy of racism is not hard to see, and we are all affected by it.

The impact of racism begins early. Even in our preschool years, we are exposed to misinformation about people different from ourselves. Many of us grew up in neighborhoods where we had limited opportunities to interact with people different from our own families. When I ask my college students, "How many of you grew up in neighborhoods where most of the people were from the same racial group as your own?" almost every hand goes up. There is still a great deal of social segregation in our communities. Consequently, most of the early information we receive about "others"—people racially, religiously, or socioeconomically different from ourselves—does not come as the result of firsthand experience. The secondhand information we do receive has often been distorted, shaped by cultural stereotypes, and left incomplete.

Some examples will highlight this process. Several years ago one of my students conducted a research project investigating preschoolers' conceptions of Native Americans.[1] Using children at a local day care center as her participants, she asked these three- and four-year-olds to draw a picture of a Native American. Most children were stumped by her request. They didn't know what a Native American was. But when she rephrased the question and asked them to draw a picture of an Indian, they readily complied. Almost every picture included one central feature: feathers. In fact, many of them also included a weapon—a knife or tomahawk—and depicted the person in violent or aggressive terms. Though this group of children, almost all of whom were White, did not live near a large Native American population and probably had had little if any personal interaction with American Indians, they all had internalized an image of what Indians were like. How did they know? Cartoon images, in particular the Disney movie *Peter Pan*, were cited by the children as their number-one source of information. At the age of three, these children already had a set of stereotypes in place. Though I would not describe three-year-olds as prejudiced, the stereotypes to which they have been exposed become the foundation for the adult prejudices so many of us have.

Sometimes the assumptions we make about others come not from what we have been told or what we have seen on television or in books, but rather from what we have *not* been told. The distortion of historical information about people of color leads young people (and older people, too) to make assumptions that may go unchallenged for a long time. Consider this conversation between two White students following a discussion about the cultural transmission of racism:

"Yeah, I just found out that Cleopatra was actually a Black woman."

"What?"

The first student went on to explain her newly learned information. The second student exclaimed in disbelief, "That can't be true. Cleopatra was beautiful!"

What had this young woman learned about who in our society is considered beautiful and who is not? Had she conjured up images of Elizabeth Taylor when she thought of Cleopatra? The new information her classmate had shared and her own deeply ingrained assumptions about who is beautiful and who is not were too incongruous to allow her to assimilate the information at that moment.

Omitted information can have similar effects. For example, another young woman, preparing to be a high school English teacher, expressed her dismay that she had never learned about any Black authors in any of her English courses. How was she to teach about them to her future students when she hadn't learned about them herself? A White male student in the class responded to this discussion with frustration in his response journal, writing "It's not my fault that Blacks don't write books." Had one of his elementary, high school, or college teachers ever told him that there were no Black writers? Probably not. Yet because he had never been exposed to Black authors, he had drawn his own conclusion that there were none.

Stereotypes, omissions, and distortions all contribute to the development of prejudice. *Prejudice* is a preconceived judgment or opinion, usually based on limited information. I assume that we all have prejudices, not because we want them, but simply because we are so continually exposed to misinformation about others. Though I have often heard students or workshop participants describe someone as not having "a prejudiced bone in his body," I usually suggest that they look again. Prejudice is one of the inescapable consequences of living in a racist society. Cultural racism—the cultural images and messages that affirm the assumed superiority of Whites and the assumed inferiority of people of color—is like smog in the air. Sometimes it is so thick it is visible, other times it is less apparent, but always, day in and day out, we are breathing it in. None of us would introduce ourselves as "smog-breathers" (and most of us don't want to be described as prejudiced), but if we live in a smoggy place, how can we avoid breathing the air? If we live in an environment in which we are bombarded with stereotypical images in the media, are frequently exposed to the ethnic jokes of friends and family members, and are rarely informed of the accomplishments of oppressed groups, we will develop the negative categorizations of those groups that form the basis of prejudice.

People of color as well as Whites develop these categorizations. Even a member of the stereotyped group may internalize the stereotypical categories about his or her own group to some degree. In fact, this process happens so frequently that it has a name, *internalized oppression*. Some of the consequences of believing the distorted messages about one's own group will be discussed in subsequent chapters.

Certainly some people are more prejudiced than others, actively embracing and perpetuating negative and hateful images of those who are different from themselves. When we claim to be free of prejudice, perhaps what we are really saying is that we are not hatemongers. But none of us is completely innocent. Prejudice is an integral part of our socialization, and it is not our fault. Just as the preschoolers my student interviewed are not to blame for the negative messages they internalized, we are not at fault for the stereotypes, distortions, and omissions that shaped our thinking as we grew up.

To say that it is not our fault does not relieve us of responsibility, however. We may not have polluted the air, but we need to take responsibility, along with others, for cleaning it up. Each of us needs to look at our own behavior. Am I perpetuating and reinforcing the negative messages so pervasive in our culture, or am I seeking to challenge them? If I have not been exposed to positive images of marginalized groups, am I seeking them out, expanding my own knowledge base for myself and my children? Am I acknowledging and examining my own prejudices, my own rigid categorizations of others, thereby minimizing the adverse impact they might have on my interactions with those I have categorized? Unless we engage in these and other conscious acts of reflection and reeducation, we easily repeat the process with our children. We teach what we were taught. The unexamined prejudices of the parents are passed on to the children. It is not our fault, but it is our responsibility to interrupt this cycle.

RACISM: A SYSTEM OF ADVANTAGE BASED ON RACE

Many people use the terms *prejudice* and *racism* interchangeably. I do not, and I think it is important to make a distinction. In his book *Portraits of White Racism*, David Wellman argues convincingly that limiting our understanding of racism to prejudice does not offer a sufficient explanation for the persistence of racism. He defines racism as a "system of advantage based on race."[2] In illustrating this definition, he provides example after example of how Whites defend their racial advantage—access to better schools, housing, jobs—even when they do not embrace overtly prejudicial thinking. Racism cannot be fully explained as an expression of prejudice alone.

This definition of racism is useful because it allows us to see that racism, like other forms of oppression, is not only a personal ideology based on racial prejudice, but a *system* involving cultural messages and institutional policies and practices as well as the beliefs and actions of individuals. In the context of the United States, this system clearly operates to the advantage of Whites and to the disadvantage of people of color. Another related definition of racism, commonly used by antiracist educators and consultants, is "prejudice plus power." Racial prejudice when combined with social power—access to social, cultural, and economic resources and decision-making—leads to the institutionalization of racist policies and practices. While I think this definition also captures the idea that racism is more than individual beliefs and attitudes, I prefer Wellman's definition because the idea of systematic advantage and disadvantage is critical to an understanding of how racism operates in American society.

In addition, I find that many of my White students and workshop participants do not feel powerful. Defining racism as prejudice plus power has little personal relevance. For some, their response to this definition is the following: "I'm not really prejudiced, and I have no power, so racism has nothing to do with me." However, most White people, if they are really being honest with themselves, can see that there are advantages to being White in the United States. Despite the current rhetoric about affirmative action and "reverse racism," every social indicator, from salary to life expectancy, reveals the advantages of being White.[3]

The systematic advantages of being White are often referred to as White privilege. In a now well-known article, "White Privilege: Unpacking the Invisible Knapsack," Peggy McIntosh, a White feminist scholar, identified a long list of societal privileges that she received simply because she was White.[4] She did not ask for them, and it is important to note that she hadn't always noticed that she was receiving them. They included major and minor advantages. Of course she enjoyed greater access to jobs and housing. But she also was able to shop in department stores without being followed by suspicious salespeople and could always find appropriate hair care products and makeup in any drugstore. She could send her child to school confident that the teacher would not discriminate against him on the basis of race. She could also be late for meetings, and talk with her mouth full, fairly confident that these behaviors would not be attributed to the fact that she was White. She could express an opinion in a meeting or in print and not have it labeled the "White" viewpoint. In other words, she was more often than not viewed as an individual, rather than as a member of a racial group.

This article rings true for most White readers, many of whom may have never considered the benefits of being White. It's one thing to have enough awareness of racism to describe the ways that people of color are disadvantaged by it. But this new understanding of racism is more elusive. In very concrete terms, it means that if a person of color is the victim of housing discrimination, the apartment that would otherwise have been rented to that person of color is still available for a White person. The White tenant is, knowingly or unknowingly, the beneficiary of racism, a system of advantage based on race. The unsuspecting tenant is not to blame for the prior discrimination, but she benefits from it anyway.

For many Whites, this new awareness of the benefits of a racist system elicits considerable pain, often accompanied by feelings of anger and guilt. These uncomfortable emotions can hinder further discussion. We all like to think that we deserve the good things we have received, and that others, too, get what they deserve. Social psychologists call this tendency a "belief in a just world."[5] Racism directly contradicts such notions of justice.

Understanding racism as a system of advantage based on race is antithetical to traditional notions of an American meritocracy. For those who have internalized this myth, this definition generates considerable discomfort. It is more comfortable simply to think of racism as a particular form of prejudice. Notions of power or privilege do not have to be addressed when our understanding of racism is constructed in that way.

The discomfort generated when a systemic definition of racism is introduced is usually quite visible in the workshops I lead. Someone in the group is usually quick to point out that this is not the definition you will find in most dictionaries. I reply, "Who wrote the dictionary?" I am not being facetious with this response. Whose interests are served by a "prejudice only" definition of racism? It is important to understand that the system of advantage is perpetuated when we do not acknowledge its existence.

RACISM: FOR WHITES ONLY?

Frequently someone will say, "You keep talking about White people. People of color can be racist, too." I once asked a White teacher what it would mean to her if a student or parent of color accused her of being racist. She said she would feel as though she had been punched in the stomach or called a "low-life scum." She is not alone in this feeling. The word *racist* holds a lot of emotional power. For many White people, to be called racist is the ultimate insult. The idea that this term might only be applied to Whites becomes highly problematic for after all, can't people of color be "low-life scum" too?

Of course, people of any racial group can hold hateful attitudes and behave in racially discriminatory and bigoted ways. We can all cite examples of horrible hate crimes which have been perpetrated by people of color as well as Whites. Hateful behavior is hateful behavior no matter who does it. But when I am asked, "Can people of color be racist?" I reply, "The answer depends on your definition of racism." If one defines racism as racial prejudice, the answer is yes. People of color can and do have racial prejudices. However, if one defines racism as a system of advantage based on race, the answer is no. People of color are not racist because they do not systematically benefit from racism. And equally important, there is no systematic cultural and institutional support or sanction for the racial bigotry of people of color. In my view, reserving the term *racist* only for behaviors committed by Whites in the context of a White-dominated society is a way of acknowledging the everpresent power differential afforded Whites by the culture and institutions that make up the system of advantage and continue to reinforce notions of White superiority. (Using the same logic, I reserve the word *sexist* for men. Though women can and do have gender-based prejudices, only men systematically benefit from sexism.)

Despite my best efforts to explain my thinking on this point, there are some who will be troubled, perhaps even incensed, by my response. To call the racially motivated acts of a person of color acts of racial bigotry and to describe similar acts committed by Whites as racist will make no sense to some people, including some people of color. To those, I will respectfully say, "We can agree to disagree." At moments like these, it is not agreement that is essential, but clarity. Even if you don't like the definition of racism I am using, hopefully you are now clear about what it is. If I also understand how you are using the term, our conversation can continue—despite our disagreement.

Another provocative question I'm often asked is "Are you saying all Whites are racist?" When asked this question, I again remember that White teacher's response, and I am conscious that perhaps the question I am really being asked is, "Are you saying all Whites are bad people?" The answer to that question is of course not. However, all White people, intentionally or unintentionally, do benefit from racism. A more relevant question is what are White people as individuals doing to interrupt racism? For many White people, the image of a racist is a hood-wearing Klan member or a name-calling Archie Bunker figure. These images represent what might be called *active racism*, blatant, intentional acts of racial bigotry and discrimination. *Passive racism* is more subtle and can be seen in the collusion of laughing when a racist joke is told, of letting exclusionary hiring practices go unchallenged, of accepting as appropriate the omissions of people of color from the curriculum, and of avoiding difficult race-related issues. Because racism is so ingrained in the fabric of American institutions, it is easily self-perpetuating.[6] All that is required to maintain it is business as usual.

I sometimes visualize the ongoing cycle of racism as a moving walkway at the airport. Active racist behavior is equivalent to walking fast on the conveyor belt. The person engaged in active racist behavior has identified with the ideology of White supremacy and is moving with it. Passive racist behavior is equivalent to standing still on the walkway. No overt effort is being made, but the conveyor belt moves the bystanders along to the same destination as those who are actively walking. Some of the bystanders may feel the motion of the conveyor belt, see the active racists ahead of them, and choose to turn around, unwilling to go to the same destination as the White supremacists. But unless they are walking actively in the opposite direction at a speed faster than the conveyor belt—unless they are actively antiracist—they will find themselves carried along with the others.

So, not all Whites are actively racist. Many are passively racist. Some, though not enough, are actively antiracist. The relevant question is not whether all Whites are racist, but how we can move more White people from a position of active or passive racism to one of active antiracism. The task of interrupting racism is obviously not the task of Whites alone. But the fact of White privilege means that Whites have greater access to the societal institutions in need of transformation. To whom much is given, much is required.

It is important to acknowledge that while all Whites benefit from racism, they do not all benefit equally. Other factors, such as socioeconomic status, gender, age, religious affiliation, sexual orientation, mental and physical ability, also play a role in our access to social influence and power. A White woman on welfare is not privileged to the same extent as a wealthy White heterosexual man. In her case, the systematic disadvantages of sexism and classism intersect with her White privilege, but the privilege is still there. This point was brought home to me in a 1994 study conducted by a Mount Holyoke graduate student, Phyllis Wentworth.[7] Wentworth interviewed a group of female college students, who were both older than their peers and were the first members of their families to attend college, about the pathways that led them to college. All of the women interviewed were White, from working-class backgrounds, from families where women were expected to graduate from high school and get married or get a job. Several had experienced abusive relationships and other personal difficulties prior to coming to college. Yet their experiences were punctuated by "good luck" stories of apartments obtained without a deposit, good jobs offered without experience or extensive reference checks, and encouragement provided by willing mentors. While the women acknowledged their good fortune, none of them discussed their Whiteness. They had not considered the possibility that being White had worked in their favor and helped give them the benefit of the doubt at critical junctures. This study clearly showed that even under difficult circumstances, White privilege was still operating.

It is also true that not all people of color are equally targeted by racism. We all have multiple identities that shape our experience. I can describe myself as a light-skinned, well-educated, heterosexual, able-bodied, Christian African American woman raised in a middle-class suburb. As an African American woman, I am systematically disadvantaged by race and by gender, but I systematically receive benefits in the other categories, which then mediate my experience of racism and sexism. When one is targeted by multiple isms—racism, sexism, classism, heterosexism, ableism, anti-Semitism, ageism—in whatever combination, the effect is intensified. The particular combination of racism and classism in many communities of color is life-threatening. Nonetheless, when I, the middle-class Black mother of two sons, read another story about a Black man's unlucky encounter with a White police officer's deadly force, I am reminded that racism by itself can kill.

NOTES

1. C. O'Toole, "The effect of the media and multicultural education on children's perceptions of Native Americans" (senior thesis, Department of Psychology and Education, Mount Holyoke College, South Hadley, MA, May 1990).

2. For an extended discussion of this point, see David Wellman, *Portraits of White racism* (Cambridge: Cambridge University Press, 1977), ch. 1.

3. For specific statistical information, see R. Farley, "The common destiny of Blacks and Whites: Observations about the social and economic status of the races," pp. 197–233 in H. Hill and J. E. Jones, Jr. (Eds.), *Race in America: The struggle for equality* (Madison: University of Wisconsin Press, 1993).

4. P. McIntosh, "White privilege: Unpacking the invisible knapsack," *Peace and Freedom* (July/August 1989): 10–12.

5. For further discussion of the concept of "belief in a just world," see M. J. Lerner, "Social psychology of justice and interpersonal attraction," in T. Huston (Ed.), *Foundations of interpersonal attraction* (New York: Academic Press, 1974).

6. For a brief historical overview of the institutionalization of racism and sexism in our legal system, see "Part V: How it happened: Race and gender issues in U.S. law," in P. S. Rothenberg (Ed.), *Race, class, and gender in the United States: An integrated study*, 3d ed. (New York: St. Martin's Press, 1995).

7. P.A. Wentworth, "The identity development of non-traditionally aged first-generation women college students: An exploratory study" (master's thesis, Department of Psychology and Education, Mount Holyoke College, South Hadley, MA, 1994).

3

THE ETHICS OF LIVING JIM CROW

An Autobiographical Sketch

■ ■ ■

Richard Wright

I

My first lesson in how to live as a Negro came when I was quite small. We were living in Arkansas. Our house stood behind the railroad tracks. Its skimpy yard was paved with black cinders. Nothing green ever grew in that yard. The only touch of green we could see was far away, beyond the tracks, over where the white folks lived. But cinders were good enough for me and I never missed the green growing things. And anyhow cinders were fine weapons. You could always have a nice hot war with huge black cinders. All you had to do was crouch behind the brick pillars of a house with your hands full of gritty ammunition. And the first woolly black head you saw pop out from behind another row of pillars was your target. You tried your very best to knock it off. It was great fun.

I never fully realized the appalling disadvantages of a cinder environment till one day the gang to which I belonged found itself engaged in a war with the white boys who lived beyond the tracks. As usual we laid down our cinder barrage, thinking that this would wipe the white boys out. But they replied with a steady bombardment of broken bottles. We doubled our cinder barrage, but they hid behind trees, hedges, and the sloping embankments of their lawns. Having no such fortifications, we retreated to the brick pillars of our homes. During the retreat a broken milk bottle caught me behind the ear, opening a deep gash which bled profusely. The sight of blood pouring over my face completely demoralized our ranks. My fellow-combatants left me standing paralyzed in the center of the yard, and scurried for their homes. A kind neighbor saw me and rushed me to a doctor, who took three stitches in my neck.

I sat brooding on my front steps, nursing my wound and waiting for my mother to come from work. I felt that a grave injustice had been done me. It was all right to throw cinders. The greatest harm a cinder could do was leave a bruise. But broken bottles were dangerous; they left you cut, bleeding, and helpless.

When night fell, my mother came from the white folks' kitchen. I raced down the street to meet her. I could just feel in my bones that she would understand. I knew she would tell me exactly what to do next time. I grabbed her hand and babbled out the whole story. She examined my wound, then slapped me.

"How come yuh didn't hide?" she asked me. "How come yuh awways fightin'?"

I was outraged, and bawled. Between sobs I told her that I didn't have any trees or hedges to hide behind. There wasn't a thing I could have used as a trench. And you couldn't throw very far when you were hiding behind the brick pillars of a house. She grabbed a barrel stave, dragged me home, stripped me naked, and beat me till I had a fever of one hundred and two. She would smack my rump with the stave, and, while the skin was still smarting, impart to me gems of Jim Crow wisdom. I was never to throw cinders any more. I was never to fight any more wars. I was never, never, under any conditions, to fight *white* folks again. And they were absolutely right in clouting me with the broken milk bottle. Didn't I know she was working hard every day in the hot kitchens of the white folks to make money to take care of me? When was I ever going to learn to be a good boy? She couldn't be bothered with my fights. She finished by telling me that I ought to be thankful to God as long as I lived that they didn't kill me.

All that night I was delirious and could not sleep. Each time I closed my eyes I saw monstrous white faces suspended from the ceiling, leering at me.

From that time on, the charm of my cinder yard was gone. The green trees, the trimmed hedges, the cropped lawns grew very meaningful, became a symbol. Even today when I think of white folks, the hard, sharp outlines of white houses surrounded by trees, lawns, and hedges are present somewhere in the background of my mind. Through the years they grew into an overreaching symbol of fear.

It was a long time before I came in close contact with white folks again. We moved from Arkansas to Mississippi. Here we had the good fortune not to live behind the railroad tracks, or close to white neighborhoods. We lived in the very heart of the local Black Belt. There were black churches and black preachers; there were black schools and black teachers; black groceries and black clerks. In fact, everything was so solidly black that for a long time I did not even think of white folks, save in remote and vague terms. But this could not last forever. As one grows older one eats more. One's clothing costs more. When I finished grammar school I had to go to work. My mother could no longer feed and clothe me on her cooking job.

There is but one place where a black boy who knows no trade can get a job, and that's where the houses and faces are white, where the trees, lawns, and hedges are green. My first job was with an optical company in Jackson, Mississippi. The morning I applied I stood straight and neat before the boss, answering all his questions with sharp yessirs and nosirs. I was very careful to pronounce my *sirs* distinctly, in order that he might know that I was polite, that I knew where I was, and that I knew he was a *white* man. I wanted that job badly.

He looked me over as though he were examining a prize poodle. He questioned me closely about my schooling, being particularly insistent about how much mathematics I had had. He seemed very pleased when I told him I had had two years of algebra.

"Boy, how would you like to try to learn something around here?" he asked me.

"I'd like it fine, sir," I said, happy. I had visions of "working my way up." Even Negroes have those visions.

"All right," he said. "Come on."

I followed him to the small factory.

"Pease," he said to a white man of about thirty-five, "this is Richard. He's going to work for us."

Pease looked at me and nodded.

I was then taken to a white boy of about seventeen.

"Morrie, this is Richard, who's going to work for us."

"Whut yuh sayin' there, boy!" Morrie boomed at me.

"Fine!" I answered.

The boss instructed these two to help me, teach me, give me jobs to do, and let me learn what I could in my spare time.

My wages were five dollars a week.

I worked hard, trying to please. For the first month I got along O.K. Both Pease and Morrie seemed to like me. But one thing was missing. And I kept thinking about it. I was not learning anything and nobody was volunteering to help me. Thinking they had forgotten that I was to learn something about the mechanics of grinding lenses, I asked Morrie one day to tell me about the work. He grew red.

"Whut yuh tryin' t' do, nigger, get smart?" he asked.

"Naw; I ain' tryin' t' git smart," I said.

"Well, don't, if yuh know whut's good for yuh!"

I was puzzled. Maybe he just doesn't want to help me, I thought. I went to Pease.

"Say, are yuh crazy, you black bastard?" Pease asked me, his gray eyes growing hard.

I spoke out, reminding him that the boss had said I was to be given a chance to learn something.

"Nigger, you think you're white, don't you?"

"Naw, sir!"

"Well, you're acting mighty like it!"

"But, Mr. Pease, the boss said . . . "

Pease shook his fist in my face.

"This is a *white* man's work around here, and you better watch yourself!"

From then on they changed toward me. They said good-morning no more. When I was just a bit slow in performing some duty, I was called a lazy black son-of-a-bitch.

Once I thought of reporting all this to the boss. But the mere idea of what would happen to me if Pease and Morrie should learn that I had "snitched" stopped me. And after all the boss was a white man, too. What was the use?

The climax came at noon one summer day. Pease called me to his work-bench. To get to him I had to go between two narrow benches and stand with my back against a wall.

"Yes, sir," I said.

"Richard, I want to ask you something," Pease began pleasantly, not looking up from his work.

"Yes, sir," I said again.

Morrie came over, blocking the narrow passage between the benches. He folded his arms, staring at me solemnly.

I looked from one to the other, sensing that something was coming.

"Yes, sir," I said for the third time.

Pease looked up and spoke very slowly.

"Richard, Mr. Morrie here tells me you called me *Pease*."

I stiffened. A void seemed to open up in me. I knew this was the show-down.

He meant that I had failed to call him Mr. Pease. I looked at Morrie. He was gripping a steel bar in his hands. I opened my mouth to speak, to protest, to assure Pease that I had never called him simply *Pease*, and that I had never had any intentions of doing so, when Morrie grabbed me by the collar, ramming my head against the wall.

"Now, be careful, nigger!" snarled Morrie, baring his teeth. "*I* heard yuh call 'im *Pease*! 'N' if yuh say yuh didn't, yuh're callin' me a *lie*, see?" He waved the steel bar threateningly.

If I had said: No, sir, Mr. Pease, I never called you *Pease*, I would have been automatically calling Morrie a liar. And if I had said: Yes, sir, Mr. Pease, I called you *Pease*, I would have been pleading guilty to having uttered the worst insult that a Negro can utter to a southern white man. I stood hesitating, trying to frame a neutral reply.

"Richard, I asked you a question!" said Pease. Anger was creeping into his voice.

"I don't remember calling you *Pease*, Mr. Pease," I said cautiously. "And if I did, I sure didn't mean . . . "

"You black son-of-a-bitch! You called me *Pease*, then!" he spat, slapping me till I bent sideways over a bench. Morrie was on top of me, demanding:

"Didn't yuh call 'im *Pease*? If yuh say yuh didn't, I'll rip yo' gut string loose with this bar, yuh black granny dodger! Yuh can't call a white man a lie 'n' git erway with it, you black son-of-a-bitch!"

I wilted. I begged them not to bother me. I knew what they wanted. They wanted me to leave.

"I'll leave," I promised. "I'll leave right *now*."

They gave me a minute to get out of the factory. I was warned not to show up again, or tell the boss.

I went.

When I told the folks at home what had happened, they called me a fool. They told me that I must never again attempt to exceed my boundaries. When you are working for white folks, they said, you got to "stay in your place" if you want to keep working.

II

My Jim Crow education continued on my next job, which was portering in a clothing store. One morning, while polishing brass out front, the boss and his twenty-year-old son got out of their car and half dragged and half kicked a Negro woman into the store. A policeman standing at the corner looked on, twirling his night-stick. I watched out of the corner of my eye, never slackening the strokes of my chamois upon the brass. After a few minutes, I heard shrill screams coming from the rear of the store. Later the woman stumbled out, bleeding, crying, and holding her stomach. When she reached the end of the block, the policeman grabbed her and accused her of being drunk. Silently, I watched him throw her into a patrol wagon.

When I went to the rear of the store, the boss and his son were washing their hands at the sink. They were chuckling. The floor was bloody and strewn with wisps of hair and clothing. No doubt I must have appeared pretty shocked, for the boss slapped me reassuringly on the back.

"Boy, that's what we do to niggers when they don't want to pay their bills," he said, laughing.

His son looked at me and grinned.

"Here, hava cigarette," he said.

Not knowing what to do, I took it. He lit his and held the match for me. This was a gesture of kindness, indicating that even if they had beaten the poor old woman, they would not beat me if I knew enough to keep my mouth shut.

"Yes, sir," I said, and asked no questions.

After they had gone, I sat on the edge of a packing box and stared at the bloody floor till the cigarette went out.

That day at noon, while eating in a hamburger joint, I told my fellow Negro porters what had happened. No one seemed surprised. One fellow, after swallowing a huge bite, turned to me and asked:

"Huh! Is tha' all they did t' her?"

"Yeah. Wasn't tha' enough?" I asked.

"Shucks! Man, she's a lucky bitch!" he said, burying his lips deep into a juicy hamburger. "Hell, it's a wonder they didn't lay her when they got through."

III

I was learning fast, but not quite fast enough. One day, while I was delivering packages in the suburbs, my bicycle tire was punctured. I walked along the hot, dusty road, sweating and leading my bicycle by the handle-bars.

A car slowed at my side.

"What's the matter, boy?" a white man called.

I told him my bicycle was broken and I was walking back to town.

"That's too bad," he said, "Hop on the running board."

He stopped the car. I clutched hard at my bicycle with one hand and clung to the side of the car with the other.

"All set?"

"Yes, sir," I answered. The car started.

It was full of young white men. They were drinking. I watched the flask pass from mouth to mouth.

"Wanna drink, boy?" one asked.

I laughed as the wind whipped my face. Instinctively obeying the freshly planted precepts of my mother, I said:

"Oh, no!"

The words were hardly out of my mouth before I felt something hard and cold smash me between the eyes. It was an empty whisky bottle. I saw stars, and fell backwards from the speeding car into the dust of the road, my feet becoming entangled in the steel spokes of my bicycle. The white men piled out and stood over me.

"Nigger, ain' yuh learned no better sense'n tha' yet?" asked the man who hit me. "Ain't yuh learned t' say *sir* t' a white man yet?"

Dazed, I pulled to my feet. My elbows and legs were bleeding. Fists doubled, the white man advanced, kicking my bicycle out of the way.

"Aw, leave the bastard alone. He's got enough," said one.

They stood looking at me. I rubbed my shins, trying to stop the flow of blood. No doubt they felt a sort of contemptuous pity, for one asked:

"Yuh wanna ride t' town now, nigger? Yuh reckon yuh know enough t' ride now?"

"I wanna walk," I said, simply.

Maybe it sounded funny. They laughed.

"Well, walk, yuh black son-of-a-bitch!"

When they left they comforted me with:

"Nigger, yuh sho better be damn glad it wuz us yuh talked t' tha' way. Yuh're a lucky bastard, 'cause if yuh'd said tha' t' somebody else, yuh might've been a dead nigger now."

IV

Negroes who have lived South know the dread of being caught alone upon the streets in white neighborhoods after the sun has set. In such a simple situation as this the plight of the Negro in America is graphically symbolized. While white strangers may be in these neighborhoods trying to get home, they can pass unmolested. But the color of a Negro's skin makes him easily recognizable, makes him suspect, converts him into a defenseless target.

Late one Saturday night I made some deliveries in a white neighborhood. I was pedaling my bicycle back to the store as fast as I could, when a police car, swerving toward me, jammed me into the curbing.

"Get down and put up your hands!" the policemen ordered.

I did. They climbed out of the car, guns drawn, faces set, and advanced slowly.

"Keep still!" they ordered.

I reached my hands higher. They searched my pockets and packages. They seemed dissatisfied when they could find nothing incriminating. Finally, one of them said:

"Boy, tell your boss not to send you out in white neighborhoods after sundown."

As usual, I said:

"Yes, sir."

V

My next job was a hall-boy in a hotel. Here my Jim Crow education broadened and deepened. When the bell-boys were busy, I was often called to assist them. As many of the rooms in the hotel were occupied by prostitutes, I was constantly called to carry them liquor and cigarettes. These women were nude most of the time. They did not bother about clothing, even for bell-boys. When you went into their rooms, you were supposed to take their nakedness for granted, as though it startled you no more than a blue vase or a red rug. Your presence awoke in them no sense of shame, for you were not regarded as human. If they were alone, you could steal sidelong glimpses at them. But if they were receiving men, not a flicker of your eyelids could show. I remember one incident vividly. A new woman, a huge, snowy-skinned blonde, took a room on my floor. I was sent to wait upon her. She was in bed with a thick-set man; both were nude and uncovered. She said she wanted some liquor and slid out of bed and waddled across the floor to get her money from a dresser drawer. I watched her.

"Nigger, what in hell you looking at?" the white man asked me, raising himself upon his elbows.

"Nothing," I answered, looking miles deep into the blank wall of the room.

"Keep your eyes where they belong, if you want to be healthy!" he said.

"Yes, sir."

VI

One of the bell-boys I knew in this hotel was keeping steady company with one of the Negro maids. Out of a clear sky the police descended upon his home and arrested him, accusing him of bastardy. The poor boy swore he had had no intimate relations with the girl. Nevertheless, they forced him to marry her. When the child arrived, it was found to be much lighter in complexion than either of the two supposedly legal parents. The white men around the hotel made a great joke of it. They spread the rumor that some white cow must have scared the poor girl while she was carrying the baby. If you were in their presence when this explanation was offered, you were supposed to laugh.

VII

One of the bell-boys was caught in bed with a white prostitute. He was castrated and run out of town. Immediately after this all the bell-boys and hall-boys were called together and warned. We were given to understand that the boy who had been castrated was a "mighty, mighty lucky bastard." We were impressed with the fact that next time the management of the hotel would not be responsible for the lives of "trouble-makin' niggers." We were silent.

VIII

One night, just as I was about to go home, I met one of the Negro maids. She lived in my direction, and we fell in to walk part of the way home together. As we passed the white night-watchman, he slapped the maid on her buttock. I turned around, amazed. The watchman looked at me with a long, hard, fixed-under stare. Suddenly he pulled his gun and asked:

"Nigger, don't yuh like it?"

I hesitated.

"I asked yuh don't yuh like it?" he asked again, stepping forward.

"Yes, sir," I mumbled.

"Talk like it, then!"

"Oh, yes sir!" I said with as much heartiness as I could muster.

Outside, I walked ahead of the girl, ashamed to face her. She caught up with me and said:

"Don't be a fool! Yuh couldn't help it!"

This watchman boasted of having killed two Negroes in self-defense.

Yet, in spite of all this, the life of the hotel ran with an amazing smoothness. It would have been impossible for a stranger to detect anything. The maids, the hallboys, and the bell-boys were all smiles. They had to be.

IX

I had learned my Jim Crow lessons so thoroughly that I kept the hotel job till I left Jackson for Memphis. It so happened that while in Memphis I applied for a job at a branch of the optical company. I was hired. And for some reason, as long as I worked there, they never brought my past against me.

Here my Jim Crow education assumed quite a different form. It was no longer brutally cruel, but subtly cruel. Here I learned to lie, to steal, to dissemble. I learned to play that dual role which every Negro must play if he wants to eat and live.

For example, it was almost impossible to get a book to read. It was assumed that after a Negro had imbibed what scanty schooling the state furnished he had no further need for books. I was always borrowing books from men on the job. One day I mustered enough courage to ask one of the men to let me get books from the library in his name. Surprisingly, he consented. I cannot help but think that he consented because he was a Roman Catholic and felt a vague sympathy for Negroes, being himself an object of hatred. Armed with a library card, I obtained books in the following manner: I would write a note to the librarian, saying: "Please let this nigger boy have the following books." I would then sign it with the white man's name.

When I went to the library, I would stand at the desk, hat in hand, looking as unbookish as possible. When I received the books desired I would take them home. If the books listed in the note happened to be out, I would sneak into the lobby and forge a new one. I never took any chances guessing with the white librarian about what the fictitious white man would want to read. No doubt if any of the white patrons had suspected that some of the volumes they enjoyed had been in the home of a Negro, they would not have tolerated it for an instant.

The factory force of the optical company in Memphis was much larger than that in Jackson, and more urbanized. At least they liked to talk, and would engage the Negro help in conversation whenever possible. By this means I found that many subjects were taboo from the white man's point of view. Among the topics they did not like to discuss with Negroes were the following: American white women; the Ku Klux Klan; France, and how Negro soldiers fared while there; French women; Jack Johnson; the entire northern part of the United States; the Civil War; Abraham Lincoln; U. S. Grant; General Sherman; Catholics; the Pope; Jews; the Republican Party; slavery; social equality; Communism; Socialism; the 13th and 14th Amendments to the Constitution; or any topic calling for positive knowledge or manly self-assertion on the part of the Negro. The most accepted topics were sex and religion.

There were many times when I had to exercise a great deal of ingenuity to keep out of trouble. It is a southern custom that all men must take off their hats when they enter an elevator. And especially did this apply to us blacks with rigid force. One day I stepped into an elevator with my arms full of packages. I was forced to ride with my hat on. Two white men stared at me coldly. Then one of them very kindly lifted my hat and placed it upon my armful of packages. Now the most accepted response for a Negro to make under such circumstances is to look at the white man out of the corner of his eye and grin. To have said: "Thank you!" would have made the white man *think* that you *thought* you were receiving from him a personal service. For such an act I have seen Negroes take a blow in the mouth. Finding the first alternative distasteful, and the second dangerous, I hit upon an acceptable course of action which fell safely between these two poles. I immediately—no sooner than my hat was lifted—pretended that my packages were about to spill, and appeared deeply distressed with keeping them in my arms. In this fashion I evaded having to acknowledge his service, and, in spite of adverse circumstances, salvaged a slender shred of personal pride.

How do Negroes feel about the way they have to live? How do they discuss it when alone amongst themselves? I think this question can be answered in a single sentence. A friend of mine who ran an elevator once told me:

"Lawd, man! Ef it wuzn't fer them polices 'n' them ol' lynch-mobs, there wouldn't be nothin' but uproar down here!"

HISTORIC ORIGINS:
How It Happened in the U.S.

1. *Dred Scott v. Sandford*, 1857

2. Emancipation Proclamation by Abraham Lincoln

3. The 13th, 14th, and 15th Amendments to the *U.S. Constitution*

4. *Plessy v. Ferguson*, 1896

5. The Three-Fifths Compromise

6. *Brown v. Board of Education of Topeka*, 1954

1

DRED SCOTT V. SANDFORD, 1857

■ ■ ■

The question is simply this: Can a negro, whose ancestors were imported into this country, and sold as slaves, become a member of the political community formed and brought into existence by the Constitution of the United States, and as such become entitled to all the rights, and privileges, and immunities, guarantied by that instrument to the citizen? One of which rights is the privilege of suing in a court of the United States in the cases specified in the Constitution.

It will be observed, that the plea applies to that class of persons only whose ancestors were negroes of the African race, and imported into this country, and sold and held as slaves. The only matter in issue before this court, therefore, is whether the descendants of such slaves, when they shall be emancipated, or who are born of parents who had become free before their birth, are citizens of a State, in the sense in which the word citizen is used in the Constitution of the United States. And this being the only matter in dispute on the pleadings, the court must be understood as speaking in his opinion of that class only, that is, of those persons who are the descendants of Africans who were imported into this country, and sold as slaves.

It becomes necessary, therefore, to determine who were citizens of the several States when the Constitution was adopted. And in order to do this, we must recur to the Governments and institutions of the thirteen colonies, when they separated from Great Britain and formed new sovereignties, and took their places in the family of independent nations. We must inquire

From Benjamin C. Howard, *Report of the Decision of the Supreme Court of the United States in the Case Dred Scott* . . . (Washington, 1857), 9, 13–14, 15–17, 60.

who, at that time, were recognised as the people or citizens of a State, whose rights and liberties had been outraged by the English Government; and who declared their independence, and assumed the powers of Government to defend their rights by force of arms.

In the opinion of the court, the legislation and histories of the times, and the language used in the Declaration of Independence, show, that neither the class of persons who had been imported as slaves, nor their descendants, whether they had become free or not, were then acknowledged as a part of the people, nor intended to be included in the general words used in that memorable instrument.

It is difficult at this day to realize the state of public opinion in relation to that unfortunate race, which prevailed in the civilized and enlightened portions of the world at the time of the Declaration of Independence, and when the Constitution of the United States was formed and adopted. But the public history of every European nation displays it in a manner too plain to be mistaken.

They had for more than a century before been regarded as beings of an inferior order, and altogether unfit to associate with the white race, either in social or political relations; and so far inferior, that they had no rights which the white man was bound to respect; and that the negro might justly and lawfully be reduced to slavery for his benefit. He was bought and sold, and treated as an ordinary article of merchandise and traffic, whenever a profit could be made by it. This opinion was at that time fixed and universal in the civilized portion of the white race. It was regarded as an axiom in morals as well as in politics, which no one thought of disputing, or supposed to be open to dispute; and men in every grade and position in society daily and habitually acted upon it in their private pursuits, as well as in matters of public concern, without doubting for a moment the correctness of this opinion.

And in no nation was this opinion more firmly fixed or more uniformly acted upon than by the English Government and English people. They not only seized them on the coast of Africa, and sold them or held them in slavery for their own use, but they took them as ordinary articles of merchandise to every country where they could make a profit on them, and were far more extensively engaged in this commerce than any other nation in the world.

The opinion thus entertained and acted upon in England was naturally impressed upon the colonies they founded on this side of the Atlantic. And, accordingly, a negro of the African race was regarded by them as an article of property, and held, and bought and sold as such, in every one of the thirteen colonies which united in the Declaration of Independence, and afterwards formed the Constitution of the United States. The slaves were more or less numerous in the different colonies, as slave labor was found more or less profitable. But no one seems to have doubted the correctness of the prevailing opinion of the time.

The legislation of the different colonies furnishes positive and indisputable proof of this fact.

The language of the Declaration of Independence is equally conclusive:

It begins by declaring that, "when in the course of human events it becomes necessary for one people to dissolve the political bands which have connected them with another, and to assume among the powers of the earth the separate and equal station to which the laws of nature and nature's God entitle them, a decent respect for the opinions of mankind requires that they should declare the causes which impel them to the separation."

It then proceeds to say: "We hold these truths to be self-evident: that all men are created equal; that they are endowed by their Creator with certain unalienable rights; that among them is life, liberty, and the pursuit of happiness; that to secure these rights, Governments are instituted, deriving their just powers from the consent of the governed."

The general words above quoted would seem to embrace the whole human family, and if they were used in a similar instrument at this day would be so understood. But it is too clear for dispute, that the enslaved African race were not intended to be included, and formed no part of the people who framed and adopted this declaration; for if the language, as understood in that day, would embrace them, the conduct of the distinguished men who framed the Declaration of Independence would have been utterly and flagrantly inconsistent with the principles they asserted; and instead of the sympathy of mankind, to which they so confidently appealed, they would have deserved and received universal rebuke and reprobation.

Yet the men who framed this declaration were great men—high in literary acquirements—high in their sense of honor, and incapable of asserting principles inconsistent with those on which they were acting. They perfectly understood the meaning of the language they used, and how it would be understood by others; and they knew that it would not in any part of the civilized world be supposed to embrace the negro race, which, by common consent, had been excluded from civilized Governments and the family of nations, and doomed to slavery. They spoke and acted according to the then established doctrines and principles, and in the ordinary language of the day, and no one misunderstood them. The unhappy black race were separated from the white by indelible marks, and laws long before established, and were never thought of or spoken of except as property, and when the claims of the owner or the profit of the trader were supposed to need protection.

The state of public opinion had undergone no change when the Constitution was adopted, as is equally evident from its provisions and language.

This brief preamble sets forth by whom it was formed, for what purposes, and for whose benefit and protection. It declares that it is formed by the *people* of the United States; that is to say, by those who were members of the different political communities in the several States; and its great object is declared to be to secure the blessings of liberty to themselves and their posterity. It speaks in general terms of the *people* of the United States, and of *citizens* of the several States, when it is providing for the exercise of the powers granted or the privileges secured to the citizen. It does not define what description of persons are intended to be included under these terms, or who shall be regarded as a citizen and one of the people. It uses them as terms so well understood, that no further description or definition was necessary.

But there are two clauses in the Constitution which point directly and specifically to the negro race as a separate class of persons, and show clearly that they were not regarded as a portion of the people or citizens of the Government then formed.

One of these clauses reserves to each of the thirteen States the right to import slaves until the year 1808, if it thinks proper. And the importation which it thus sanctions was unquestionably of persons of the race of which we are speaking, as the traffic in slaves in the United States had always been confined to them. And by the other provision the States pledge themselves to each other to maintain the right of property of the master, by delivering up to him any slave who may have escaped from his service, and be found within their respective territories. By the first above-mentioned clause, therefore, the right to purchase and hold this property is directly sanctioned and authorized for twenty years by the people who framed the Constitution. And by the second, they pledge themselves to maintain and uphold the right of the master in the manner specified, as long as the Government they then formed should endure. And these two provisions show, conclusively, that neither the description of persons therein referred to, nor their descendants, were embraced in any of the other provisions of the Constitution, for certainly these two clauses were not intended to confer on them or their posterity the blessings of liberty, or any of the personal rights so carefully provided for the citizen.

Upon the whole, therefore, it is the judgment of this court, that it appears by the record before us that the plaintiff in error is not a citizen of Missouri, in the sense in which that word is used in the Constitution; and that the Circuit Court of the United States, for that reason, had no jurisdiction in the case, and could give no judgment in it. Its judgment for the defendant must, consequently, be reversed, and a mandate issued, directing the suit to be dismissed for want of jurisdiction.

2

THE EMANCIPATION PROCLAMATION

■ ■ ■

Abraham Lincoln

EMANCIPATION PROCLAMATION BY THE PRESIDENT OF THE UNITED STATES OF AMERICA: A PROCLAMATION

January 1, 1863

Whereas, on the twenty-second day of September, in the year of our Lord one thousand eight hundred and sixty two, a proclamation was issued by the President of the United States, containing, among other things, the following, to wit:

"That on the first day of January, in the year of our Lord one thousand eight hundred and sixty-three, all persons held as slaves within any State or designated part of a State, the people whereof shall then be in rebellion against the United States, shall be then, thenceforward, and forever free; and the Executive Government of the United States, including the military and naval authority thereof, will recognize and maintain the freedom of such persons, and will do no act or acts to repress such persons, or any of them, in any efforts they may make for their actual freedom.

"That the Executive will, on the first day of January aforesaid, by proclamation, designate the States and parts of States, if any, in which the people thereof, respectively, shall then be in rebellion against the United States; and the fact that any State, or the people thereof, shall on that day be, in good faith, represented in the Congress of the United States by members chosen thereto at elections wherein a majority of the qualified voters of such State shall have participated, shall, in the absence of strong countervailing testimony, be deemed conclusive evidence that such State, and the people thereof, are not then in rebellion against the United States."

Now, therefore I, Abraham Lincoln, President of the United States, by virtue of the power in me vested as Commander-in-Chief, of the Army and Navy of the United States in time of actual armed rebellion against authority and government of the United States, and as a fit and necessary war measure for suppressing said rebellion, do, on this first day of January, in the year of our Lord one thousand eight hundred and sixty-three, and in accordance with my purpose so to do publicly proclaimed for the full period of one hundred days, from the day first above mentioned, order and designate as the States and parts of States wherein the people there of respectively, are this day in rebellion against the United States, the following, to wit:

Arkansas, Texas, Louisiana (except the Parishes of St. Bernard, Plaquemines, Jefferson, St. Johns, St. Charles, St. James[,] Ascension, Assumption, Terrebonne, Lafourche, St. Mary, St. Martin, and Orleans, including the City of New-Orleans), Mississippi, Alabama, Florida, Georgia, South-Carolina, North-Carolina, and Virginia (except the forty-eight counties designated as West Virginia, and also the counties of Berkley, Accomac, Northampton, Elizabeth-City, York, Princess Ann, and Norfolk, including the cities of Norfolk & Portsmouth [)]; and which excepted parts are, for the present, left precisely as if this proclamation were not issued.

And by virtue of the power, and for the purpose aforesaid, I do order and declare that all persons held as slaves within said designated States, and parts of States, are, and henceforward shall be free; and that the Executive Government of the United States, including the military and naval authorities thereof, will recognize and maintain the freedom of said persons.

And I hereby enjoin upon the people so declared to be free to abstain from all violence, unless in necessary self-defence; and I recommend to them that, in all cases when allowed, they labor faithfully for reasonable wages.

And I further declare and make known, that such persons of suitable condition, will be received into the armed service of the United States to garrison forts, positions, stations, and other places, and to man vessels of all sorts in said service.

And upon this act, sincerely believed to be an act of justice, warranted by the Constitution, upon military necessity, I invoke the considerate judgment of mankind, and the gracious favor of Almighty God.

In witness whereof, I have hereunto set my hand and caused the seal of the United States to be affixed.

Done at the City of Washington, this first day of January, in the year of our Lord one thousand eight hundred and sixty-three, and of the Independence of the United States of America the eighty-seventh.

By the President:
Abraham Lincoln

William H. Steward,
Secretary of State

3

UNITED STATES CONSTITUTION

Thirteenth (1865), Fourteenth (1868), and Fifteenth (1870) Amendments

■ ■ ■

Amendment XIII (Ratified December 6, 1865). *Section 1.* Neither slavery nor involuntary servitude, except as a punishment for crime whereof the party shall have been duly convicted, shall exist within the United States, or any place subject to their jurisdiction.

Section 2. Congress shall have power to enforce this article by appropriate legislation.

Amendment XIV (Ratified July 9, 1868). *Section 1.* All persons born or naturalized in the United States, and subject to the jurisdiction thereof, are citizens of the United States and of the state wherein they reside. No State shall make or enforce any law which shall abridge the privileges or immunities of citizens of the United States; nor shall any State deprive any person of life, liberty, or property, without due process of law; nor deny to any person within its jurisdiction the equal protection of the laws.

Section 2. Representatives shall be apportioned among the several states according to their respective numbers, counting the whole number of persons in each state, excluding Indians not taxed. But when the right to vote at any election for the choice of Electors for President and Vice-President of the United States, Representatives in Congress, the executive and judicial officers of a State, or the members of the Legislature thereof, is denied to any of the male inhabitants of such State, being twenty-one years of age, and, citizens of the United States, or in any way abridged, except for participation in rebellion, or other crime, the basis of representation therein shall be reduced in the proportion which the number of such male citizens shall bear to the whole number of male citizens twenty-one years of age in such State.

Section 3. No person shall be a Senator or Representative in Congress, or elector of President and Vice-President, or hold any office, civil or military, under the United States, or under any State, who, having previously taken an oath, as a member of Congress, or as an officer of the United States, or as an executive or judicial officer of any State, to support the Constitution of the United States, shall have engaged in insurrection or rebellion against the same, or given aid or comfort to the enemies thereof. But Congress may by a vote of two-thirds of each House, remove such disability.

Section 4. The validity of the public debt of the United States, authorized by law, including debts incurred for payment of pensions and bounties for services in suppressing insurrection or rebellion, shall not be questioned. But neither the United States nor any State shall assume or pay any debt or obligation incurred in aid of insurrection or rebellion against the United States, or any claim for the loss or emancipation of any slave; but all such debts, obligations, and claims, shall be held illegal and void.

Section 5. The Congress shall have power to enforce, by appropriate legislation, the provisions of this article.

Amendment XV (Ratified February 3, 1870). *Section 1.* The right of citizens of the United States to vote shall not be denied or abridged by the United States or by any State on account of race, color, or previous condition of servitude.

Section 2. The Congress shall have power to enforce this article by appropriate legislation.

4

PLESSY V. FERGUSON, 1896

■ ■ ■

After the collapse of Reconstruction governments, Southern whites began gradu-
ally to legalize the informal practices of segregation which obtained in the South.
One such law was passed by the Louisiana legislature in 1890 and provided that
"all railway companies carrying passengers . . . in this State shall provide separate
but equal accommodations for the white and colored races."

Plessy v. Ferguson *tested the constitutionality of this recent trend in Southern*
legislation. Plessy was a mulatto who, on June 7, 1892, bought a first-class ticket on
the East Louisiana Railway for a trip from New Orleans to Covington, Louisiana,
and sought to be seated in the "white" coach. Upon conviction of a violation of the
1890 statute, he appealed to the Supreme Court of Louisiana, which upheld his
conviction, and finally to the U.S. Supreme Court, which pronounced the Louisiana
law constitutional, on May 18, 1896. The defense of Plessy and attack on the
Louisiana statute was in the hands of four men, the most famous of whom was Albion
W. Tourgée. M. J. Cunningham, attorney general of Louisiana, was assisted by two
other lawyers in defending the statute. The majority opinion of the Court was
delivered by Justice Henry B. Brown. John Marshall Harlan dissented and Justice
David J. Brewer did not participate, making it a 7–1 decision.

In his dissent to this decision Harlan asserted that "Our Constitution is color-
blind, and neither knows nor tolerates classes among citizens. In respect of civil
rights, all citizens are equal before the law." He offered the prophecy that "the
judgment rendered this day will, in time, prove to be quite as pernicious as the
decision made by this tribunal in the Dred Scott case."

The constitutionality of this act is attacked upon the ground that it conflicts
both with the Thirteenth Amendment of the Constitution, abolishing
slavery, and the Fourteenth Amendment, which prohibits certain restrictive
legislation on the part of the States.

1. That it does not conflict with the Thirteenth Amendment, which
abolished slavery and involuntary servitude, except as a punishment for

From *Plessy* v. *Ferguson*, 163 U.S. 537 *United States Reports: Cases Adjudged in the Supreme Court*
(New York, Banks & Brothers, 1896).

crime, is too clear for argument. Slavery implies involuntary servitude—a state of bondage: the ownership of mankind as a chattel, or at least the control of the labor and services of one man for the benefit of another, and the absence of a legal right to the disposal of his own person, property and services. . . .

A statute which implies merely a legal distinction between the white and colored races—a distinction which is founded in the color of the two races, and which must always exist so long as white men are distinguished from the other race by color—has no tendency to destroy the legal equality of the two races, or reestablish a state of involuntary servitude. Indeed, we do not understand that the Thirteenth Amendment is strenuously relied upon by the plaintiff in error in this connection.

2. By the Fourteenth Amendment, all persons born or naturalized in the United States, and subject to the jurisdiction thereof, are made citizens of the United States and of the State wherein they reside; and the States are forbidden from making or enforcing any law which shall abridge the privileges or immunities of citizens of the United States, or shall deprive any person of life, liberty or property without due process of law, or deny to any person within their jurisdiction the equal protection of the laws. . . .

The object of the amendment was undoubtedly to enforce the absolute equality of the two races before the law, but in the nature of things it could not have been intended to abolish distinctions based upon color, or to enforce social, as distinguished from political equality, or a commingling of the two races upon terms unsatisfactory to either. Laws permitting, and even requiring, their separation in places where they are liable to be brought into contact do not necessarily imply the inferiority of either race to the other, and have been generally, if not universally, recognized as within the competency of the state legislatures in the exercise of their police power. The most common instance of this is connected with the establishment of separate schools for white and colored children, which has been held to be a valid exercise of the legislative power even by courts of States where the political rights of the colored race have been longest and most earnestly enforced. . . .

While we think the enforced separation of the races, as applied to the internal commerce of the State, neither abridges the privileges or immunities of the colored man, deprives him of his property without due process of law, nor denies him the equal protection of the laws, within the meaning of the Fourteenth Amendment, we are not prepared to say that the conductor, in assigning passengers to the coaches according to their race, does not act at his peril, or that the provision of the second section of the act, that denies to the passenger compensation in damages for a refusal to receive him into the coach in which he properly belongs, is a valid exercise of the legislative power. Indeed, we understand it to be conceded by the State's attorney, that such part of the act as exempts from liability the railway company and its officers is unconstitutional. The power to assign to a particular coach obviously implies the power to determine to which race the passenger belongs, as well as the power to determine who, under the laws of the particular State, is to be deemed a white, and who a colored person. . . .

It is claimed by the plaintiff in error that, in any mixed community, the reputation of belonging to the dominant race, in this instance the white race, is *property*, in the same sense that a right of action, or of inheritance, is property. Conceding this to be so, for the purposes of this case, we are unable to see how this statute deprives him of, or in any way affects his right to, such property. If he be a white man and assigned to a colored coach, he may have his action for damages against the company for being deprived of his so called property. Upon the other hand, if he be a colored man and be so assigned, he has been deprived of no property, since he is not lawfully entitled to the reputation of being a white man.

In this connection, it is also suggested by the learned counsel for the plaintiff in error that the same argument that will justify the state legislature in requiring railways to provide separate accommodations for the two races will also authorize them to require separate cars to be provided for the people whose hair is of a certain color, or who are aliens, or who belong to certain nationalities, or to enact laws requiring colored people to walk upon one side of the street, and white people upon the other, or requiring white men's houses to be painted white, and colored men's black, or their vehicles or business signs to be of different colors, upon the theory that one side of the street is as good as the other, or that a house or vehicle of one color is as good as one of another color. The reply to all this is that every exercise of the police power must be reasonable, and extend only to such laws as are enacted in good faith for the promotion for the public good, and not for the annoyance or oppression of a particular class. . . .

We consider the underlying fallacy of the plaintiff's argument to consist in the assumption that the enforced separation of the two races stamps the colored race with a badge of inferiority. If this be so, it is not by reason of anything found in the act, but solely because the colored race chooses to put that construction upon it. The argument necessarily assumes that if, as has been more than once the case, and is not unlikely to be so again, the colored race should become the dominant power in the state legislature, and should enact a law in precisely similar terms, it would thereby relegate the white race to an inferior position. We imagine that the white race, at least, would not acquiesce in this assumption. The argument also assumes that social prejudices may be overcome by legislation, and that equal rights cannot be secured to the negro except by an enforced commingling of the two races. We cannot accept this proposition. If the two races are to meet upon terms of social equality, it must be the result of natural affinities, a mutual appreciation of each other's merits and a voluntary consent of individuals.

5

THE "THREE-FIFTHS COMPROMISE"

The U.S. Constitution, Article I, Section 2

∎ ∎ ∎

One of the major debates in the Constitutional Convention hinged on the use of slaves in computing taxes and fixing representation. Southern delegates held that slaves should be computed in determining representation in the House, but that they should not be counted in determining a state's share of the direct tax burden. The northern delegates' point of view was exactly the opposite. A compromise was reached whereby three-fifths of the slaves were to be counted in apportionment of representation and in direct taxes among the states. Thus the South was victorious in obtaining representation for its slaves, even though delegate Luther Martin might rail that the Constitution was an insult to the Deity "who views with equal eye the poor African slave and his American master." The "three-fifths compromise" appears in Article I, Section 2.

Representatives and direct Taxes shall be apportioned among the several States which may be included within this Union, according to their respective Numbers, which shall be determined by adding to the whole Number of free Persons, including those bound to Service for a Term of Years, and excluding Indians not taxed, three fifths of all other Persons.

6

BROWN V. BOARD OF EDUCATION OF TOPEKA, 1954

■ ■ ■

Mr. Chief Justice Warren delivered the opinion of the Court.

These cases come to us from the States of Kansas, South Carolina, Virginia, and Delaware. They are premised on different facts and different local conditions, but a common legal question justifies their consideration together in this consolidated opinion.[1]

In each of the cases, minors of the Negro race, through their legal representatives, seek the aid of the courts in obtaining admission to the public schools of their community on a nonsegregated basis. In each instance, they had been denied admission to schools attended by white children under laws requiring or permitting segregation according to race. This segregation was alleged to deprive the plaintiffs of the equal protection of the laws under the Fourteenth Amendment. In each of the cases other than the Delaware case, a three-judge federal district court denied relief to the plaintiffs on the so-called "separate but equal" doctrine announced by this Court in Plessy v. Ferguson, 163 U.S. 537. Under that doctrine, equality of treatment is accorded when the races are provided substantially equal facilities, even though these facilities be separate. In the Delaware case, the Supreme Court of Delaware adhered to that doctrine, but ordered that the plaintiffs be admitted to the white schools because of their superiority to the Negro schools.

The plaintiffs contend that segregated public schools are not "equal" and cannot be made "equal," and that hence they are deprived of the equal protection of the laws. Because of the obvious importance of the question presented, the Court took jurisdiction.[2] Argument was heard in the 1952 Term, and reargument was heard this Term on certain questions propounded by the Court. . . .[3]

In approaching this problem, we cannot turn the clock back to 1868 when the Amendment was adopted, or even to 1896 when Plessy v. Ferguson was written. We must consider public education in the light of its full development and its present place in American life throughout the Nation. Only in this way can it be determined if segregation in public schools deprives these plaintiffs of the equal protection of the laws.

Today, education is perhaps the most important function of state and local governments. Compulsory school attendance laws and the great expenditures for education both demonstrate our recognition of the importance of education to our democratic society. It is required in the performance of our most basic public responsibilities, even service in the armed forces. It is the very foundation of good citizenship. Today it is a principal instrument in awakening the child to cultural values, in preparing him for later professional training, and in helping him to adjust normally to his environment. In these days, it is doubtful that any child may reasonably be expected to succeed in life if he is denied the opportunity of an education. Such an opportunity, where the state has undertaken to provide it, is a right which must be made available to all on equal terms.

We come then to the question presented: Does segregation of children in public schools solely on the basis of race, even though the physical facilities and other "tangible" factors may be equal, deprive the children of the minority group of equal educational opportunities? We believe that it does.

In Sweatt v. Painter, in finding that a segregated law school for Negroes could not provide them equal educational opportunities, this Court relied in large part on "those qualities which are incapable of objective measurement but which make for greatness in a law school." In McLaurin v. Oklahoma State Regents, the Court, in requiring that a Negro admitted to a white graduate school be treated like all other students, again resorted to intangible considerations: " . . . his ability to study, to engage in discussions and exchange views with other students, and in general, to learn his profession." Such considerations apply with added force to children in grade and high schools. To separate them from others of similar age and qualifications solely because of their race generates a feeling of inferiority as to their status in the community that may affect their hearts and minds in a way unlikely ever to be undone. The effect of this separation on their educational opportunities was well stated by a finding in the Kansas case by a court which nevertheless felt compelled to rule against the Negro plaintiffs:

> Segregation of white and colored children in public schools has a detrimental effect upon the colored children. The impact is greater when it has the sanction of the law; for the policy of separating the races is usually interpreted as denoting the inferiority of the negro group. A sense of inferiority

affects the motivation of a child to learn. Segregation with the sanction of law, therefore, has a tendency to [retard] the educational and mental development of negro children and to deprive them of some of the benefits they receive in a racial[ly] integrated school system.[4]

Whatever may have been the extent of psychological knowledge at the time of Plessy v. Ferguson, this finding is amply supported by modern authority.[5] Any language in Plessy v. Ferguson contrary to this finding is rejected.

We conclude that in the field of public education the doctrine of "separate but equal" has no place. Separate educational facilities are inherently unequal. Therefore, we hold that the plaintiffs and others similarly situated for whom the actions have been brought are, by reason of the segregation complained of, deprived of the equal protection of the laws guaranteed by the Fourteenth Amendment. This disposition makes unnecessary any discussion whether such segregation also violates the Due Process Clause of the Fourteenth Amendment.

Because these are class actions, because of the wide applicability of this decision, and because of the great variety of local conditions, the formulation of decrees in these cases presents problems of considerable complexity. On reargument, the consideration of appropriate relief was necessarily subordinated to the primary question—the constitutionality of segregation in public education. We have now announced that such segregation is a denial of the equal protection of the laws. In order that we may have the full assistance of the parties in formulating decrees, the cases will be restored to the docket, and the parties are requested to present further argument on Questions 4 and 5 previously propounded by the Court for the reargument this Term.[6] The Attorney General of the United States is again invited to participate. The Attorneys General of the states requiring or permitting segregation in public education will also be permitted to appear as amici curiae upon request to do so by September 15, 1954, and submission of the briefs by October 1, 1954.

It is so ordered.

NOTES

1. In the Kansas case, Brown v. Board of Education, the plaintiffs are Negro children of elementary school age residing in Topeka. They brought this action in the United States District Court for the District of Kansas to enjoin enforcement of a Kansas statute which permits, but does not require, cities of more than 15,000 population to maintain separate school facilities for Negro and white students. Kan. Gen. Stat. §72–1724 (1949). Pursuant to that authority, the Topeka Board of Education elected to establish segregated elementary schools. Other public schools in the community, however, are operated on a nonsegregated basis. The three-judge District Court, convened under 28 U.S.C. §§2281 and 2284, found that segregation in public education

has a detrimental effect upon Negro children, but denied relief on the ground that the Negro and white schools were substantially equal with respect to buildings, transportation, curricula, and educational qualifications of teachers. 98 F. Supp. 797. The case is here on direct appeal under 28 U.S.C. §1253. [The Topeka, Kansas, case would be analogous to a northern school case inasmuch as the school segregation that existed in Topeka was not mandated by state law, and some of the system was integrated. It would be eighteen years before the Court would accept another such case for review. Keyes v. School District No. 1, Denver, 445 F.2d 990 (10th Cir. 1971), *cert. granted*, 404 U.S. 1036 (1972)].

In the South Carolina case, Briggs v. Elliot, the plaintiffs are Negro children of both elementary and high school age residing in Clarendon County. They brought this action in the United States District Court for the Eastern District of South Carolina to enjoin enforcement of provisions in the state constitution and statutory code which require the segregation of Negroes and whites in public schools. S.C. Const., Art. XI, §7; S.C. Code §5377 (1942). The three-judge District Court, convened under 28 U.S.C. §§2281 and 2284, denied the requested relief. The court found that the Negro schools were inferior to the white schools and ordered the defendants to begin immediately to equalize the facilities. But the court sustained the validity of the contested provisions and denied the plaintiffs admission to the white schools during the equalization program. 98 F. Supp. 529. This Court vacated the District Court's judgment and remanded the case for the purpose of obtaining the court's views on a report filed by the defendants concerning the progress made in the equalization program. 342 U.S. 350. On remand, the District Court found that substantial equality had been achieved except for buildings and that the defendants were proceeding to rectify this inequality as well. 103 F. Supp. 920. The case is again here on direct appeal under 28 U.S.C. §1253.

In the Virginia case, Davis v. Country School Board, the plaintiffs are Negro children of high school age residing in Prince Edward Country. They brought this action in the United States District Court for the Eastern District of Virginia to enjoin enforcement of provisions in the state constitution and statutory code which require the segregation of Negroes and whites in public schools. Va. Const., §140; Va. Code §22–221 (1950). The three-judge District Court, convened under 28 U.S.C. §§2281 and 2284, denied the requested relief. The court found the Negro school inferior in physical plant, curricula, and transportation, and ordered the defendants forthwith to provide substantially equal curricula and transportation and to "proceed with all reasonable diligence and dispatch to remove" the inequality in physical plant. But, as in the South Carolina case, the court sustained the validity of the contested provisions and denied the plaintiffs admission to the white schools during the equalization program. 103 F. Supp. 337. The case is here on direct appeal under 28 U.S.C. §1253.

In the Delaware case, Gebhart v. Belton, the plaintiffs are Negro children of both elementary and high school age residing in New Castle Country. They brought this action in the Delaware Court of Chancery to enjoin enforcement of provisions in the state constitution and statutory code which require the segregation of Negroes and whites in public schools. Del. Const., Art. X, §2; Del. Rev. Code §2631 (1935). The Chancellor gave judgment for the plaintiffs and ordered their immediate admission to schools previously attended only by white children, on the ground that the Negro schools were inferior with respect to teacher training, pupil-teacher ratio, extracurricular activities, physical plant, and time and distance involved in travel. 87 A.2d 862. The Chancellor also found that segregation itself results in an inferior education for

Negro children (see note 4, infra), but did not rest his decision on that ground. Id., at 865. The Chancellor's decree was affirmed by the Supreme Court of Delaware, which intimated, however, that the defendants might be able to obtain a modification of the decree after equalization of the Negro and white schools had been accomplished. 91 A.2d 137, 152. The defendants, contending only that the Delaware courts had erred in ordering the immediate admission of the Negro plaintiffs to the white schools, applied to this Court for certiorari. The writ was granted, 344 U.S. 891. The plaintiffs, who were successful below, did not submit a cross-petition.

2. 344 U.S. 1, 141, 891.

3. 345 U.S. 972. The Attorney General of the United States participated both Terms as amicus curiae.

4. A similar finding was made in the Delaware case: "I conclude from the testimony that in our Delaware Society, State-imposed segregation in education itself results in the Negro children, as a class, receiving educational opportunities which are substantially inferior to those available to white children otherwise similarly situated." 87 A.2d 862, 865.

5. K. B. Clark, Effect of Prejudice and Discrimination on Personality Development (Midcentury White House Conference on Children and Youth, 1950); Witmer and Kotinsky, Personality in the Making (1952), c. VI; Deutscher and Chein, The Psychological Effects of Enforced Segregation: A Survey of Social Science Opinion, 26 J. Psychol. 259 (1948); Chein, What Are the Psychological Effects of Segregation Under Conditions of Equal Facilities?, 3 Int. J. Opinion and Attitude Res. 229 (1949); Brameld, Educational Costs, in Discrimination and National Welfare (MacIver, ed., 1949), 44–48; Frazier, The Negro in the United States (1949), 674–681. And see generally Myrdal, An American Dilemma (1944).

6. "4. Assuming it is decided that segregation in public schools violates the Fourteenth Amendment

  "(a) would a decree necessarily follow providing that, within the limits set by normal geographic school districting, Negro children should forthwith be admitted to schools of their choice, or

  "(b) may this Court, in the exercise of its equity powers, permit an effective gradual adjustment to be brought about from existing segregated systems to a system not based on color distinctions?

  "5. On the assumption on which questions 4(a) and (b) are based, and assuming further that this Court will exercise its equity powers to the end described in question 4(b),

  "(a) should this Court formulate detailed decrees in these cases;

  "(b) if so, what specific issues should the decrees reach;

  "(c) should this Court appoint a special master to hear evidence with a view to recommending specific terms for such decrees;

  "(d) should this Court remand to the courts of first instance with directions to frame decrees in these cases, and if so what general directions should the decrees of this Court include and what procedures should the courts of first instance follow in arriving at the specific terms of more detailed decrees?"

EVERYDAY DISCRIMINATION

1

THE PROBLEM

Discrimination

■ ■ ■

U.S. Commission on Civil Rights

Making choices is an essential part of everyday life for individuals and organizations. These choices are shaped in part by social structures that set standards and influence conduct in such areas as education, employment, housing, and government. When these choices limit the opportunities available to people because of their race, sex, or national origin, the problem of discrimination arises.

Historically, discrimination against minorities and women was not only accepted but it was also governmentally required. The doctrine of white supremacy used to support the institution of slavery was so much a part of American custom and policy that the Supreme Court in 1857 approvingly concluded that both the North and the South regarded slaves "as beings of an inferior order, and altogether unfit to associate with the white race, either in social or political relations; and so far inferior, that they had no rights which the white man was bound to respect."[1] White supremacy survived the passage of the Civil War amendments to the Constitution and continued to dominate legal and social institutions in the North as well as the South to disadvantage not only blacks,[2] but other racial and ethnic groups as well—American Indians, Alaskan Natives, Asian and Pacific Islanders and Hispanics.[3]

From *Affirmative Action in the 1980s.* U.S. Commission on Civil Rights 65 (January 1981): 9–15.

While minorities were suffering from white supremacy, women were suffering from male supremacy. Mr. Justice Brennan has summed up the legal disabilities imposed on women this way:

> [T]hroughout much of the 19th century the position of women in our society was, in many respects, comparable to that of blacks under the pre–Civil War slave codes. Neither slaves nor women could hold office, serve on juries, or bring suit in their own names, and married women traditionally were denied the legal capacity to hold or convey property or to serve as legal guardians of their own children.[4]

In 1873 a member of the Supreme Court proclaimed, "Man is, or should be, woman's protector and defender. The natural and proper timidity and delicacy which belongs to the female sex evidently unfits it for many of the occupations of civil life."[5] Such romantic paternalism has alternated with fixed notions of male superiority to deny women in law and in practice the most fundamental of rights, including the right to vote, which was not granted until 1920;[6] the Equal Rights Amendment has yet to be ratified.[7]

White and male supremacy are no longer popularly accepted American values. The blatant racial and sexual discrimination that originated in our conveniently forgotten past, however, continues to manifest itself today in a complex interaction of attitudes and actions of individuals, organizations, and the network of social structures that make up our society.

INDIVIDUAL DISCRIMINATION

The most common understanding of discrimination rests at the level of prejudiced individual attitudes and behavior. Although open and intentional prejudice persists, individual discriminatory conduct is often hidden and sometimes unintentional.[8] Some of the following are examples of deliberately discriminatory actions by consciously prejudiced individuals. Some are examples of unintentionally discriminatory actions taken by persons who may not believe themselves to be prejudiced but whose decisions continue to be guided by deeply ingrained discriminatory customs.

- Personnel officers whose stereotyped beliefs about women and minorities justify hiring them for low level and low paying jobs exclusively, regardless of their potential experience or qualifications for higher level jobs.[9]
- Administrators, historically white males, who rely on "word-of-mouth" recruiting among their friends and colleagues, so that only their friends and protégés of the same race and sex learn of potential job openings.[10]
- Employers who hire women for their sexual attractiveness or potential sexual availability rather than their competence, and

employers who engage in sexual harassment of their female employees.[11]

- Teachers who interpret linguistic and cultural differences as indications of low potential or lack of academic interest on the part of minority students.[12]
- Guidance counselors and teachers whose low expectations lead them to steer female and minority students away from "hard" subjects, such as mathematics and science, toward subjects that do not prepare them for higher paying jobs.[13]
- Real estate agents who show fewer homes to minority buyers and steer them to minority or mixed neighborhoods because they believe white residents would oppose the presence of black neighbors.[14]
- Families who assume that property values inevitably decrease when minorities move in and therefore move out of their neighborhoods if minorities do move in.[15]
- Parole boards that assume minority offenders to be more dangerous or more unreliable than white offenders and consequently more frequently deny parole to minorities than to whites convicted of equally serious crimes.[16]

These contemporary examples of discrimination may not be motivated by conscious prejudice. The personnel manager is likely to deny believing that minorities and women can only perform satisfactorily in low level jobs and at the same time allege that other executives and decisionmakers would not consider them for higher level positions. In some cases, the minority or female applicants may not be aware that they have been discriminated against—the personnel manager may inform them that they are deficient in experience while rejecting their applications because of prejudice; the white male administrator who recruits by word-of-mouth from his friends or white male work force excludes minorities and women who never learn of the available positions. The discriminatory results these activities cause may not even be desired. The guidance counselor may honestly believe there are no other realistic alternatives for minority and female students.

Whether conscious or not, open or hidden, desired or undesired, these acts build on and support prejudicial stereotypes, deny their victims opportunities provided to others, and perpetuate discrimination, regardless of intent.

ORGANIZATIONAL DISCRIMINATION

Discrimination, though practiced by individuals, is often reinforced by the well-established rules, policies, and practices of organizations. These actions are often regarded simply as part of the organization's way of doing business and are carried out by individuals as just part of their day's work.

Discrimination at the organizational level takes forms that are similar to those on the individual level. For example:

- Height and weight requirements that are unnecessarily geared to the physical proportions of white males and, therefore, exclude females and some minorities from certain jobs.[17]
- Seniority rules, when applied to jobs historically held only by white males, make more recently hired minorities and females more subject to layoff—the "last hired, first fired" employee—and less eligible for advancement.[18]
- Nepotistic membership policies of some referral unions that exclude those who are not relatives of members who, because of past employment practices, are usually white.[19]
- Restrictive employment leave policies, coupled with prohibitions on part-time work or denials of fringe benefits to part-time workers, that make it difficult for the heads of single parent families, most of whom are women, to get and keep jobs and meet the needs of their families.[20]
- The use of standardized academic tests or criteria, geared to the cultural and educational norms of the middle-class or white males, that are not relevant indicators of successful job performance.[21]
- Preferences shown by many law and medical schools in the admission of children of wealthy and influential alumni, nearly all of whom are white.[22]
- Credit policies of banks and lending institutions that prevent the granting of mortgage monies and loans in minority neighborhoods, or prevent the granting of credit to married women and others who have previously been denied the opportunity to build good credit histories in their own names.[23]

Superficially "color blind" or "gender neutral," these organizational practices have an adverse effect on minorities and women. As with individual actions, these organizational actions favor white males, even when taken with no conscious intent to affect minorities and women adversely, by protecting and promoting the status quo arising from the racism and sexism of the past. If, for example, the jobs now protected by "last hired, first fired" provisions had always been integrated, seniority would not operate to disadvantage minorities and women. If educational systems from kindergarten through college had not historically favored white males, many more minorities and women would hold advanced degrees and thereby be included among those involved in deciding what academic tests should test for. If minorities had lived in the same neighborhoods as whites, there would be no minority neighborhoods to which mortgage money could be denied on the basis of their being minority neighborhoods.

In addition, these barriers to minorities and women too often do not fulfill legitimate needs of the organization, or these needs can be met through other means that adequately maintain the organization without discriminating. Instead of excluding all women on the assumption that they are too weak or should be protected from strenuous work, the organization can implement a reasonable test that measures the strength actually needed to perform the job or, where possible, develop ways of doing the work that require less physical effort. Admissions to academic and professional schools can be decided not only on the basis of grades, standardized test scores, and the prestige of the high school or college from which the applicant graduated, but also on the basis of community service, work experience, and letters of recommendation. Lending institutions can look at the individual and his or her financial ability rather than the neighborhood or marital status of the prospective borrower.

Some practices that disadvantage minorities and women are readily accepted aspects of everyday behavior. Consider the "old boy" network in business and education built on years of friendship and social contact among white males, or the exchanges of information and corporate strategies by business acquaintances in racially or sexually exclusive country clubs and locker rooms paid for by the employer.[24] These actions, all of which have a discriminatory impact on minorities and women, are not necessarily acts of conscious prejudice. Because such actions are so often considered part of the "normal" way of doing things, people have difficulty recognizing that they are discriminating and therefore resist abandoning these practices despite the clearly discriminatory results. Consequently, many decision-makers have difficulty considering, much less accepting, nondiscriminatory alternatives that may work just as well or better to advance legitimate organizational interests but without systematically disadvantaging minorities and women.

This is not to suggest that all such discriminatory organizational actions are spurious or arbitrary. Many may serve the actual needs of the organization. Physical size or strength at times may be a legitimate job requirement; sick leave and insurance policies must be reasonably restricted; educational qualifications are needed for many jobs; lending institutions cannot lend to people who cannot reasonably demonstrate an ability to repay loans. Unless carefully examined and then modified or eliminated, however, these apparently neutral rules, policies, and practices will continue to perpetuate age-old discriminatory patterns into the structure of today's society.

Whatever the motivation behind such organizational acts, a process is occurring, the common denominator of which is unequal results on a very large scale. When unequal outcomes are repeated over time and in numerous societal and geographical areas, it is a clear signal that a discriminatory process is at work.

Such discrimination is not a static, one-time phenomenon that has a clearly limited effect. Discrimination can feed on discrimination in self-perpetuating cycles.[25]

- The employer who recruits job applicants by word-of-mouth within a predominantly white male work force reduces the chances of receiving applications from minorities and females for open positions. Since they do not apply, they are not hired. Since they are not hired, they are not present when new jobs become available. Since they are not aware of new jobs, they cannot recruit other minority or female applicants. Because there are no minority or female employees to recruit others, the employer is left to recruit on his own from among his predominantly white and male work force.[26]
- The teacher who expects poor academic performance from minority and female students may not become greatly concerned when their grades are low. The acceptance of their low grades removes incentives to improve. Without incentives to improve, their grades remain low. Their low grades reduce their expectations, and the teacher has no basis for expecting more of them.[27]
- The realtor who assumes that white home owners do not want minority neighbors "steers" minorities to minority neighborhoods. Those steered to minority neighborhoods tend to live in minority neighborhoods. White neighborhoods then remain white, and realtors tend to assume that whites do not want minority neighbors.[28]
- Elected officials appoint voting registrars who impose linguistic, geographic, and other barriers to minority voter registration. Lack of minority registration leads to low voting rates. Lower minority voting rates lead to the election of fewer minorities. Fewer elected minorities leads to the appointment of voting registrars who maintain the same barriers.[29]

STRUCTURAL DISCRIMINATION

Such self-sustaining discriminatory processes occur not only within the fields of employment, education, housing, and government but also between these structural areas. There is a classic cycle of structural discrimination that reproduces itself. Discrimination in education denies the credentials to get good jobs. Discrimination in employment denies the economic resources to buy good housing. Discrimination in housing confines minorities to school districts providing inferior education, closing the cycle in a classic form.[30]

With regard to white women, the cycle is not as tightly closed. To the extent they are raised in families headed by white males, and are married to or live with white males, white women will enjoy the advantages in housing and other areas that such relationships to white men can confer. White women lacking the sponsorship of white men, however, will be unable to avoid gender-based discrimination in housing, education, and employment. White women can thus be the victims of discrimination produced by social structures that is comparable in form to that experienced by minorities.

This perspective is not intended to imply that either the dynamics of discrimination or its nature and degree are identical for women and minorities. But when a woman of any background seeks to compete with men of any group, she finds herself the victim of a discriminatory process. Regarding the similarities and differences between the discrimination experienced by women and minorities, one author has aptly stated:

> [W]hen two groups exist in a situation of inequality, it may be self-defeating to become embroiled in a quarrel over which is more unequal or the victim of greater oppression. The more salient question is how a condition of inequality for both is maintained and perpetuated—through what means is it reinforced?[31]

The following are additional examples of the interaction between social structures that affect minorities and women:

- The absence of minorities and women from executive, writing, directing, news reporting, and acting positions in television contributes to unfavorable stereotyping on the screen, which in turn reinforces existing stereotypes among the public and creates psychological roadblocks to progress in employment, education, and housing.[32]
- Living in inner-city high crime areas in disproportionate numbers, minorities, particularly minority youth, are more likely to be arrested and are more likely to go to jail than whites accused of similar offenses, and their arrest and conviction records are then often used as bars to employment.[33]
- Because of past discrimination against minorities and women, female and minority-headed businesses are often small and relatively new. Further disadvantaged by contemporary credit and lending practices, they are more likely than white male–owned businesses to remain small and be less able to employ full-time specialists in applying for government contracts. Because they cannot monitor the availability of government contracts, they do not receive such contracts. Because they cannot demonstrate success with government contracts, contracting officers tend to favor other firms that have more experience with government contracts.[34]

Discriminatory actions by individuals and organizations are not only pervasive, occurring in every sector of society, but also cumulative with effects limited neither to the time nor the particular structural area in which they occur. This process of discrimination, therefore, extends across generations, across organizations, and across social structures in self-reinforcing cycles, passing the disadvantages incurred by one generation in one area to future generations in many related areas.[35]

These interrelated components of the discriminatory process share one basic result: the persistent gaps seen in the status of women and minorities relative to that of white males. These unequal results themselves have real consequences. The employer who wishes to hire more minorities and women may be bewildered by charges of racism and sexism when confronted by what appears to be a genuine shortage of qualified minority and female applicants. The guidance counselor who sees one promising minority student after another drop out of school or give up in despair may be resentful of allegations of racism when there is little he or she alone can do for the student. The banker who denies a loan to a female single parent may wish to do differently, but believes that prudent fiscal judgment requires taking into account her lack of financial history and inability to prove that she is a good credit risk. These and other decisionmakers see the results of a discriminatory process repeated over and over again, and those results provide a basis for rationalizing their own actions, which then feed into that same process.

When seen outside the context of the interlocking and intertwined effects of discrimination, complaints that many women and minorities are absent from the ranks of qualified job applicants, academically inferior and unmotivated, poor credit risks, and so forth, may appear to be justified. Decisionmakers like those described above are reacting to real social problems stemming from the process of discrimination. But many too easily fall prey to stereotyping and consequently disregard those minorities and women who have the necessary skills or qualifications. And they erroneously "blame the victims" of discrimination,[36] instead of examining the past and present context in which their own actions are taken and the multiple consequences of these actions on the lives of minorities and women.

THE PROCESS OF DISCRIMINATION

Although discrimination is maintained through individual actions, neither individual prejudices nor random chance can fully explain the persistent national patterns of inequality and underrepresentation. Nor can these patterns be blamed on the persons who are at the bottom of our economic, political, and social order. Overt racism and sexism as embodied in popular notions of white and male supremacy have been widely repudiated, but our history of discrimination based on race, sex, and national origin has not been readily put aside. Past discrimination continues to have present effects. The task today is to identify those effects and the forms and dynamics of the discrimination that produced them.

Discrimination against minorities and women must now be viewed as an interlocking process involving the attitudes and actions of individuals and the organizations and social structures that guide individual behavior. That process, started by past events, now routinely bestows privileges, favors, and advantages on white males and imposes disadvantages and penalties on minorities and women. This process is also self-perpetuating. Many normal, seemingly neutral, operations of our society create stereotyped expectations that justify unequal results; unequal results in one area foster inequalities in opportunity and accomplishment in others; the lack of opportunity and accomplishment confirms the original prejudices or engenders new ones that fuel the normal operations generating unequal results.

As we have shown, the process of discrimination involves many aspects of our society. No single factor sufficiently explains it, and no single means will suffice to eliminate it. Such elements of our society as our history of *de jure* discrimination, deeply ingrained prejudices,[37] inequities based on economic and social class,[38] and the structure and function of all our economic, social, and political institutions[39] must be continually examined in order to understand their part in shaping today's decisions that will either maintain or counter the current process of discrimination.

It may be difficult to identify precisely all aspects of the discriminatory process and assign those parts their appropriate importance. But understanding discrimination starts with an awareness that such a process exists and that to avoid perpetuating it, we must carefully assess the context and consequences of our everyday actions. . . .

NOTES

1. Dred Scott v. Sandford, 60 U.S. (19 How.) 393, 408 (1857).
2. For a concise summary of this history, see U.S. Commission on Civil Rights, *Twenty Years After Brown*, pp. 4–29 (1975); *Freedom to the Free: 1863, Century of Emancipation* (1963).
3. The discriminatory conditions experienced by these minority groups have been documented in the following publications by the U.S. Commission on Civil Rights: *The Navajo Nation: An American Colony* (1975); *The Southwest Indian Report* (1973); *The Forgotten Minority: Asian Americans in New York City* (State Advisory Committee Report 1977); *Success of Asian Americans: Fact or Fiction?* (1980); *Stranger in One's Land* (1970); *Toward Quality Education for Mexican Americans* (1974); *Puerto Ricans in the Continental United States: An Uncertain Future* (1976).
4. Frontiero v. Richardson, 411 U.S. 677, 684–86 (1973), citing L. Kanowitz, *Women and the Law: The Unfinished Revolution*, pp. 5–6 (1970), and G. Myrdal, *An American Dilemma* 1073 (20th Anniversary Ed., 1962). Justice Brennan wrote the opinion of the

Court, joined by Justices Douglas, White, and Marshall. Justice Stewart concurred in the judgment. Justice Powell, joined by Chief Justice Burger and Justice Blackmun, wrote a separate concurring opinion. Justice Rehnquist dissented. See also H. M. Hacker, "Women as a Minority Group," *Social Forces*, vol. 30 (1951), pp. 60–69; W. Chafe, *Women and Equality: Changing Patterns in American Culture* (New York: Oxford University Press, 1977).

5. Bradwell v. State, 83 U.S. (16 Wall) 130, 141 (1873) (Bradley, J., concurring), quoted in *Frontiero, supra* note 4.

6. U.S. Const. amend. XIX.

7. See U.S. Commission on Civil Rights, *Statement on the Equal Rights Amendment* (December 1978).

8. See, e.g., R. K. Merton, "Discrimination and the American Creed," in R. K. Merton, *Sociological Ambivalence and Other Essays* (New York: The Free Press, 1976), pp. 189–216. In this essay on racism, published for the first time more than 30 years ago, Merton presented a typology which introduced the notion that discriminatory actions are not always directly related to individual attitudes of prejudice. Merton's typology consisted of the following: Type I—the unprejudiced nondiscriminator; Type II—the unprejudiced discriminator; Type III—the prejudiced nondiscriminator; Type IV—the prejudiced discriminator. In the present context, Type II is crucial in its observation that discrimination is often practiced by persons who are not themselves prejudiced, but who respond to, or do not oppose, the actions of those who discriminate because of prejudiced attitudes (Type IV). See also D. C. Reitzes, "Prejudice and Discrimination: A Study in Contradictions," in *Racial and Ethnic Relations*, ed. H. M. Hughes (Boston: Allyn and Bacon, 1970), pp. 56–65.

9. See R. M. Kanter and B. A. Stein, "Making a Life at the Bottom," in *Life in Organizations, Workplaces as People Experience Them*, ed. Kanter and Stein (New York: Basic Books, 1976), pp. 176–90; also L. K. Howe, "Retail Sales Worker," ibid., pp. 248–51; also R. M. Kanter, *Men and Women of the Corporation* (New York: Basic Books, 1977).

10. See M. S. Granovetter, *Getting a Job: A Study of Contract and Careers* (Cambridge: Harvard University Press, 1974), pp. 6–11; also A. W. Blumrosen, *Black Employment and the Law* (New Brunswick, N.J.: Rutgers University Press, 1971), p. 232.

11. See U.S. Equal Employment Opportunity Commission, "Guidelines on Discrimination Because of Sex," 29 C.F.R. §1604.4 (1979); L. Farley, *Sexual Shakedown: The Sexual Harassment of Women on the Job* (New York: McGraw-Hill, 1978), pp. 92–96, 176–79; C. A. Mackinnon, *Sexual Harassment of Working Women* (New Haven: Yale University Press, 1979), pp. 25–55.

12. See R. Rosenthal and L. F. Jacobson, "Teacher Expectations for the Disadvantaged," *Scientific American*, 1968 (b) 218, 219–23; also D. Bar Tal, "Interactions of Teachers and Pupils," in *New Approaches to Social Problems*, ed. I. H. Frieze, D. Bar Tal, and J. S. Carrol (San Francisco: Jossey Bass, 1979), pp. 337–58; also U.S. Commission on Civil Rights, *Teachers and Students, Report V: Mexican American Education Study. Differences in Teacher Interaction with Mexican American and Anglo Students* (1973), pp. 22–23.

13. Ibid.

14. U.S. Department of Housing and Urban Development, "Measuring Racial Discrimination in American Housing Markets: The Housing Market Practices Survey" (1979); D. M. Pearce, "Gatekeepers and Home Seekers: Institutional Patterns in Racial Steering," *Social Problems*, vol. 26 (1979), pp. 325–42; "Benign Steering and Benign Quotas: The Validity of Race Conscious Government Policies to Promote Residential Integration," 93 *Harv. L. Rev.* 938, 944 (1980).

15. See M. N. Danielson, *The Politics of Exclusion* (New York: Columbia University Press, 1976), pp. 11–12; U.S. Commission on Civil Rights, *Equal Opportunity in Suburbia* (1974).

16. See L. L. Knowles and K. Prewitt, eds., *Institutional Racism in America* (Englewood Cliffs, N.J.: Prentice Hall, 1969), pp. 58–77, and E. D. Wright, *The Politics of Punishment* (New York: Harper and Row, 1973). Also, S. V. Brown, "Race and Parole Hearing Outcomes," in *Discrimination in Organizations*, ed. R. Alvarez and K. G. Lutterman (San Francisco: Jossey Bass, 1979), pp. 355–74.

17. Height and weight minimums that disproportionately exclude women without a showing of legitimate job requirement constitute unlawful sex discrimination. See Dothard v. Rawlinson, 433 U.S. 321 (1977); Bowe v. Colgate Palmolive Co., 416 F.2d 711 (7th Cir. 1969). Minimum height requirements used in screening applicants for employment have also been held to be unlawful where such a requirement excludes a significantly higher percentage of Hispanics than other national origin groups in the labor market and no job relatedness is shown. See Smith v. City of East Cleveland, 520 F.2d 492 (6th Cir. 1975).

18. U.S. Commission on Civil Rights, *Last Hired, First Fired* (1976); Tangren v. Wackenhut Servs., Inc., 480 F. Supp. 539 (D. Nev. 1979).

19. U.S. Commission on Civil Rights, *The Challenge Ahead, Equal Opportunity in Referral Unions* (1977), pp. 84–89.

20. A. Pifer, "Women Working: Toward a New Society," pp. 13–34, and D. Pearce, "Women, Work and Welfare: The Feminization of Poverty," pp. 103–24, both in K. A. Fernstein, ed., *Working Women and Families* (Beverly Hills: Sage Publications, 1979). Disproportionate numbers of single-parent families are minorities.

21. See Griggs v. Duke Power Company, 401 U.S. 424 (1971); U.S. Commission on Civil Rights, *Toward Equal Educational Opportunity: Affirmative Admissions Programs at Law and Medical Schools* (1978), pp. 10–12; I. Berg, *Education and Jobs: The Great Training Robbery* (Boston: Beacon Press, 1971), pp. 58–60.

22. See U.S. Commission on Civil Rights, *Toward Equal Educational Opportunity: Affirmative Admissions Programs at Law and Medical Schools* (1978), pp. 14–15.

23. See U.S. Commission on Civil Rights, *Mortgage Money: Who Gets It? A Case Study in Mortgage Lending Discrimination in Hartford, Conn.* (1974); J. Feagin and C. B. Feagin, *Discrimination American Style, Institutional Racism and Sexism* (Englewood Cliffs, N.J.: Prentice Hall, 1976), pp. 78–79.

24. See *Club Membership Practices by Financial Institutions: Hearing before the Comm. on Banking, Housing and Urban Affairs, United States Senate*, 96th Cong., 1st Sess. (1979). The Office of Federal Contract Compliance Programs of the Department of Labor has proposed a rule that would make the payment or reimbursement of membership fees in a private club that accepts or rejects persons on the basis of race, color, sex, religion, or national origin a prohibited discriminatory practice. 45 Fed. Reg. 4954 (1980) (to be codified in 41 C.F.R. §60–1.11).

25. See U.S. Commission on Civil Rights, *For All the People . . . By All the People* (1969), pp. 122–23.

26. See note 10.

27. See note 12.

28. See notes 14 and 15.

29. See Statement of Arthur S. Flemming, Chairman, U.S. Commission on Civil Rights, before the Subcommittee on Constitutional Rights of the Committee on the Judiciary of the U.S. Senate on S.407, S.903, and S.1279, Apr. 9, 1975, pp. 15–18, based on U.S. Commission on Civil Rights, *The Voting Rights Act: Ten Years After* (January 1975).

30. See, e.g., U.S. Commission on Civil Rights, *Equal Opportunity in Suburbia* (1974).

31. Chafe, *Women and Equality*, p. 78.

32. U.S. Commission on Civil Rights, *Window Dressing on the Set* (1977).

33. See note 16; Gregory v. Litton Systems, Inc., 472 F.2d 631 (9th Cir. 1972); Green v. Mo.-Pac. R.R., 523 F.2d 1290 (8th Cir. 1975).

34. See U.S. Commission on Civil Rights, *Minorities and Women as Government Contractors*, pp. 20, 27, 125 (1975).

35. See, e.g., A. Downs, *Racism in America and How to Combat It* (U.S. Commission on Civil Rights, 1970); "The Web of Urban Racism," in *Institutional Racism in America*, ed. Knowles and Prewitt (Englewood Cliffs, N.J.: Prentice Hall, 1969), pp. 134–76. Other factors in addition to race, sex, and national origin may contribute to these interlocking institutional patterns. In *Equal Opportunity in Suburbia* (1974), this Commission documented what it termed "the cycle of urban poverty" that confines minorities in central cities with declining tax bases, soaring educational and other public needs, and dwindling employment opportunities, surrounded by largely white, affluent suburbs. This cycle of poverty, however, started with and is fueled by discrimination against minorities. See also W. Taylor, *Hanging Together, Equality in an Urban Nation* (New York: Simon & Schuster, 1971).

36. The "self-fulfilling prophecy" is a well-known phenomenon. "Blaming the victim" occurs when responses to discrimination are treated as though they were the causes rather than the results of discrimination. See Chafe, *Women and Equality*, (pp. 76–78; W. Ryan, *Blaming the Victim* (New York: Pantheon Books, 1971).

37. See, e.g., J. E. Simpson and J. M. Yinger, *Racial and Cultural Minorities* (New York: Harper and Row, 1965), pp. 49–79; J. M. Jones, *Prejudice and Racism* (Reading, Mass.: Addison Wesley, 1972), pp. 60–111; M. M. Tumin, "Who Is Against Desegregation?" in *Racial and Ethnic Relations*, ed. H. Hughes (Boston: Allyn and Bacon, 1970), pp. 76–85; D. M. Wellman, *Portraits of White Racism* (Cambridge: Cambridge University Press, 1977).

38. See, e.g., D. C. Cox, *Caste, Class and Race: A Study in Social Dynamics* (Garden City, N.Y.: Doubleday, 1948); W. J. Wilson, *Power, Racism and Privilege* (New York: Macmillan, 1973).

39. H. Hacker, "Women as a Minority Group," *Social Forces*, vol. 30 (1951), pp. 60–69; J. Feagin and C. B. Feagin, *Discrimination American Style*; Chafe, *Women and Equality*; J. Feagin, "Indirect Institutionalized Discrimination," *American Politics Quarterly*, vol. 5 (1977), pp. 177–200; M. A. Chesler, "Contemporary Sociological Theories of Racism," in *Towards the Elimination of Racism*, ed. P. Katz (New York: Pergamon Press, 1976); P. Van den Berghe, *Race and Racism: A Comparative Perspective* (New York: Wiley, 1967); S. Carmichael and C. Hamilton, *Black Power* (New York: Random House, 1967); Knowles and Prewitt, *Institutional Racism in America*; Downs, *Racism in America and How to Combat It*.

2

ON THE NATURE
OF CONTEMPORARY
PREJUDICE

The Causes, Consequences, and
Challenges of Aversive Racism

■ ■ ■

John F. Dovidio
Samuel L. Gaertner

Race relations in the United States are better now than ever before. Or are they? On one hand, the dramatic positive impact of the civil rights legislation of the 1960s is undeniable. Before this legislation, in many parts of the country, it was customary for whites to limit the freedom of blacks (e.g., limiting blacks to the back of buses), to demand deference from blacks (e.g., requiring blacks to give up their seats to whites on buses), and to restrict residential, educational, and employment opportunities for blacks. Under the civil rights legislation, discrimination and segregation became no longer simply immoral, but also illegal. As a consequence, black Americans currently have greater access to political, social, and economic opportunities than ever before in our history. On the other hand, there are new signals of

From "On the Nature of Contemporary Prejudice," in *Confronting Racism: The Problem and the Responses*. Jennifer L. Eberhardt and Susan T. Fiske, eds. Copyright © 1998. Reprinted by permission of Sage Publications. Inc.

AUTHOR'S NOTE: The work presented in this chapter was supported by NIMH Grant MH-48721. We express our appreciation to Jennifer Eberhardt and Susan Fiske for their thoughtful comments on earlier versions of the chapter. Correspondence regarding this chapter should be addressed to John F. Dovidio. Department of Psychology. Colgate University, Hamilton, NY 13346.

deteriorating race relations. Symptoms of racial tension, which emerged in the 1960s, are reappearing. As the 1990s began, riots in Miami, Tampa, New Jersey, Washington, D.C., and Los Angeles reflected large-scale and violent racial unrest. Over the past 5 years, over 300 colleges have reported significant racial incidents and protests. In the first 6 months of 1996, there were 27 suspicious fires, presumed to be racially motivated arson, across the South (Morganthau, 1996). The majority of blacks in the United States today have a profound distrust of the police and the legal system, and about a third are overtly distrustful of whites in general (Anderson, 1996). Middle-class blacks are very worried about the future for blacks and for the nation (Hochschild, 1995). . . .

RACIAL ATTITUDES IN THE UNITED STATES

Across time, the attitudes of whites toward minorities, in general, and blacks, in particular, are becoming less negative and more accepting. Negative stereotypes are declining. For example, in 1933, 75% of white respondents described blacks as lazy; in 1993, that figure declined to just 5% (Dovidio, Brigham, Johnson, & Gaertner, 1996). White America is also becoming more accepting of black leaders. In 1958, the majority of whites reported that they would not be willing to vote for a well-qualified black presidential candidate; in 1994, over 90% said that they would (Davis & Smith, 1994). In addition, the increase in tolerance of white Americans extends beyond blacks to other racial and ethnic minority groups as well (American National Election Survey, 1995).

Despite these encouraging trends in the intergroup attitudes of white Americans, there are still reasons for concern. One reason is that, across a variety of surveys and polls, 10%–15% of the white population still expresses the old-fashioned, overt form of bigotry. These respondents consistently describe blacks as innately less intelligent than whites, say that they will not vote for a well-qualified presidential candidate simply because of that person's race, and oppose programs designed to ensure full integration and equal opportunity. Another reason for concern is that a substantial portion of the white population expressed merely racial tolerance but not true openness to enthusiasm for full racial equality. A third reason for concern, which is our current focus, is that there is also evidence that many of the people who are part of the 85%–90% of the white population who say and probably believe that they are not prejudiced may nonetheless be practicing a modern, subtle form of bias.

We believe that the existence of this subtle form of bias helps to account, in part, for the persistence of racism in our society. In a 1988 nationwide poll (Gelman, 1988), 25% of the black respondents said that they believed that white people "want to hold" black people down; 44% of all respondents said that they believed that society is holding blacks down. In a more recent poll, 32% of blacks reported that discrimination is the primary obstacle to achieving equality in the United States (Anderson, 1996). Furthermore, despite dramatic improvements in whites' expressed racial attitudes over time, racial disparities persist in the United States. Gaps between black and white Americans in physiological areas (e.g., infant mortality, life expectancy) and economic areas (e.g., employment, income, poverty) have continued to exist; and, in many cases, these disparities have actually increased over the past 30 years (Hacker, 1995).

AVERSIVE RACISM

Over the past 20 years, we, with a number of our colleagues, have investigated a prevalent type of modern racial bias, called *aversive racism* (Dovidio & Gaertner, 1991; Gaertner & Dovidio, 1986; Gaertner et al., 1997; Kovel 1970). In contrast to "old fashioned" racism, which is expressed directly and openly, aversive racism represents a subtle, often unintentional, form of bias that characterizes many white Americans who possess strong egalitarian values and who believe that they are non-prejudiced. Aversive racists also possess negative racial feelings and beliefs of which they are unaware or that they try to dissociate from their nonprejudiced self-images. The negative feelings that aversive racists have for blacks do not reflect open hostility or hate. Instead, their reactions involve discomfort, uneasiness, disgust, and sometimes fear. That is, they find blacks "aversive," while, at the same time, they find any suggestion that they might be prejudiced aversive as well. . . .

The aversive racism framework helps to identify when discrimination against blacks and other minority groups will or will not occur. The ambivalence involving both positive and negative feelings that aversive racists experience creates psychological tension that leads to behavioral instability. Thus, unlike the consistent and overt pattern of discrimination that might be expected from old-fashioned racists, aversive racists sometimes discriminate (manifesting their negative feelings) and sometimes do not (reflecting their egalitarian beliefs). Our research has provided a framework for understanding this pattern of discrimination.

Because aversive racists consciously recognize and endorse egalitarian values – they truly want to be fair and just people – they will not discriminate in situations in which they recognize that discrimination would be obvious to others and themselves. Specifically, we propose that when people are presented with a situation in which the appropriate response is clear, in which right and wrong is clearly defined, aversive racists will not discriminate against blacks. Wrongdoing, which would directly threaten their nonprejudiced self-image, would be too obvious. Because aversive racists still possess negative feelings, however, these negative feelings will eventually be expressed, but they will be expressed in subtle, indirect, and rationalizable ways. For instance, discrimination will occur when appropriate (and thus inappropriate) behavior is not obvious or when an aversive racist can justify or rationalize a negative response on the basis of some factor other than race. Under these circumstances, aversive racists may discriminate, but in a way that insulates them from ever having to believe that their behavior was racially motivated.

Aversive racists may be identified by a constellation of characteristic responses to racial issues and interracial situations. First, aversive racists, in contrast to old-fashioned racists, endorse fair and just treatment of all groups. Second, despite their conscious good intentions, aversive racists unconsciously harbor negative feelings towards blacks, and thus try to avoid interracial interaction. Third, when interracial interaction is unavoidable, aversive racists experience anxiety and discomfort, and consequently they try to disengage from the interaction as quickly as possible. As we noted earlier, the negative feelings that aversive racists have toward blacks involve discomfort rather than hostility or hatred. Fourth, because part of the discomfort that aversive racists experience is due to a concern about acting inappropriately and appearing prejudiced, aversive racists strictly adhere to established rules and codes of behavior in the interracial situations that they cannot avoid. They also frequently assert that they are color-blind; if they do not see race, then it follows that no one can accuse them of being racist. Finally, their negative feelings will get expressed, but in subtle, rationalizable ways that may ultimately disadvantage minorities or unfairly benefit the majority group. . . .

SUBTLE, RATIONALIZABLE BIAS

Because of the ambivalence that characterizes their attitudes toward blacks, aversive racists' interracial behavior is more variable than that of old-fashioned racists. In this section, we illustrate support for our framework concerning how aversive racism operates. We first examine spontaneous reactions to blacks, and then we compare the effects of aversive racism to old-fashioned racism in more deliberative decisions.

Reactions in an Emergency

In one of the early tests of our framework (Gaertner & Dovidio, 1977), we tried to take advantage of a naturally occurring event and model it in the laboratory. The event was the Kitty Genovese incident, which occurred in New York City in 1964. Kitty Genovese was returning home one evening.

As she entered the parking lot of her building, a man drove up, jumped out of his car, and began to stab her. She screamed. Lights went on in her building. The brutal attack continued for 45 minutes, but no one intervened or even called the police. After he was sure she was dead, the assailant calmly got into his car and drove away.

We know so much about this case because when the police arrived a short time later, they found that there were 38 witnesses who watched the event from beginning to end. How could it happen that none of these people helped, either directly or indirectly? One explanation that psychologists have developed concerns the bystander's sense of responsibility (Darley & Latané, 1968). When a person is the only witness to an emergency, that bystander bears 100% of the responsibility for helping and 100% of the guilt and blame for not helping. The appropriate behavior in this situation, helping, is clearly defined. If, however, a person witnesses an emergency but believes that somebody else is around who can help or will help, then that bystander's personal responsibility is less clearly defined. Under these circumstances, the bystander could rationalize not helping by coming to believe that someone else will intervene. Of course, if everyone believes that someone else will help, no one will intervene. That presumably was what occurred in the Kitty Genovese incident. . . .

We predicted that when people were the only witness to the emergency, aversive racists would not discriminate against the black victim. In this situation, appropriate behavior is clearly defined. Not to help a black victim could easily be interpreted, by oneself or others, as racial bias. We predicted, however, that because aversive racists have unconscious negative feeling toward blacks, they would discriminate when they could justify their behavior on the basis of some factor other than race – such as the belief that someone else would help the victim. Specifically, we expected that blacks would be helped less than whites only when white bystanders believed that there were other witnesses to the emergency.

The results of the study supported our predictions. When white bystanders were the only witnesses to the emergency, they helped very frequently and equivalently for black and white victims. In fact, they even helped black victims somewhat more often than white victims (95% vs. 83%, respectively). There was no evidence of old-fashioned racism. In contrast, when white bystanders were given an opportunity to rationalize not helping on the basis of the belief that one of the two other witnesses could intervene, they were less likely to help, particularly when the victim was African American. When participants believed that there were two other bystanders, they helped the black victim half as often as they helped the white victim (38% vs. 75%). If this situation were real, the white victim would have died 25% of the time; the black victim would have died 62% of the time. As we hypothesized, the nature of the situation determines whether discrimination does or does not occur. This principal applies in more considered decision-making situations, often with equally severe consequences for blacks. Next we consider the roles of subtle and overt biases in juridic decisions.

Is Justice Color Blind?

Traditionally, blacks and whites have not been treated equally under the law. Across time and locations in the United States, blacks have been more likely to be convicted of crimes, and, if convicted, sentenced to longer terms for similar crimes, particularly if the victim is white (see Johnson, 1985; Nickerson, Mayo & Smith, 1986). In addition, blacks are more likely to receive the death penalty (General Accounting Office, 1990). Baldus, Woodsworth, and Pulaski (1990) examined over 2,000 murder cases in Georgia and found that a death sentence was returned in 22% of the cases in which black defendants were convicted of killing a white victim, but in only 8% of the cases in which the defendant and the victim were white. Although differences in judicial outcomes have tended to persist, paralleling the trends in overt expressions of bias, racial disparities in sentencing are declining over time, and the effects are becoming more indirect (Nickerson et al., 1986).

Although the influence of old-fashioned racism in juridic judgments may be waning, aversive racism appears to have a continuing, subtle influence. That is, bias does occur, but mainly when it can be justified on the basis of some other – ostensibly nonrace-related – basis. For example, in a laboratory simulation study, Johnson, Whitestone, Jackson, and Gatto (1995) examined the effect of the introduction of inadmissible evidence, which was damaging to a defendant's case, on whites' judgments of a black or white defendant's guilt. No differences in judgments of guilt occurred as a function of defendant race when all the evidence presented was admissible. Consistent with the aversive racism framework, however, the presentation of inadmissible evidence increased judgment of guilt when the defendant was black, but not when the defendant was white. Furthermore, suggesting the unconscious or unintentional nature of the bias, participants' self-reports indicated that they believed that the inadmissible evidence had less effect on their decisions when the defendant was black than when the defendant was white, Johnson et al. (1995) conclude that these results "are clearly consistent with the modern racism perspective, which suggests that discriminatory behavior will occur only when it can be justified on nonracial ground" (p. 896). . . .

Recently, we have also found laboratory evidence of direct and indirect patterns of racial discrimination among whites scoring high and low in self-reported prejudice in recommending the death penalty (Dovidio, Smith, Donnella, & Gaertner, 1997). High-and low-prejudice-scoring white college students read a summary of facts associated with a case in which the offender was found guilty of murdering a white police officer following a robbery. The race of the defendant, black or white, was systematically varied.

After reading the case and before making a decision, participants viewed five other jurors on videotape individually presenting their decisions to vote for the death penalty in the case. In half of the conditions, all of these jurors were white; in the other half of the conditions, the second juror presenting a decision was a black male student. The main measure of interest was how strongly the participant subsequently recommended the death penalty....

As predicted, high-prejudice-scoring whites showed a straightforward pattern of bias against black defendants: Regardless of the other jurors, they gave generally stronger recommendations for the death penalty for black defendants than for white defendants. Low-prejudice-scoring white participants, in contrast, demonstrated a more complicated pattern of responses. Their strongest recommendations for the death penalty occurred when the defendant was black and a black juror advocated the death penalty. Under these conditions, in which their response could not necessarily be interpreted as racial bias, low-prejudice whites were as discriminating as high-prejudice whites. When, however, all of the jurors were white and thus their responses could potentially be attributed to racial antipathy, low-prejudice scoring whites exhibited the strongest recommendations *against* the death penalty when the defendant was black. Consistent with the aversive racism framework, aversive racism is expressed subtly, indirectly, and in rationalizable ways. Although the bias may be subtle. The consequences may still be of great consequence, potentially influencing life or death decisions. In the next section of the chapter, we examine how aversive racism is reflected in the conscious and nonconscious manifestations of attitudes and beliefs about blacks.

BIAS IN WORDS AND THOUGHT

We believe that aversive racism has relevance to the way that whites express their racial attitudes. When we ask people directly, as in surveys, "Do you support integration?" "Would you vote for a well-qualified black presidential candidate?" the socially acceptable answer is very obvious to people. To say anything but "yes" could be interpreted by other people and oneself as racial bias. As a consequence, we believe that many of the nationwide surveys over represent the racially tolerant response.

Blacks are Not Worse Than Whites, But . . .

To examine how aversive racism relates to questionnaire or survey responses, we conducted an experiment in which we asked people on 1 to 7 scales (e.g., good to bad) to describe blacks and whites (Dovidio & Gaertner, 1991). These white respondents demonstrated no racial difference in their evaluative ratings. A biased response (e.g., "bad") is obvious, and respondents consistently rated both blacks and whites on the positive ends of the scales. When, however, we varied the instrument slightly by placing positive and negative characteristics in separate scales (e.g., bad, from *not at all* to *extremely*), we found that bias does exist, but in a subtle form. Although the ratings of blacks and whites on the negative scales showed no racial bias, the ratings on the positive scales did reveal a significant difference. Whereas blacks were not rated more negatively than whites, whites were evaluated more positively than blacks. Apparently, aversive racists resist believing that blacks are bad or even that they are worse than whites, remarks easily interpreted as racial bias. Subtle bias is displayed, however, in respondents' willingness to believe that whites are better than blacks. Again, this is not the old-fashioned, overt type of bias associated with the belief about black inferiority. Instead, it is a modern, subtle form of bias that reflects a belief about white superiority. . . .

The identification of aversive racists who say that they are not prejudiced, but who have these unconscious negative associations, is important to our understanding of contemporary racism. For example, in a recent study (Dovidio, 1995), unconscious racial attitudes were used to predict and understand the development of conflict in interracial communication. The study examined the possibility that whites and blacks attend to different aspects in social interactions. A black person and a white person first interacted and then completed questionnaires that asked how friendly they felt they behaved during the conversation and how friendly their partner acted. In general, whites' perceptions of their own friendliness correlated with their self-reported prejudice scores: Those who said they were less prejudiced said that they behaved in a more friendly manner with the black partner in the subsequent interaction. These perceptions were apparently guided by the conscious attitudes of whites; at this level, they seemed to be behaving consistently. In contrast, the perceptions of black partners about the friendliness of these same white participants were more strongly associated with the whites' response latency measure of bias (see also Fazio et al., 1995). That is, in assessing how friendly the white person was, blacks may have been considering not only the overt, consciously controlled behavior of the partner, but also concentrating on the nonconscious behaviors (such as eye contact, nonverbal expression of discomfort) that whites were unable to monitor or control. These findings suggest that although whites may intend to convey a positive and friendly attitude to their black partner and believe that they have succeeded, in the same interaction the black partner may be attuned to the negative or mixed messages inadvertently sent by whites (see Devine. Evett. & Vasquez-Suson, 1996). These unintended messages can produce a very different, potentially conflicting, perspective that can contribute to racial tension and distrust. . . .

What does all this have to do with behavior? If the decisions that people make are biased in systematic ways, they will have biased outcomes for minorities and nonminorities. Attitudes translate into the way people think, and the way people think translates into the way people behave, sometimes as discrimination. In the next section we consider a relatively unique prediction of the aversive racism framework – that more bias is expressed toward higher status blacks. Regarding discrimination, it may also be that it is not that blacks are worse than whites, but that whites are better than blacks.

HIGHER STATUS, GREATER BIAS

We investigated the relationship between status and bias in the context of an important decision for our participants (Kline & Dovidio, 1982). We recruited participants to help us make admissions decisions for their university. Because students believed that their decisions would have direct implications for them, partially determining who would attend their college, we hypothesized that bias against blacks would be expressed, but in subtle ways (Dovidio & Mullen, 1992). Participants were presented with information about an applicant whose qualifications were systematically varied. Some participants evaluated a poorly qualified applicant, some rated a moderately qualified candidate, and others judged a highly qualified applicant. In addition, the race of the applicant was manipulated by a photograph attached to the file. The central question concerned how this picture would affect students' admission decisions.

Discrimination against the black applicant occurred, but, as expected, it did not occur equally in all conditions. Participants rated the poorly qualified black and white applicants equally low. They showed some bias when they evaluated the moderately qualified white applicant slightly higher than the comparable black candidate. Discrimination against the black applicant was most apparent, however, when the applicants were highly qualified. Consistent with our other studies, there was no bias on the "low" end; Poorly qualified black applicants were not rated worse than poorly qualified white applicants. As in the previous studies, discrimination occurred at the "high" end. Although white participants evaluated the highly qualified black applicant very positively, they judged the highly qualified white applicant, with exactly the same credentials, as even better. . . .

[In another study,] white male undergraduates were introduced to a black or white male confederate who was presented as either the participant's supervisor or subordinate. In addition, the confederate was described as being higher or lower than the participant in an intellectual ability that was relevant to the dyad's task. The dependent measure was an incidental helping task, picking up pencils that the confederate "accidentally" knocked to the floor.

Overall, participants helped black partners more than white partners. The effect of race, however, was moderated by status and ability. Specifically, the results indicated that relative status, rather than relative ability was the primary determinant of helping behavior toward blacks. Black supervisors were helped less than black subordinates, whereas white supervisors were helped somewhat more than white subordinates. Relative ability, in contrast, did not affect prosocial behavior toward blacks. In general, high- and low-ability blacks were helped more frequently than were low-ability white partners. Thus, ability, not status, was instrumental in determining helping toward whites, but status, not ability, was the major factor influencing prosocial behavior toward blacks. Given that there were no significant effects involving participants' self-reports of prejudice, it seems that even well-intentioned whites will respond negatively to a black supervisor compared to a black subordinate, regardless of apparent qualifications.

How could people in this experiment rationalize not responding positively to competent blacks? Subjects' post experimental evaluations of their partners revealed that their behaviors may have been mediated by perceptions of relative intelligence (competence). Although participants' ratings indicated that they accepted high-ability white partners as being somewhat more intelligent than themselves, the ratings revealed that participants described even high-ability black partners as significantly less intelligent than themselves. Blacks may be regarded as intelligent, but not as intelligent as whites. It therefore appears that although whites may accept that a black person is intelligent on an absolute dimension, white participants are reluctant to believe that a black person is higher or equal in intelligence compared to themselves. . . .

Across organizations as diverse as the armed forces, federal government, and Fortune 1000 companies, we find data consistent with our prediction of greater racial disparities at higher-statues levels. In addition, these patterns persist over the past decade. Within the Navy, for example, blacks represent 13% of the force, but only 5% of the officers and 1.5% of the admirals. Furthermore, these differences cannot be accounted for by vastly different backgrounds. A recent study by the General Accounting Office (1995) found that, over a 5-year period, the success rate of blacks who qualified for promotions was systematically below the rate of whites across all of the military services. Consistent with our model, the disparities in promotion rates tended to increase with higher ranks for enlisted personnel and up through ranks equivalent to Major for officers (Hudson, 1995). We have also examined patterns of disparities for various segments of federal employees and found evidence consistent with our model: Blacks are generally less well represented in higher grades (e.g., GS 16–18) than in lower grades. Furthermore, these disparities have remained relatively stable across time. A study of industry provides independent evidence of the "glass ceiling effect" for minorities (Federal Glass Ceiling Commission, 1995). Representations of minorities consistently decline with higher occupational status. Fewer than 1% of the top-level executives in

Fortune 1000 industrial and Fortune 500 service firms are black. Independent research reveals that not only are blacks promoted less frequently than whites, they have less access to training and development opportunities (Greenhaus, Parasuraman, & Wormley, 1990). . . .

CONCLUSION

In summary, despite apparent consistent improvements in expressed racial attitudes over time, aversive racism continues to exert a subtle but pervasive influence on the lives of black Americans. This bias is expressed in indirect and rationalizable ways that restrict opportunities for blacks while insulating aversive racists from ever having to confront their prejudices. It is an elusive phenomenon: When aversive racists monitor their interracial behaviors, they do not discriminate. In fact, they may respond even more favorably to blacks than to whites as a way of reaffirming their nonprejudiced self-images. When they are not conscious of their actions, however, bias is subtly expressed, usually in ways that can be justified on the basis of some factor other than race. Although the expression of bias may be more subtle, the consequences of aversive racism are comparable to that of old-fashioned racism – the restriction of opportunity to other groups and support for a system that is believed to be fair in principle but that perpetuates the social and economic advantages of the majority group over minority groups.

Even though these negative feelings, which aversive racists harbor toward blacks, may be unconscious and rooted in normal processes, this does not imply that this bias is either excusable or immutable. Having the potential for bias is not an acceptable excuse for being biased. In addition, what is unconscious can, with increased awareness and commitment, be made conscious and replaced by truly egalitarian beliefs and feelings. Racial bias, whether subtle or blatant, is inconsistent with standards of fairness and justice. The unfulfilled potential of human lives as well as the expense of violence and other crimes that arise out of disaffection with the system and personal despair, make racism costly to both blacks and whites. Thus, recognition of this subtle racism may be an essential step in moving a significant segment of white America from feeling nonprejudiced to actually being nonprejudiced.

REFERENCES

American National Election Survey Studies 1948–1994. (1995). Ann Arbor, MI: Interuniversity Consortium for Political and Social Research.

Anderson, J. (1996, April 29/May 6). Black and blue, *New Yorker*, 62–64.

Baldus. D., Woodsworth, G., & Pulaski, C. (1990). *Equal justice and the death penalty: A legal and empirical analysis.* Boston: Northeastern University Press.

Darley, J. M., & Latané, B. (1968), Bystander intervention in emergencies: Diffusion of responsibility. *Journal of Personality and Social Psychology, 8,* 377–383.

Davis, J. A., & Smith, T.W. (1994). *General social surveys, 1972–1994: Cumulative codebook.* Chicago: National Opinion Research Center.

Devine, P. G., Evett, S. R., & Vasquez-Suson, K. A. (1996). Exploring the interpersonal dynamics of intergroup contact. In R. M. Sorrentino & E. T. Higgins (Eds.), *Handbook of motivation and cognition: The interpersonal context* (Vol. 3, pp. 423–464). New York: Guilford.

Dovidio, J. F. (1995, August), *Stereotypes, prejudice, and discrimination: Automatic and controlled processes.* Paper presented at the annual meeting of the American Psychological Society, New York.

Dovidio, J. F., Brigham, J. C., Johnson, B. T., & Gaertner, S. L. (1996). Stereotyping, prejudice, and discrimination: Another look. In N. Macrae, C. Stangor, & M. Hewstonc (Eds.), *Foundations of stereotypes and stereotyping* (pp. 276–319), New York: Guilford.

Dovidio, J. F., & Gaertner, S. L. (1991). Changes in the nature and expression of racial prejudice. In H. Knopke, J. Norrell, & R. Rogers (Eds.), *Opening doors: An appraisal of race relations in contemporary America* (pp. 201–241). Tuscaloosa: University of Alabama Press.

Dovidio, J. F., & Mullen, B. (1992). *Race, physical handicap, and response amplification.* Unpublished manuscript, Colgate University, Hamilton, NY.

Dovidio, J. F., Smith, J. K., Donnella, A. G., & Gaertner, S. L. (1997). Racial attitudes and the death penalty. *Journal of Applied Social Psychology, 27,* 1468–1487.

Fazio, R. H., Jackson, J. R., Dunton, B. C., & Williams, C. J. (1995). Variability in automatic activation as an unobtrusive measure of racial attitudes: A bona fide pipeline? *Journal of Personality and Social Psychology, 69,* 1013–1027.

Federal Glass Ceiling Commission. (1995). *Good for business: Making full use of the nation's human capital.* Washington, DC: Government Printing Office.

Gaertner, S. L., & Dovidio, J. F. (1977). The subtlety of white racism, arousal, and helping behavior. *Journal of Personality and Social Psychology, 35,* 691–707.

Gaertner, S. L., & Dovidio, J. F., (1986). The aversive form of racism. In J. F. Dovidio & S. L. Gaertner (Eds.), *Prejudice, discrimination, and racism* (pp. 61–89). Orlando, FL: Academic Press.

Gaertner, S. L., Dovidio, J. F., Banker, B., Rust, M., Nier, J., Mottola, G., & Ward, C. (1997). Does racism necessarily mean antiblackness? Aversive racism and pro-whiteness. In M. Fine, L. Powell, L. Weis, & M. Wong (Eds.), *Off white* (pp. 167–168). London: Routledge.

Gelman, D. (1988, March 7). Black and white in America. *Newsweek, 111,* 24–43.

General Accounting Office, (1990). *Death penalty sentencing: Research indicates patterns of racial disparities* (GAO/GGD-90-57). Washington DC: Author.

General Accounting Office, (1995). *Military equal opportunity: Certain trends in racial and gender data may warrant further analysis* (GAO/NSIAD Report No. 96-17). Washington DC: Author.

Greenhaus, J. H., Parasuraman, S., & Wormley, W. M. (1990). Effects of race on organizational experiences, job performance evaluations, and career outcomes. *Academy of Management Journal, 33*(1), 64–86.

Hacker, A. (1995). *Two nations: Black and white, separate, hostile, unequal.* New York: Ballantine.

Hochschild, J. L. (1995). *Facing up to the American dream: Race, class, and the soul of the nation.* Princeton, NJ: Princeton University Press.

Hudson, N. (1995, December 4). Study: Races differ in promotion rates. *Navy Times,* p. 8.

Johnson, J. D., Whitestone, E., Jackson, L. E., & Gatto, L. (1995). Justice is still not color-blind: Differential racial effects of exposure to inadmissible evidence. *Personality and Social Psychology Bulletin, 21*, 893–898.

Johnson, S. L. (1985). Black innocence and the white jury. *Michigan Law Review, 83*, 1611–1708.

Klinc, B. B., Dovidio, J. F. (1982, April). *Effects of race, sex, and qualifications on predictions of a college applicant's performance.* Paper presented at the annual meeting of the Eastern Psychological Association, Baltimore. MD.

Kovel, J. (1970). *White racism: A psychohistory.* New York: Pantheon.

Morganthau, T. (1996, June 24). Fires in the night. *Newsweek, 127*, 28–38.

Nickerson, S., Mayo, C., & Smith, A. (1986). Racism in the courtroom. In J. F. Dovidio & S. L. Gaertner (Eds.), *Prejudice, discrimination, and racism* (pp. 255–278). Orlando, FL: Academic Press.

3

COMBATTING INTENTIONAL BIGOTRY AND INADVERTENTLY RACIST ACTS

■ ■ ■

Fletcher A. Blanchard

What you say about racial discrimination matters: Your vocal opinions affect what others think and say. A series of experiments that I and my students and colleagues conducted demonstrate that racial prejudice is much more malleable than many researchers, policy makers, and educational leaders believe. In the wake of the verdict in the case of four

From *The Chronicle of Higher Education* (May 13, 1992). Reprinted by permission of the author.

Los Angeles policemen accused of beating Rodney King and the violence that followed it, the search for ways to lessen the devastating consequences of racism in America has intensified. If we understand that simply over-hearing others condemn or condone racial harassment dramatically affects people's reactions to racism, we may be able to help find solutions to tensions and bigotry—both on campuses and in the larger society.

In the experiments we conducted, the first two of which are described in an article in *Psychological Science* (March, 1991), we briefly interviewed students as they walked between classes. In some portions of the experi-ment, the interviewer also stopped a second person, ostensibly another student but in reality a member of the research team, who offered her programmed opinions first. After hearing someone else condemn racism, college students expressed anti-racist sentiments much more strongly than those who heard someone express equivocal views. However, students who first heard someone condone racism then voiced views that reflected strong acceptance of racism.

The large differences that we observed appeared both when research participants spoke their views publicly and when we measured their opinions more anonymously by asking them to complete a questionaire and return it to the researcher in a sealed envelope. The elasticity of privately held views regarding racism appears to reveal a lack of knowl-edge about the nature of racism and uncertainty about how institutions and individuals might appropriately respond to expressions of racism.

I suspect that one of the reasons that opinions about racism are so easily influenced derives from the high level of racial segregation that still characterizes contemporary American society. Indeed, one wonders just how much people's ignorance about racism and lack of contact with other races contributed to the verdict in the King case. Although a recent survey by People for the American Way indicated that many young Americans say they have a friend of another race, most still know little about other racial and ethnic groups.

Public-opinion polls over the last several decades portray largely favor-able trends regarding whites' attitudes toward African Americans, but those attitudes and opinions derive from little direct experience. Few white college students have grown up in integrated neighborhoods, attended schools with integrated classrooms, or observed their parents interact in a friendly manner with people of color.

Even fewer of the white students entering college today have had the chance to learn from black teachers, work for black employers, or partici-pate in voluntary activities and organizations where the adult leaders, coaches, or advisers were black. America's campuses constitute the first multiracial social setting encountered by many young people.

As a result, few of the many whites who have reached an honest com-mitment to egalitarian values have had the opportunity to acquire the full range of interpersonal skills, sensibilities, and knowledge that might allow them to fulfill that commitment. Few, for example, have vicariously experienced the pain felt by a friend who has suffered racial harassment. Few have discovered the ways that everyday language may communicate disrespect for a particular group. Thus the elasticity of reactions to racism appears to reflect the uncertainty that the inexperienced, but well intentioned, bring to their first interracial setting.

Although there has been an alarming increase in racial harassment on campuses and in society at large, the results of opinion polls showing a trend toward more egalitarian racial attitudes among Americans make it difficult to attribute the racist attacks to any increase in racial prejudice among the many. Instead, much of the harassment should be understood to represent open hostility expressed by the strongly prejudiced few. Efforts to reduce racial harassment and enhance tolerance must acknowledge the many who are naive, inexperienced, and often well intentioned, on the one hand, and the few who are genuinely mean spirited, on the other. Strategies that are effective for one group may be less so for the other.

Many colleges and universities are responding to the current wave of racist attacks by creating policies that attempt to define and regulate racial harassment. However, none of the new codes of conduct acknowledges the important differences between the intentional behavior of the committed bigot and the inadvertent behavior of the profoundly inexperienced.

The least controversial variety of code, aimed squarely at the committed bigot, borrows language from federal and state civil-rights statutes and anti-harassment regulations. By narrowly framing the boundaries of unacceptable behavior, this approach provides a basis for punishing some behavior of the mean-spirited few.

Unfortunately, the federal and state regulations that define and bar racial harassment are neither as articulate nor as encompassing as those governing sexual harassment. Until state and federal rules barring racial harassment recognize how seemingly less-odious behaviors can accumulate to produce an atmosphere of intimidation, codes of conduct that rely on them will restrain only the most flagrant forms of attack.

A second approach to regulating racial harassment, aimed squarely at the well-intentioned many, consists of urging civility. Instead of defining the limits of impropriety and barring behavior that oversteps those bounds, civility codes encourage general tolerance and acceptance, leaving it to administrators and adjudicating bodies to apply the rules to particular instances of unacceptable behavior.

These policies rarely offer the specific guidance required by those inexperienced with racism. Little controversy follows the promulgation of such codes. Rather, it more often attends their application to particular instances of objectionable behavior—behavior that falls somewhere between civility and clearly illegal harassment.

A third variety of code attempts to define and forbid a much broader range of impropriety than currently is addressed by federal and most state regulations. The prohibitions often embrace both the intentional behavior of the committed bigot and the careless behavior of those inexperienced with interracial contacts. Although both classes of behavior cause harm, the new policies fail to acknowledge the different motivations of the actors, and thus the need for different remedies.

Most important, it is difficult to write such codes so that they enhance freedom from discrimination but also preserve the broader freedom of speech. These are the policies that have generated the most interesting debate and the most belligerent contention. Some of the opposition has been raised by those who would safeguard the use of racial epithets under the guise of defending First Amendment freedoms. Other opponents have resorted to ridicule and name calling, perhaps to avoid acknowledging the prevalence of racial harassment and bias in our society. The principled portions of the discussion undoubtedly have enhanced both our understanding of the boundaries of free speech and of the causes of contemporary racism.

The principal virtue of all of the codes I have outlined is that each encourages consensus regarding proper conduct. It is this consensus—the shared sense of what is right and what is wrong—that steers social behavior much more effectively than mere rules and regulations. Articulate codes that are widely distributed and discussed can contribute to a consensus that rejects bigotry.

No one of these three strategies for regulating racism is complete, however. The most effective policies must combine elements of all three approaches. The best policies must proscribe illegal racial harassment, thereby providing punishment for the mean-spirited few, as well as prescribe expectations for tolerance and respect, thereby providing guidance for the inexperienced many. The best policies also will step beyond the boundaries of current statutes, recognizing, for example, that racial epithets directed at individuals are intolerable in humane society.

By linking codes of conduct with statements of academic mission, effective policies signal a strong institutional commitment to the protection of civil rights. Yet no code of conduct, no matter how comprehensively it is framed, can create by itself the sort of accepting and respectful communities that we need.

Other forms of attention to the discriminatory consequences of behavior are required if colleges and universities are to become the sort of educational settings where everyone can thrive. The fact that people of color often find themselves numerically underrepresented in academic institutions exaggerates the discomfort and pain that arise out of insensitive acts.

Consider an organization in which 10 percent of the people are black and 90 percent are white. Imagine a department of that organization in which 10 people work, nine of whom are white and one of whom is black. Imagine further that all nine of the whites perceive themselves to be unprejudiced and have adopted a genuine commitment to egalitarian values. If each of those well-intentioned whites makes only one insensitive "mistake" a month, the one black target of the nine naive whites would experience, on average, some hurtful and isolating behavior every third day.

The well-intentioned white is aware of only one insensitive event over the last month—if, in fact, he or she has been informed of that lapse. But the personal experience of the person of color reflects a high rate of discriminatory behavior. Reduce the proportion of African Americans or add an intentional racist and the resulting setting becomes even more intolerable. This imbalance in perceptions of the rate of discrimination and insensitivity exacerbates the potential for misunderstanding.

Until college students bring with them from high school more extensive experience with interracial interaction, massive commitments to remedial education and training will be required to reduce the rate of unintentional harm caused by these "interracially incompetent" people. I suspect that the best educational techniques will take advantage of the positive motivation to "do the right thing" that characterizes most entering students—by emphasizing vivid and concrete examples of the hurtful and harmful behavior of the naive. One-shot "workshops" presented during first-year orientation probably will not be sufficient. Rather, activities or programs that foster the early formation of strong interracial friendships will contribute most to intergroup understanding.

Until inexperienced students master the behaviors that reflect their egalitarian commitments, we must maintain havens for minority students that protect them from intentional harassment and naive disrespect, including cultural centers and organizations for particular minority groups. By also introducing programs and activities that foster formation of strong interracial friendships, it may be possible, over time, to reduce the need for safe havens.

It is solid interracial friendships that help insulate targets of harassment from the most devastating consequences of anonymous racist attacks and exaggerated feelings of isolation. Such friendships also will provide the basis for the sort of interracial learning that has been absent from the experience of many who enter college today.

The research that I described at the outset suggests that each of us can affect others' concern for eliminating racism by taking strong public stands condemning bigotry on campuses. Just as anti-smoking attitudes among non-smokers eventually led to regulations banning smoking in public places, a broad consensus that eschews bigotry surely can reduce the display of intentional bias and inadvertent discriminatory behavior on campuses.

Our research suggests that no one need wait for administrators to take the lead. Each of us can influence each other by criticizing the willful bigotry of the mean-spirited few and gently guiding the well-intentioned efforts of the inexperienced many.

4

WHITE PRIVILEGE: UNPACKING THE INVISIBLE KNAPSACK

■ ■ ■

Peggy McIntosh

"I was taught to see racism only in individual acts of meanness, not in invisible systems conferring dominance on my group"

Through work to bring materials from women's studies into the rest of the curriculum, I have often noticed men's unwillingness to grant that they are overprivileged, even though they may grant that women are disadvantaged. They may say they will work to improve women's status, in the society, the university, or the curriculum, but they can't or won't support the idea of lessening men's. Denials that amount to taboos surround the subject of advantages that men gain from women's disadvantages. These denials protect male privilege from being fully acknowledged, lessened, or ended.

Thinking through unacknowledged male privilege as a phenomenon, I realized that, since hierarchies in our society are interlocking, there was most likely a phenomenon of while privilege that was similarly denied and protected. As a white person, I realized I had been taught about racism as something that puts others at a disadvantage, but had been taught not to see one of its corollary aspects, white privilege, which puts me at an advantage.

I think whites are carefully taught not to recognize white privilege, as males are taught not to recognize male privilege. So I have begun in an untutored way to ask what it is like to have white privilege. I have come to see white privilege as an invisible package of unearned assets that I can count on cashing in each day, but about which I was "meant" to remain oblivious. White privilege is like an invisible weightless knapsack of special provisions, maps, passports, codebooks, visas, clothes, tools, and blank checks.

Describing white privilege makes one newly accountable. As we in women's studies work to reveal male privilege and ask men to give up some of their power, so one who writes about having white privilege must ask, "Having described it, what will I do to lessen or end it?"

After I realized the extent to which men work from a base of unacknowledged privilege, I understood that much of their oppressiveness was unconscious. Then I remembered the frequent charges from women of color that white women whom they encounter are oppressive. I began to understand why we are justly seen as oppressive, even when we don't see ourselves that way. I began to count the ways in which I enjoy unearned skin privilege and have been conditioned into oblivion about its existence.

My schooling gave me no training in seeing myself as an oppressor, as an unfairly advantaged person, or as a participant in a damaged culture. I was taught to see myself as an individual whose moral state depended on her individual moral will. My schooling followed the pattern my colleague Elizabeth Minnich has pointed out: whites are taught to think of their lives as morally neutral, normative, and average, and also ideal, so that when we work to benefit others, this is seen as work that will allow "them" to be more like "us."

DAILY EFFECTS OF WHITE PRIVILEGE

I decided to try to work on myself at least by identifying some of the daily effects of white privilege in my life. I have chosen those conditions that I think in my case attach somewhat more to skin-color privilege than to class, religion, ethnic status, or geographic location, though of course all these other factors are intricately intertwined. As far as I can tell, my African American coworkers, friends, and acquaintances with whom I come into daily or frequent contact in this particular time, place and line of work cannot count on most of these conditions.

1. I can if I wish arrange to be in the company of people of my race most of the time.
2. I can avoid spending time with people whom I was trained to mistrust and who have learned to mistrust my kind or me.
3. If I should need to move, I can be pretty sure of renting or purchasing housing in an area which I can afford and in which I would want to live.
4. I can be pretty sure that my neighbors in such a location will be neutral or pleasant to me.
5. I can go shopping alone most of the time, pretty well assured that I will not be followed or harassed.
6. I can turn on the television or open to the front page of the paper and see people of my race widely represented.
7. When I am told about our national heritage or about "civilization," I am shown that people of my color made it what it is.
8. I can be sure that my children will be given curricular materials that testify to the existence of their race.
9. If I want to, I can be pretty sure of finding a publisher for this piece on white privilege.
10. I can be pretty sure of having my voice heard in a group in which I am the only member of my race.
11. I can be casual about whether or not to listen to another person's voice in a group in which s/he is the only member of his/her race.
12. I can go into a music shop and count on finding the music of my race represented, into a supermarket and find the staple foods which fit with my cultural traditions, into a hairdresser's shop and find someone who can cut my hair.
13. Whether I use checks, credit cards or cash, I can count on my skin color not to work against the appearance of financial reliability.
14. I can arrange to protect my children most of the time from people who might not like them.
15. I do not have to educate my children to be aware of systemic racism for their own daily physical protection.
16. I can be pretty sure that my children's teachers and employers will tolerate them if they fit school and workplace norms; my chief worries about them do not concern others' attitudes toward their race.
17. I can talk with my mouth full and not have people put this down to my color.
18. I can swear, or dress in second hand clothes, or not answer letters, without having people attribute these choices to the bad morals, the poverty or the illiteracy of my race.

19. I can speak in public to a powerful male group without putting my race on trial.

20. I can do well in a challenging situation without being called a credit to my race.

21. I am never asked to speak for all the people of my racial group.

22. I can remain oblivious of the language and customs of persons of color who constitute the world's majority without feeling in my culture any penalty for such oblivion.

23. I can criticize our government and talk about how much I fear its policies and behavior without being seen as a cultural outsider.

24. I can be pretty sure that if I ask to talk to the "person in charge," I will be facing a person of my race.

25. If a traffic cop pulls me over or if the IRS audits my tax return, I can be sure I haven't been singled out because of my race.

26. I can easily buy posters, post-cards, picture books, greeting cards, dolls, toys and children's magazines featuring people of my race.

27. I can go home from most meetings of organizations I belong to feeling somewhat tied in, rather than isolated, out-of-place, out-numbered, unheard, held at a distance or feared.

28. I can be pretty sure that an argument with a colleague of another race is more likely to jeopardize her/his chances for advancement than to jeopardize mine.

29. I can be pretty sure that if I argue for the promotion of a person of another race, or a program centering on race, this is not likely to cost me heavily within my present setting, even if my colleagues disagree with me.

30. If I declare there is a racial issue at hand, or there isn't a racial issue at hand, my race will lend me more credibility for either position than a person of color will have.

31. I can choose to ignore developments in minority writing and minority activist programs, or disparage them, or learn from them, but in any case, I can find ways to be more or less protected from negative consequences of any of these choices.

32. My culture gives me little fear about ignoring the perspectives and powers of people of other races.

33. I am not made acutely aware that my shape, bearing or body odor will be taken as a reflection on my race.

34. I can worry about racism without being seen as self-interested or self-seeking.

35. I can take a job with an affirmative action employer without having my co-workers on the job suspect that I got it because of my race.

36. If my day, week or year is going badly, I need not ask of each negative episode or situation whether it had racial overtones.

37. I can be pretty sure of finding people who would be willing to talk with me and advise me about my next steps, professionally.

38. I can think over many options, social, political, imaginative or professional, without asking whether a person of my race would be accepted or allowed to do what I want to do.

39. I can be late to a meeting without having the lateness reflect on my race.

40. I can choose public accommodation without fearing that people of my race cannot get in or will be mistreated in the places I have chosen.

41. I can be sure that if I need legal or medical help, my race will not work against me.

42. I can arrange my activities so that I will never have to experience feelings of rejection owing to my race.

43. If I have low credibility as a leader I can be sure that my race is not the problem.

44. I can easily find academic courses and institutions which give attention only to people of my race.

45. I can expect figurative language and imagery in all of the arts to testify to experiences of my race.

46. I can choose blemish cover or bandages in "flesh" color and have them more or less match my skin.

47. I can travel alone or with my spouse without expecting embarrassment or hostility in those who deal with us.

48. I have no difficulty finding neighborhoods where people approve of our household.

49. My children are given texts and classes which implicitly support our kind of family unit and do not turn them against my choice of domestic partnership.

50. I will feel welcomed and "normal" in the usual walks of public life, institutional and social.

ELUSIVE AND FUGITIVE

I repeatedly forgot each of the realizations on this list until I wrote it down. For me white privilege has turned out to be an elusive and fugitive subject. The pressure to avoid it is great, for in facing it I must give up the myth of meritocracy. If these things are true, this is not such a free country; one's life is not what one makes it; many doors open for certain people through no virtues of their own.

In unpacking this invisible knapsack of white privilege, I have listed conditions of daily experience that I once took for granted. Nor did I think of any of these perquisites as bad for the holder. I now think that we need a more finely differentiated taxonomy of privilege, for some of these varieties are only what one would want for everyone in a just society, and others give license to be ignorant, oblivious, arrogant, and destructive.

I see a pattern running through the matrix of white privilege, a pattern of assumptions that were passed on to me as a white person. There was one main piece of cultural turf; it was my own turn, and I was among those who could control the turf. My skin color was an asset for any move I was educated to want to make. I could think of myself as belonging in major ways and of making social systems work for me. I could freely disparage, fear, neglect, or be oblivious to anything outside of the dominant cultural forms. Being of the main culture, I could also criticize it fairly freely.

In proportion as my racial group was being made confident, comfortable, and oblivious, other groups were likely being made unconfident, uncomfortable, and alienated. Whiteness protected me from many kinds of hostility, distress, and violence, which I was being subtly trained to visit, in turn, upon people of color.

For this reason, the word "privilege" now seems to me misleading. We usually think of privilege as being a favored state, whether earned or conferred by birth or luck. Yet some of the conditions I have described here work systematically to over empower certain groups. Such privilege simply confers dominance because of one's race or sex.

EARNED STRENGTH, UNEARNED POWER

I want, then, to distinguish between earned strength and unearned power conferred privilege can look like strength when it is in fact permission to escape or to dominate. But not all of the privileges on my list are inevitably damaging. Some, like the expectation that neighbors will be decent to you, or that your race will not count against you in court, should be the norm in a just society. Others, like the privilege to ignore less powerful people, distort the humanity of the holders as well as the ignored groups.

We might at least start by distinguishing between positive advantages, which we can work to spread, and negative types of advantage, which unless rejected will always reinforce our present hierarchies. For example, the feeling that one belongs within the human circle, as Native Americans say, should not be seen as privilege for a few. Ideally it is an unearned entitlement. At present, since only a few have it, it is an unearned advantage for them. This paper results from a process of coming to see that some of the power that I originally saw as attendant on being a human being in the United States consisted in unearned advantage and conferred dominance.

I have met very few men who truly distressed about systemic, unearned male advantage and conferred dominance. And so one question for me and others like me is whether we will be like them, or whether we will get truly distressed, even outraged, about unearned race advantage and conferred dominance, and, if so, what we will do to lessen them. In any case, we need to do more work in identifying how they actually affect our daily lives. Many, perhaps most, of our white students in the United States think that racism doesn't affect them because they are not people of color; they do not see "whiteness" as a racial identity. In addition, since race and sex are not the only advantaging systems at work, we need similarly to examine the daily experience of having age advantage, or ethnic advantage, or physical ability, or advantage related to nationality, religion, or sexual orientation.

Difficulties and dangers surrounding the task of finding parallels are many. Since racism, sexism, and heterosexism are not the same, the advantages associated with them should not be seen as the same. In addition, it is hard to disentangle aspects of unearned advantage that rest more on social class, economic class, race, religion, sex, and ethnic identity than on other factors. Still, all of the oppressions are interlocking, as the members of the Combahee River Collective pointed out in their "Black Feminist Statement" of 1977.

One factor seems clear about all of the interlocking oppressions. They take both active forms, which we can see, and embedded forms, which as a member of the dominant groups one is taught not to see. In my class and place, I did not see myself as a racist because I was taught to recognize racism only in individual acts of meanness by members of my group, never in invisible systems conferring unsought racial dominance on my group from birth.

Disapproving of the systems won't be enough to change them. I was taught to think that racism could end if white individuals changed their attitudes. But a "white" skin in the United States opens many doors for whites whether or not we approve of the way dominance has been conferred on us. Individual acts can palliate but cannot end, these problems.

To redesign social systems we need first to acknowledge their colossal unseen dimensions. The silences and denials surrounding privilege are the key political surrounding privilege are the key political tool here. They keep the thinking about equality or equity incomplete, protecting unearned advantage and conferred dominance by making these subjects taboo. Most talk by whites about equal opportunity seems to me now to be about equal opportunity to try to get into a position of dominance while denying that systems of dominance exist.

It seems to me that obliviousness about white advantage, like obliviousness about male advantage, is kept strongly inculturated in the United States so as to maintain the myth of meritocracy, the myth that democratic choice is equally available to all. Keeping most people unaware that freedom of confident action is there for just a small number of people props up those in power and serves to keep power in the hands of the same groups that have most of it already.

Although systemic change takes many decades, there are pressing questions for me and, I imagine, for some others like me if we raise our daily consciousness on the perquisites of being light-skinned. What will we do with such knowledge? As we know from watching men, it is an open question whether we will choose to use unearned advantage, and whether we will use any of our arbitrarily awarded power to try to reconstruct power systems on a broader base.

Peggy McIntosh is associate director of the Wellesley Collage Center for Research on Women. This essay is excerpted from Working Paper 189. "White Privilege and Male Privilege: A Personal Account of Coming To See Correspondences through Work in Women's Studies" (1988), by Peggy McIntosh; available for $4.00 from the Wellesley College Center for Research on Women, Wellesley MA 02181 The working paper contains a longer list of privileges.

This excerpted essay is reprinted from the Winter 1990 issue of Independent School.

5

MASKED RACISM

Reflections on the Prison Industrial Complex

■ ■ ■

Angela Davis

Imprisonment has become the response of first resort to far too many of the social problems that burden people who are ensconced in poverty. These problems often are veiled by being conveniently grouped together under the category "crime" and by the automatic attribution of criminal behavior to people of color. Homelessness, unemployment, drug addiction, mental illness, and illiteracy are only a few of the problems that disappear from

From *Colorlines* (Fall, 1998).

public view when the human beings contending with them are relegated to cages.

Prisons thus perform a feat of magic. Or rather the people who continually vote in new prison bonds and tacitly assent to a proliferating network of prisons and jails have been tricked into believing in the magic of imprisonment. But prisons do not disappear problems, they disappear human beings. And the practice of disappearing vast numbers of people from poor, immigrant, and racially marginalized communities has literally become big business.

The seeming effortlessness of magic always conceals an enormous amount of behind-the-scenes work. When prisons disappear human beings in order to convey the illusion of solving social problems, penal infrastructures must be created to accommodate a rapidly swelling population of caged people. Goods and services must be provided to keep imprisoned populations alive. Sometimes these populations must be kept busy and at other times—particularly in repressive super-maximum prisons and in INS detention centers—they must be deprived of virtually all meaningful activity. Vast numbers of handcuffed and shackled people are moved across state borders as they are transferred from one state or federal prison to another.

All this work, which used to be the primary province of government, is now also performed by private corporations, whose links to government in the field of what is euphemistically called "corrections" resonate dangerously with the military industrial complex. The dividends that accrue from investment in the punishment industry, like those that accrue from investment in weapons production, only amount to social destruction. Taking into account the structural similarities and profitability of business–government linkages in the realms of military production and public punishment, the expanding penal system can now be characterized as a "prison industrial complex."

THE COLOR OF IMPRISONMENT

Almost two million people are currently locked up in the immense network of U.S. prisons and jails. More than 70 percent of the imprisoned population are people of color. It is rarely acknowledged that the fastest growing group of prisoners are black women and that Native American prisoners are the largest group per capita. Approximately five million people—including those on probation and parole—are directly under the surveillance of the criminal justice system.

Three decades ago, the imprisoned population was approximately one-eighth its current size. While women still constitute a relatively small percentage of people behind bars, today the number of incarcerated women in California alone is almost twice what the nationwide women's prison population was in 1970. According to Elliott Currie, "[t]he prison has become a looming presence in our society to an extent unparalleled in our history—or that of any other industrial democracy. Short of major wars, mass incarceration has been the most thoroughly implemented government social program of our time."

To deliver up bodies destined for profitable punishment, the political economy of prisons relies on racialized assumptions of criminality—such as images of black welfare mothers reproducing criminal children—and on racist practices in arrest, conviction, and sentencing patterns. Colored bodies constitute the main human raw material in this vast experiment to disappear the major social problems of our time. Once the aura of magic is stripped away from the imprisonment solution, what is revealed is racism, class bias, and the parasitic seduction of capitalist profit. The prison industrial system materially and morally impoverishes its inhabitants and devours the social wealth needed to address the very problems that have led to spiraling numbers of prisoners.

As prisons take up more and more space on the social landscape, other government programs that have previously sought to respond to social needs—such as Temporary Assistance to Needy Families—are being squeezed out of existence. The deterioration of public education, including prioritizing discipline and security over learning in public schools located in poor communities, is directly related to the prison "solution."

PROFITING FROM PRISONERS

As prisons proliferate in U.S. society, private capital has become enmeshed in the punishment industry. And precisely because of their profit potential, prisons are becoming increasingly important to the U.S. economy. If the notion of punishment as a source of potentially stupendous profits is disturbing by itself, then the strategic dependence on racist structures and ideologies to render mass punishment palatable and profitable is even more troubling.

Prison privatization is the most obvious instance of capital's current movement toward the prison industry. While government-run prisons are often in gross violation of international human rights standards, private prisons are even less accountable. In March of this year, the Corrections Corporation of America (CCA), the largest U.S. private prison company, claimed 54,944 beds in 68 facilities under contract or development in the U.S., Puerto Rico, the United Kingdom, and Australia. Following the global trend of subjecting more women to public punishment, CCA recently opened a women's prison outside Melbourne. The company recently identified California as its "new frontier."

Wackenhut Corrections Corporation (WCC), the second largest U.S. prison company, claimed contracts and awards to manage 46 facilities in

North America, U.K., and Australia. It boasts a total of 30,424 beds as well as contracts for prisoner health care services, transportation, and security.

Currently, the stocks of both CCA and WCC are doing extremely well. Between 1996 and 1997, CCA's revenues increased by 58 percent, from $293 million to $462 million. Its net profit grew from $30.9 million to $53.9 million. WCC raised its revenues from $138 million in 1996 to $210 million in 1997. Unlike public correctional facilities, the vast profits of these private facilities rely on the employment of non-union labor.

THE PRISON INDUSTRIAL COMPLEX

But private prison companies are only the most visible component of the increasing corporatization of punishment. Government contracts to build prisons have bolstered the construction industry. The architectural community has identified prison design as a major new niche. Technology developed for the military by companies like Westinghouse are being marketed for use in law enforcement and punishment.

Moreover, corporations that appear to be far removed from the business of punishment are intimately involved in the expansion of the prison industrial complex. Prison construction bonds are one of the many sources of profitable investment for leading financiers such as Merrill Lynch. MCI charges prisoners and their families outrageous prices for the precious telephone calls which are often the only contact prisoners have with the free world.

Many corporations whose products we consume on a daily basis have learned that prison labor power can be as profitable as third world labor power exploited by U.S.-based global corporations. Both relegate formerly unionized workers to joblessness and many even wind up in prison. Some of the companies that use prison labor are IBM, Motorola, Compaq, Texas Instruments, Honeywell, Microsoft, and Boeing. But it is not only the hi-tech industries that reap the profits of prison labor. Nordstrom department stores sell jeans that are marketed as "Prison Blues," as well as t-shirts and jackets made in Oregon prisons. The advertising slogan for these clothes is "made on the inside to be worn on the outside." Maryland prisoners inspect glass bottles and jars used by Revlon and Pierre Cardin, and schools throughout the world buy graduation caps and gowns made by South Carolina prisoners.

"For private business," write Eve Goldberg and Linda Evans (a political prisoner inside the Federal Correctional Institution at Dublin, California) "prison labor is like a pot of gold. No strikes. No union organizing. No health benefits, unemployment insurance, or workers' compensation to pay. No language barriers, as in foreign countries. New leviathan prisons are being built on thousands of eerie acres of factories inside the walls. Prisoners do data entry for Chevron, make telephone reservations for TWA, raise hogs, shovel manure, make circuit boards, limousines, waterbeds, and lingerie for Victoria's Secret—all at a fraction of the cost of 'free labor.' "

DEVOURING THE SOCIAL WEALTH

Although prison labor—which ultimately is compensated at a rate far below the minimum wage—is hugely profitable for the private companies that use it, the penal system as a whole does not produce wealth. It devours the social wealth that could be used to subsidize housing for the homeless, to ameliorate public education for poor and racially marginalized communities, to open free drug rehabilitation programs for people who wish to kick their habits, to create a national health care system, to expand programs to combat HIV, to eradicate domestic abuse—and, in the process, to create well-paying jobs for the unemployed.

Since 1984 more than twenty new prisons have opened in California, while only one new campus was added to the California State University system and none to the University of California system. In 1996–97, higher education received only 8.7 percent of the State's General Fund while corrections received 9.6 percent. Now that affirmative action has been declared illegal in California, it is obvious that education is increasingly reserved for certain people, while prisons are reserved for others. Five times as many black men are presently in prison as in four year colleges and universities. This new segregation has dangerous implications for the entire country.

By segregating people labeled as criminals, prison simultaneously fortifies and conceals the structural racism of the U.S. economy. Claims of low unemployment rates—even in black communities—make sense only if one assumes that the vast numbers of people in prison have really disappeared and thus have no legitimate claims to jobs. The numbers of black and Latino men currently incarcerated amount to two percent of the male labor force. According to criminologist David Downes, "[t]reating incarceration as a type of hidden unemployment may raise the jobless rate for men by about one-third, to 8 percent. The effect on the black labor force is greater still, raising the [black] male unemployment rate from 11 percent to 19 percent."

HIDDEN AGENDA

Mass incarceration is not a solution to unemployment, nor is it a solution to the vast array of social problems that are hidden away in a rapidly growing network of prisons and jails. However, the great majority of people have been tricked into believing in the efficacy of imprisonment, even though the historical record clearly demonstrates that prisons do not work. Racism has undermined our ability to create a popular critical discourse to contest the ideological trickery that posits imprisonment as key to public safety. The focus of state policy is rapidly shifting from social welfare to social control.

Black, Latino, Native American, and many Asian youth are portrayed as the purveyors of violence, traffickers of drugs, and as envious of commodities that they have no right to possess. Young black and Latina women are represented as sexually promiscuous and as indiscriminately propagating babies and poverty. Criminality and deviance are racialized. Surveillance is thus focused on communities of color, immigrants, the unemployed, the undereducated, the homeless, and in general on those who have a diminishing claim to social resources. Their claim to social resources continues to diminish in large part because law enforcement and penal measures increasingly devour these resources. The prison industrial complex has thus created a vicious cycle of punishment which only further impoverishes those whose impoverishment is supposedly "solved" by imprisonment.

Therefore, as the emphasis of government policy shifts from social welfare to crime control, racism sinks more deeply into the economic and ideological structures of U.S. society. Meanwhile, conservative crusaders against affirmative action and bilingual education proclaim the end of racism, while their opponents suggest that racism's remnants can be dispelled through dialogue and conversation. But conversations about "race relations" will hardly dismantle a prison industrial complex that thrives on and nourishes the racism hidden within the deep structures of our society.

The emergence of a U.S. prison industrial complex within a context of cascading conservatism marks a new historical moment, whose dangers are unprecedented. But so are its opportunities. Considering the impressive number of grassroots projects that continue to resist the expansion of the punishment industry, it ought to be possible to bring these efforts together to create radical and nationally visible movements that can legitimize anti-capitalist critiques of the prison industrial complex. It ought to be possible to build movements in defense of prisoners' human rights and movements that persuasively argue that what we need is not new prisons, but new health care, housing, education, drug programs, jobs, and education. To safeguard a democratic future, it is possible and necessary to weave together the many and increasing strands of resistance to the prison industrial complex into a powerful movement for social transformation.

6

BLACKS' PRESUMED GUILT HITS A LITTLE TOO CLOSE TO HOME

■ ■ ■

Leonard Pitts, Jr.

My youngest son was arrested last year.

Police came to my house looking for an armed robbery suspect, 5-foot-8-inches with long hair. They took my son, 6-foot-3 with short braids. They made my daughter, 14, fresh from the shower and dressed for bed, lie facedown in wet grass and handcuffed her. They took my grandson, 8, from the bed where he slept and made him sit on the sidewalk beside her.

My son, should it need saying, hadn't done a damn thing. In fact, I was talking to him long-distance—I was in New Orleans—at the time of the alleged crime. Still, he spent almost two weeks in jail. The prosecutor asked for a high bail, citing the danger my son supposedly posed.

A few weeks later, the prosecutor declined to press charges, finally admitting there was no evidence. The alleged perpetrator of the alleged crime, a young man who was staying with us, did go on trial. There was no robbery, he said. The alleged victim had picked a fight with him, lost and concocted a tale. A surveillance video backed him up. The jury returned an acquittal in a matter of hours.

But the damage was done. The police took a picture of my son the night he was arrested. He is on his knees, hands cuffed behind him, eyes fathomless and dead. I cannot see that picture without feeling a part of me die.

So I take personally what William Bennett said. For those who missed it, Bennett, former education secretary and self-appointed arbiter of all things moral, said on his radio program that if you wanted to reduce crime,

From the *Miami Herald*. Reprinted with permission.

"you could . . . abort every black baby in this country, and your crime rate would go down. That would be an impossible, ridiculous and morally reprehensible thing to do, but your crime rate would go down."

The comment has been widely denounced. Bennett says critics are quoting him out of context, leaving out his denunciation of the idea and the fact that he was criticizing a thesis that holds that making abortion readily available to low-income women in the '70s led the U.S. crime rate to drop in the '90s.

Fine. I get all that. But see, my anger doesn't stem from any mistaken belief that Bennett wants to practice eugenics on black mothers. No, what bothers me is his easy, almost causal conflation of race and crime. Not class and crime, not culture and crime, but race and crime. As if black, solely and of itself, equals felony.

It's a conflation that comes too readily to too many. The results of which can be read in studies like the one the Justice Department co-sponsored in 2000 that found that black offenders receive substantially harsher treatment at every step along the way than white ones with similar records.

They can also be read in that picture of my son, eyes lifeless and dull with this realization of How Things Are.

I once asked a black cop who was uninvolved in the case how his colleagues could have arrested a 6-foot-3 man while searching for a 5-foot-8 suspect. They were looking for a black man, he said. Any black man would do.

So how do I explain that to my son? Should I tell him to content himself with the fact that to some people, all black men look alike, all look like criminals?

Actually I don't have to explain it at all. A few months back, my son was stopped by police and cited for driving with an obstructed windshield. The "obstruction" was one of those air fresheners shaped like a Christmas tree.

So my son gets it now. Treatment he once found surprising he now recognizes as the price he pays for being. He understands what the world expects of him.

I've watched that awful knowledge take root in three sons now. In a few years, I will watch it take root in my grandson, who is in fifth grade.

The conflation of black and crime may be easy for William Bennett, but it never gets any easier for me.

7

ARSONIST SENTENCED FOR HATE CRIMES

■ ■ ■

Tom Kertscher

In a case that invoked the Vietnam War, America's promise of freedom and the tragedy of Sept. 11, a 23-year-old Manitowoc man who helped burn a house down was sentenced Tuesday to nearly 19 years in prison.

The Hmong victims and the judge spoke eloquently about what the crimes, and the punishment, said about this country.

Andrew Franz, the first of the seven white perpetrators to be sentenced in the hate crimes case, stayed silent.

Franz, a two-time burglar who has served prison time, had pleaded guilty in October to two hate crimes and a gun charge in the Hmong case. He said at the time that the 1998 arson, as well as an unfulfilled murder plot, were meant to "send a message" that Asians in the Manitowoc area should leave him and his friends alone.

On Tuesday in Milwaukee, U.S. District Judge Charles Clevert also spoke of sending a message, but first he listened to three of the victims.

Chao Lee, 43, began to cry before finishing her first thought. On July 28, 1998, she recalled, she, her husband and their six children ran into the night as their home went up in flames. Franz had ignited gasoline that he and one of his friends had poured on the porch.

"All that came out was our bodies," Lee said.

All of the family's possessions, including the sacred Hmong clothing she was saving for her burial, were lost.

Like other victims in the case, Lee and her family had resettled in the Manitowoc area from their native Laos after the war in Vietnam. Many

Hmong fought with Americans and faced almost certain death had they remained in their homeland after the Communists took over.

"We came here seeking peace, but this is not peace," Lee said.

After the fire, the family had to live for a time with Lee's parents, a total of 12 in a tiny home.

"Every night one of the kids asked us, 'When can we go home?' But there is no home . . . nothing but ashes," said Lee, whose family moved into a new home.

Lee's testimony was translated by her oldest child, 20-year-old Xiong Lee. The last to escape the home, he said he would have perished had his mother not gone back inside to find him.

One who saw combat with the CIA in Vietnam was Humphrey Chang, 57, who was wounded twice during the war. Three days before the Lee fire, Franz and two of his co-defendants, armed with shotguns, had gone to Two Rivers intending to shoot Asians. They ignited an explosive outside Chang's home, hoping it would flush people out, but no one fled and no shots were fired.

"America is a country where freedom began," Chang said. Americans cannot allow such racial terrorism, "the act of killing innocent life for the only reason of hate," he said.

Franz and his friends said they had planned the arson and the shooting as revenge for an earlier fight between Asians and whites at a Manitowoc park. His father, Michael Franz, said that he and his son were sorry "for what happened" and that since the crimes his son had "really turned his life around."

Bobbi Bernstein, a civil rights prosecutor from Washington, D.C., and local Assistant U.S. Attorney Brian Pawlak said Franz's assistance to the FBI was pivotal in bringing charges against the six co-defendants. They recommended a roughly 17-year sentence.

Franz, who remained composed as he watched the victims speak, shed tears as he spoke with family and friends during a break in the hearing. But after Franz refused a second offer to speak, the judge told him he had seen no sign of remorse and spoke of the need to deter "this despicable" type of crime.

"Last Friday night in Salt Lake, a tattered American flag was paraded into the Olympic stadium as a reminder that this country had been attacked and that hate, unrelenting hate and total disregard for life, can have very tragic and lasting consequences," Clevert said.

"Given those considerations, it is important that this court impose a sentence as a reminder, a lifetime reminder for you and anyone who learns of your crime, that this court and our courts will deal with this type of crime very strongly and with the firm belief that we have to stamp out the kind of hate displayed in your case."

Franz will serve at least 85% of his 19-year term before being eligible for probation.

Later in the day, Judge J.P. Stadtmueller sentenced 21-year-old Augustine LaBarge of Manitowoc to 10 years in prison, one month less than the maximum for this lesser role in both crimes.

Four more adults will be sentenced. The record of the seventh defendant, a juvenile, is sealed.

SOCIAL CHANGE

1

CENSUS BUREAU PREDICTS DIVERSE U.S. FUTURE

■ ■ ■

Genaro C. Armas

IN 2050, MINORITIES WILL MAKE UP HALF THE POPULATION, SENIORS 21%

WASHINGTON For as long as there has been an America, whites have made up a clear majority. But that will change by 2050 when minority groups will be 49.9 percent of the population, the Census Bureau says.

Asians and Hispanics will see the most dramatic increases between now and midcentury, when the U.S. population will have grown by almost 50 percent to reach 420 million, according to bureau projections being released today.

America will get older, too. Nearly 21 percent of its residents will be age 65 or older, compared with 12 percent now.

The data highlight trends long predicted. But racial and ethnic changes are taking shape faster than expected, due in large part to higher-than-forecast immigration rates for Asians and Hispanics, said Greg Spencer, a bureau demographer.

Whites now represent 69 percent of the population, but their growth is slowing because of low rates of birth and immigration. Their total will grow 7 percent to 210 million, or 50.1 percent of the population, in 2050.

Those figures do not include Hispanics. The Census Bureau counts "Hispanic" or "Latino" as an ethnicity rather than a race, so they can be of any race, including white.

Between 2040 and 2050, the Census Bureau expects the non-Hispanic white population actually will decline slightly because of a large number of expected deaths of Baby Boomers, who by 2040 will be at least 76.

Meantime, the Hispanic and Asian populations are expected to continue their explosive growth.

The Asian population is expected to more than triple to 33 million by 2050. Hispanics will increase their ranks by 188 percent to 102.6 million, or roughly one-quarter of the population.

"Historically, we've been a black-and-white country. That's not true any longer, and even less true in the future," said Roderick Harrison, a demographer with the Joint Center for Political and Economic Studies in Washington, which studies issues of concern to minorities.

"A good deal of social history in the next several decades will be reflected in how we sort that out, whether we achieve greater degrees of equality in these populations," he said.

The projections—the first released by the bureau since the 2000 head count—also show a burgeoning older population as healthier lifestyles and better medical treatment increase longevity. By 2050, 5 percent of the country will be 85 or older, compared with 1.5 percent now.

"This poses very interesting challenges. Institutions are going to be transformed—and Social Security is the obvious one," said demographer Martha Farnsworth Riche, a former Census Bureau director. She pointed to education and health care as other affected areas.

Factors such as how multiracial Americans are counted could drastically alter these predictions, Riche and Harrison said.

Prior census data show that most Hispanics choose white as their race. Riche said that could be a sign that future generations of U.S.-born Latinos would select white rather than Hispanic as their background as they move further from the generation that first immigrated to the United States.

"When you look at 2050 and possibly see a large Hispanic population that doesn't speak Spanish anymore, being Hispanic might be something very different from today," Harrison said.

The bureau expects the black population will rise 71 percent to more than 61 million, or about 15 percent of the population, compared with nearly 13 percent now. Blacks would remain the second-largest minority.

Asians would comprise 8 percent of the population in 2050, compared with 4 percent now.

"This means more of a mix of cultures and ethnic backgrounds, said Edward Kwanhun Rim, president of the Pacific Rim Cultural Foundation Inc. in Barrington, Ill., and a member of a citizen advisory panel to the Census Bureau on the Asian population. "It will be a more colorful and bright future—we can hope."

Asian, Hispanic Population to Triple by 2050

The Hispanic and Asian population will triple over the next half-century and whites will account for about one-half of the total population by 2050 nationwide, according to projections by the Census Bureau.

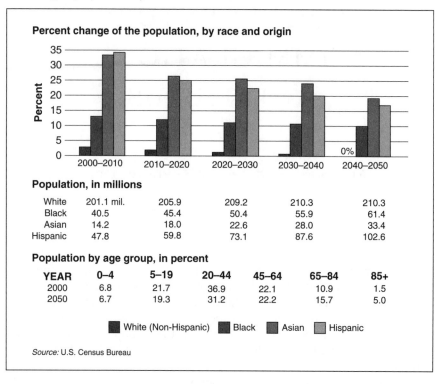

Percent change of the population, by race and origin

Population, in millions

White	201.1 mil.	205.9	209.2	210.3	210.3
Black	40.5	45.4	50.4	55.9	61.4
Asian	14.2	18.0	22.6	28.0	33.4
Hispanic	47.8	59.8	73.1	87.6	102.6

Population by age group, in percent

YEAR	0–4	5–19	20–44	45–64	65–84	85+
2000	6.8	21.7	36.9	22.1	10.9	1.5
2050	6.7	19.3	31.2	22.2	15.7	5.0

White (Non-Hispanic)   Black   Asian   Hispanic

Source: U.S. Census Bureau

2

A NEW CENTURY: IMMIGRATION AND THE US

■ ■ ■

MPI Staff, updated by Kevin Jernegan

Immigration, perhaps more than any other social, political, or economic process, has shaped the United States over the past century. As the next decades of the 21st century unfold, the rate of immigrant-driven transformation, which began in earnest in the 1960s, will continue to accelerate. Never before has the Statue of Liberty, long the symbol of America's rich immigrant heritage, lifted her torch over so many foreign-born individuals and families.

In short, America's profound demographic and cultural transformation continues—and the policies that govern who can enter the US, and how, will affect every aspect of American life in the new century. Just how to minimize the challenges confronting this "nation of immigrants" while maximizing the attendant opportunities will continue to animate the US immigration policy discourse in the years to come.

MANAGING IMMIGRATION

The United States has a long history of regulating immigration, dating back to the 1860s. Early legislation, such as the 1945 National Origins Act and the Immigration and Nationality Act of 1952, sought overall limits in immigration, but strongly favored immigrants from Europe over other regions of the world.

Originally published on the Migration Information Source, a project of the Migration Policy Institute.

It was the Immigration and Nationality Act Amendments of 1965, however, which set in motion a powerful set of forces that are still shaping the United States today. The 1965 Amendments ushered in sweeping changes to immigration policy by abolishing the national origins quota system as the basis for immigration and replacing it with a seven-category preference system for the allocation of immigrant visas.

In addition, numerical limits were increased from 154,000 to 290,000, of which 120,000 were reserved for immigrants from the Western Hemisphere. The 290,000-person limit did not include "immediate family members" of US citizens (spouses, minor children, or parents), who were exempt from numerical limitations.

In this period, the United States first began to witness the transformation from predominantly European immigration to Latin American and Asian flows that continue to characterize today's immigration patterns.

The Immigration and Nationality Act, as amended by the Refugee Act of 1980, brought US policy in line with the 1967 Protocol to the 1951 UN Refugee Convention. The protocol, together with the 1969 Organization of African Unity (OAU) Convention, expanded the number of persons considered refugees. Whereas previously the definition of refugee had centered on those affected by World War II, the new framework took into account other global conflicts contributing to the refugee population.

In another change, in response to the growing undocumented population in the US, Congress passed the Immigration Reform and Control Act (IRCA) of 1986. IRCA resulted in large part from the recommendations of the Select Commission on Immigration and Refugee Policy, which was created in 1977 to study illegal aliens and other aspects of immigration and refugee policy. The commission's final report in 1981 included over 100 recommendations.

In an attempt to "close the back door while opening the front door," IRCA granted amnesty to illegal immigrants who had resided in the United States for a certain period of time. That period varied depending on whether or not the immigrant worked in agriculture. At the same time, it attempted to curtail incentives for future undocumented immigration by creating a system of employer sanctions. The system criminalized the facilitation of illegal immigration by placing steep penalties on those who would harbor or hire unauthorized residents. The third components of IRCA—enhanced border control—did not begin in earnest until the mid-1990s.

The Immigration Act of 1990 rounded out this set of legislation by adjusting admissions categories and restructuring employment-based entry categories for both permanent and temporary entries. The goal has been to increase the skills and education levels of these entrants.

The decade of the 1990s was marked by state and federal legislation that limited immigrants' access to a range of social services and benefits. In 1994, California passed Proposition 187, one of the most controversial pieces of state law. Specifically, Proposition 187 denied undocumented immigrants in California access to public schools, medical care, and other social services, and required public employees and law enforcement officials to report suspected undocumented immigrants to the Immigration and Naturalization Service.

In 1996, Congress passed three new federal laws that limited access to public benefits and legal protections for non-citizens. Under the Personal Responsibility and Work Opportunity Reconciliation Act (PRWORA), commonly known as the Welfare Reform Act, legal and undocumented immigrants no longer had access to federal public benefits, such as Medicaid, Supplemental Security Income (SSI), and food stamps.

The Illegal Immigration Reform and Immigrant Responsibility Act (IIRIRA) hastened deportation of illegal immigrants who committed crimes. It also made it more difficult for immigrants to make legal appeals following executive branch decisions.

The last in the three pieces of legislation, the Anti-Terrorism and Effective Death Penalty Act (AEDPA), made it easier to arrest, detain, and deport non-citizens.

By the end of the decade, Congress' attention had shifted to the booming economy's increasing need for highly skilled immigrants who could fill technology jobs. The American Competitiveness in the Twenty-First Century Act, passed in 2000, increased the number of temporary work visas (H-lBs) available per year from 65,000 to 115,00 in fiscal year 2000, then to 195,000 for FY 2001, 2002 and 2003.

The most far-reaching changes in US immigration may stem from the events of September 11, 2001, and related concerns about the growing undocumented population in the country. These issues are discussed in detail below.

PARTING THE WAVES

Non-citizens entering the United States are divided among three streams: "lawful permanent residents (LPRs)," "non-immigrants," and "undocumented migrants."

Lawful permanent residents are foreign-born individuals who have been admitted to reside permanently in the United States. Such immigrants may enter the US through family-sponsored immigration, employment-based immigration, or through refugee and asylum admissions.

Family-sponsored immigration accounts for more than three-quarters of all regular immigration into the United States. In some cases, permanent residents may be admitted through the diversity visa lottery program, which allots additional immigration visas to countries that are underrepresented in US immigration streams.

According to the Department of Homeland Security (DHS), legal immigration in fiscal year 2003 was 705,827, coming mainly from Mexico (115,864),

India (50,379), the Philippines (45,397), China (40,659), El Salvador (28,296), the Dominican Republic (26,205) and Vietnam (22,133). Together, these seven countries accounted for nearly half of all legal immigration.

Overall immigrant admissions and adjustments of status for fiscal year 2003 fell by approximately a third, from 1,063,732 in fiscal year 2002, primarily as a consequence of heightened security precautions introduced after the September 11, 2001, terrorist attacks.

In addition to those non-citizens who arrive to take up permanent residence, some enter lawfully as "non-immigrants"—foreigners who are in the United States temporarily. Totaling more than 27.8 million in fiscal year 2003, this category includes tourists as well as those who enter to help fill the temporary needs of US employers—often on visas that allow stays of greater than a year.

There are dozens of non-immigrant visa classifications, including the F-1 category for students in academic or language programs, the J visa for those who enter for cultural exchange purposes, and the TN category for professionals from Canada or Mexico who enter under North American Free Trade Agreement (NAFTA) regulations.

Work-entitled non-immigrants, such as holders of various types of H and other visas, play an increasing role in the US economy. The H-1B visa category provides for the temporary admission of workers with specialized knowledge and skills. Congress determines the number of H-1B visas available each year. The number of H-1B visas Congress approves has declined substantially in recent years, from a high of 195,000 in 2001–2003 to 65,000 for fiscal year 2005.

For six of the last eight years, the number of H-1B visas authorized each year has fallen short of US employers' demand, with the annual cap typically being filled within the first few months or even weeks of the fiscal year. For fiscal year 2005, the cap of 65,000 H-1B visas was depleted on October 1, 2004, the first day of the fiscal year. Despite the high demand, non-immigrant admissions have declined in recent years with a commensurate reduction in tourism, foreign student enrollments at US universities, cultural and scholarly exchange, and business travel.

"Illegal" or "unauthorized" immigrants enter the US by avoiding official inspection, passing through inspection with fraudulent documents, entering legally but overstaying the terms of their temporary visas, or somehow violating other terms of their visa. Under IRCA in 1986, roughly 2.7 million unauthorized migrants were legalized.

While it is notoriously difficult to measure the undocumented population, the US Census Bureau and most independent analysts estimate the figure to be between 9 and 10 million as of 2003, and growing at a rate between 300,000 and 500,000 each year. Mexico remains the leading country of origin, claiming nearly half of the total, with several Central American and European countries also strongly represented.

CLOSER LOOK AT NEW FACES

Since the 1960s, the number of foreign-born people in the US has increased. In terms of absolute numbers, this number is at its highest point in history. According to US Census Bureau 2003 Current Population Survey (CPS) data, 33.5 million foreign born lived in the US, representing about 11.7 percent of the entire population. However, this percentage remains well below the historic highs of almost 15 percent in both 1890 and 1910.

Approximately 53.3 percent of these foreign-born persons originate from Latin America (including Central America, South America and the Caribbean), 25.0 percent from Asia, 13.7 percent from Europe, and 8.0 percent from other regions of the world, such as Africa and Oceania.

Migrants from Central America (including, for data purposes, Mexico) account for nearly one-third of the entire foreign-born population. Mexicans, the largest single group, now compose 27 percent of all foreign born.

Mexicans account for the largest proportion of the illegal immigrant population by far, with El Salvador and Guatemala running a distant second and third place. Hispanics now comprise the largest ethnic minority group in the US, at 12.5 percent.

SPREADING OUT

Data from the US Census Bureau 2004 Current Population Survey reveal that the foreign-born population is geographically concentrated, with 67 percent residing in only six of the 50 states—29 percent in California alone. The other immigrant-heavy states are New York (11 percent), Texas (9 percent), Florida (9 percent), New Jersey (5 percent), and Illinois (4 percent).

While the six states mentioned above continue to attract and retain the bulk of the foreign-born population, there is a growing trend toward broader dispersal across the United States. Economic conditions, such as cost of living and employment opportunities, are increasingly motivating immigrants to move to states such as Georgia, Nevada, North Carolina, Arizona, Arkansas, and Oregon. These nontraditional receiving states have seen significant growth in their foreign-born populations, ushering in a new era of integration challenges across the country. . . .

AT THE BORDERS

The US borders with Mexico and Canada are among the most active in the world. Canada is the United States' largest trading partner, with an average of US$1.2 billion traded every day, according to the US Trade Representative. Mexico claims second place, with an average of US$733 million traded per day. With 132 legal ports of entry along the Canadian border and 25 along the Mexican border, cross-border traffic is bustling.

Ninety percent of Canadians live within 100 miles of the US-Canada border. It is estimated that every day, about 250,000 people arrive in the US from Canada for a variety of reasons.

With Mexicans constituting roughly a quarter of the foreign-born population in the United States—far outnumbering other source countries—the southern border is extremely important for the futures of both the United States and Mexico.

In 2001, according to the US Embassy in Mexico City, the US processed 2,650,912 non-immigrant visa applications in Mexico, an increase of 17.65 percent over the 2,252,594 applications processed in 2000, which represented a 37 percent increase over the 1,635,309 applications in 1999.

These numbers indicate that the US is growing more dependent on Mexican labor, and that the two economies are becoming more integrated.

BECOMING AMERICAN

Of the 33.5 million foreign born residing in the US in 2003, approximately 38 percent have obtained US citizenship through naturalization. Applications for naturalization increased dramatically in the 1990s in response to legislative developments restricting access to public benefits and legal protections for noncitizens, including Proposition 187 in California (1994), the Personal Responsibility and Work Opportunity Act (1996), and the Illegal Immigration Reform and Immigrant Responsibility Act (IIRIRA, 1996).

Between 1994 and 1997, the number of naturalization applications filed nearly tripled, from 543,353 to 1,412,712. Since 1999, there have been, on average, slightly more than half a million applications for naturalization received every year.

Increases in the number of applications filed for benefits such as citizenship and immigrant visas, coupled with increased security precautions following the events of September 11, have resulted in historically high backlogs of pending applications.

By the end of fiscal year 2003, the Department of Homeland Security's (DHS) bureau of Citizenship and Immigration Services (CIS) had a backlog of 6.1 million pending applications. Recent efforts to deal with the backlog have reduced it to 4.1 million pending applications at the close of fiscal year 2004.

The US Citizenship and Immigration Service Office (USCIS) is reviewing citizenship testing procedures to standardize testing criteria, eliminate questions based upon rote memorization, and add more interpretative questions. USCIS is conducting pilot studies and planning to offer the new test in late 2006.

21st CENTURY CHALLENGES

Two challenges are clearly front and center on the immigration horizon: security concerns resulting from the events of September 11, 2001, and comprehensive US immigration reform. The latter involves satisfying security concerns about illegal immigration, preventing future unauthorized immigration to the fullest extent possible, and providing adequate legal means for needed immigrants (close family members and workers) to enter the United States. Both challenges stand to reshape immigrations's impact on the United States in the next two decades.

SOURCES

De Jong, Gordon F. and Tran, Quynh-Giang. 2001. "Warm Welcome, Cool Welcome: Mapping Receptivity Toward Immigrants in the US." Population Today (November/December). Population Reference Bureau. **Available online**.

Fix, Michael and Jeffrey Passel. 2001. "US Immigration at the Beginning of the 21st Century." Testimony before the Subcommittee on Immigration and Claims Hearing on "The US Population and Immigration." Committee on the Judiciary US House of Representatives. **Available online**.

Guzman, Betsy. 2001. "The Hispanic Population." Census 2000 Brief. **Available online**.

Kramer, Roger. 2001. "Developments in International Migration to the United States: 2001." SOPEMI report (30 November). Paris: OECD.

Lapham, Susan J. September 1993. "We the American Foreign Born." Washington, DC: US Department of Commerce, US Census Bureau.

Lollock, Lisa. 2001. "The Foreign-Born Population in the United States: Population Characteristics." Current Population Reports (January). Washington, DC: US Department of Commerce, US Census Bureau.

National Immigration Forum. 2001. "Fast Facts on Today's Newcomers."

OECD. 2001. Trends in International Migration. SOPEMI report. Paris: OECD.

Papademetriou, Demetrios. 2001. "An Immigration and National Security Grand Bargain with Mexico" (30 November). **Available online**.

Papademetriou, Demetrios and Deborah Meyers. 2001. "Caught in the Middle: Border Communities in an Era of Globalization." Washington, DC: Carnegie Endowment for International Peace.

Passel, Jeffrey. 2002. "New Estimates of the Undocumented Population in the United States." Migration Information Source. **Available online**.

Population Reference Bureau. 1999. "Main Region of Origin in US Shifts to Latin America." **Available online**.

Schmidley, Dianne. 2001. "Profile of the Foreign Born in the United States: 2000." US Census Bureau, Special Studies/Current Population Reports. **Available online**.

US Bureau of Transportation Statistics. **Available online**.

US Census Bureau. Current Population Survey. US Census Bureau website. **Available online**.

US Citizenship and Immigration Services, Department of Homeland Security. "Who Gets In: Four Main Immigration Laws." **Available online**.

US Citizenship and Immigration Services, Department of Homeland Security. "Eligibility Information: Who May Apply to Change to a New Non-immigrant Status?" **Available online**.

3

WHERE "ENGLISH ONLY" FALLS SHORT

■ ■ ■

Stacy A. Teicher

COMPANIES SCRAMBLE TO COPE WITH MULTIPLE LANGUAGES IN THE WORKPLACE

They were the go-to people when customers needed advice in Spanish about eyeshadow or perfume. But when Hispanic employees wanted to speak Spanish to one another, they say it was forbidden—even on lunch breaks.

Five women who worked for the cosmetics store Sephora in New York filed, complaints, and the Equal Employment Opportunity Commission (EEOC) sued last fall on their behalf. They argue the policy is too restrictive and amounts to national-origin discrimination, which is illegal under the Civil Rights Act of 1964.

"All of the [women say] how hurtful it is to be told that you can't speak your own language," says EEOC attorney Raechel Adams. "Language is so closely tied to their culture and their ethnicity. [Ironically,] they were expected to assist Spanish-speaking customers."

As companies hire from an ever more diverse labor pool, they reap the benefits of bilingualism, but they're also running into a Babel of problems. Already, a fifth of the nation's population speaks something other than English as their primary language (in some areas, it's two-fifths). Many of them have limited English proficiency that can lead to costly mistakes or low productivity. Managers worry about compromised safety or the quality of customer service. And if some workers use a foreign language to mock others, morale can break down.

There's no quick fix. Some employers go to the expense of offering classes to improve workers' English. Others turn the tables and train supervisors in languages most often spoken by workers in their industry. What seems the simplest answer to some—an English-only policy—is tricky because conflicts between court rulings and EEOC guidelines leave a lot of gray areas.

In the case of the five New York Hispanics, Sephora denied that it had an English-only rule or discriminated in any way. The court is awaiting the store's answer to the complaint.

English-only policies generate few official grievances. In 2002, the EEOC received 228 such complaints out of about 9,000 claims of national-origin discrimination. But observers say that many more workers who feel silenced don't take action for fear of losing their jobs.

Often what determines fairness is how a policy is implemented and whether there's an atmosphere of ethnic tension. In a case settled recently for $1.5 million, Hispanic housekeepers at a casino were not allowed to speak Spanish. A janitor reported that he had to hide in closets to train new employees who understood only Spanish. Others told of harassment by supervisors who called them "wetbacks," accused them of stealing, and fired them for objecting to the English policy. The Colorado Central Station Casino in Black Hawk did not return calls seeking comment. In the settlement, it denied wrongdoing but agreed to remedies such as posting notices declaring there is no English-only rule.

For bilingual people, suppressing the tendency to talk in both languages can be difficult. They may know enough English to get by in their jobs, but to talk about family or other topics with friends, their primary language offers them a much richer vocabulary.

"It's called code-switching," says Nina Perales, regional counsel of the Mexican-American Legal Defense Fund (MALDEF), which joined the EEOC in the suit against the casino. "You might switch languages for reason of emphasis or because you're more comfortable explaining certain things in one language versus the other." And sometimes it's even done uncon-sciously, linguists say.

But when conversations are restricted, "there's almost an issue of dehu-manization," says Karl Krahnke, a linguistics professor at Colorado State University. "They are not being viewed as humans with the same social needs as anybody else."

Some insist those complexities shouldn't keep employers from creating a language policy if they think it's good for business. "I speak four languages . . . but a business has the right to establish rules for whatever reason—it could be safety, it could be social . . . so other [workers] won't feel insulted," says Mauro E. Mujica, chairman of U.S. English in Washington, D.C. His organization promotes official-English policies, which exist in 27 states and apply only to government, not the private sector. But workplace policies, he says, should not extend to people's personal time.

NO NAVAJO

Another case takes the debate out of the immigration context. At R.D.'s Drive-In in Page, Ariz., it wasn't a "foreign" language that the boss restrict-ed, but a native one: Navajo.

The town borders the Navajo Nation reservation, and nearly 90 percent of the restaurant's employees are Navajo, though the owners, the Kidman family, are not.

Speaking on the Kidman's behalf, Joe Becker of the Mountain States Legal Foundation in Denver says the family asked employees to sign a language policy in the summer of 2000. Their reason: There were complaints from customers and staff about rude comments being made in Navajo.

The agreement read: "The owner of this business can speak and under-stand only English. While the owner is paying you as an employee, you are required to use English at all times . . . [except] when the customer cannot understand English. If you feel unable to comply with this requirement, you may find another job."

Elva Josley and three others took exception to the rule. Ms. Josley had worked for the Kidmans for nearly three years and their families were close friends. But this, she says, was hurtful. She says the Kidmans never told her there had been complaints about things being said in Navajo.

LEGACY OF SUPPRESSION

"A lot of Native American people were sent to boarding schools and told not to speak their own language . . . and they were trying to make Christians out of these 'savages,'" she says. "I [said to the Kidmans]: 'It's not fair, because you people are the ones who came to our land and you can't tell us not to be who we are.'" Without native languages, she says, the US wouldn't have had the help of the code talkers during World War II.

The EEOC sued the diner, and Josley hopes the case will be settled soon and will send a message to employers: "Everyone's human and deserves to be respected . . . and next time people will think twice before doing something like this."

4

BLACKS VS. LATINOS AT WORK

■ ■ ■

Miriam Jordan

LOS ANGELES Donnie Gaut, an African-American with 12 years of warehouse experience, applied for a job in 2002 at Farmer John Meats, a large Los Angeles pork processor. When he was turned down for the position, a job stocking goods that paid $7 an hour, Mr. Gaut decided the problem wasn't his résumé—it was his race. He filed a complaint with the U.S. Equal Employment Opportunity Commission, the federal agency that enforces antidiscrimination laws in the workplace.

Last October, the EEOC secured a $110,000 settlement from the company to be shared by Mr. Gaut and six other black applicants who were rejected for production jobs at Farmer John based on their race, according to the agency.

The EEOC says it found that the pork packer, owned by Clougherty Packing Co., had been almost exclusively hiring Hispanics for warehouse, packing and production jobs. Clougherty was acquired by Hormel Foods Corp. in 2004.

In response to questions, Clougherty Packing said in a statement that settlement of the case "in no way suggests the company did anything wrong." It said the packer wanted to avoid "what would have been costly and protracted litigation."

A new wave of race-discrimination cases is appearing in the workplace: African-Americans who feel that they are being passed over for Hispanics.

This kind of case marks a shift from years past, when blacks were likely to seek legal action against employers who showed preferential treatment toward whites. The cases highlight mounting tension between Hispanics and blacks as they compete for resources and job opportunities.

Recently, the federal agency announced it also secured a $180,000 settlement from Zenith National Insurance Corp., a national workers-compensation specialist, to be divided among 10 blacks who applied for a mailroom job at its headquarters in Woodland Hills, Calif. The job was offered to a Latino man with no mailroom experience, according to the EEOC.

Henry Shields, an attorney for Zenith, said the insurance company had adopted EEOC recommendations for improving its hiring practices "as a means of furthering its goals of equal opportunity." Mr. Shields declined to comment on the specifics of the case.

"There used to be a reluctance to bring cases against other minorities," says Anna Park, the EEOC regional attorney who oversaw both the Zenith and the Farmer John cases. "It's no longer a white-black paradigm. This is a new trend."

The situation is exacerbated by strong stereotypes that have set in among some employers about the pluses and minuses of hiring from each pool of minority workers. "There is a perception that Latinos closer to the immigrant experience might work harder than black persons," says Joe Hicks, who is African-American and vice president of Community Advocates, a nonpartisan group that aims to advance interracial dialogue.

John Trasvina, vice president for law and policy at the Mexican-American Defense League, an advocacy group that works on civil rights issues, says that some Latinos may be viewed as "preferred applicants." He believes there is a feeling among some employers that Latinos can be exploited because, in their view, they tend to be immigrants who are more likely to accept low wages and be less aware of their rights than blacks. Says Mr. Trasvina: "Employers sometimes pit one group of employees against the other."

California—where Hispanic immigrants have been moving into black working-class pockets of the state's cities for decades—is at the leading edge of this growing trend. As Latinos migrate eastward, to such states as Louisiana, Georgia and North Carolina, the competition with blacks for blue-collar jobs is likely to grow.

Hispanics have become the second-largest population group in the U.S.—ahead of African-Americans but behind Caucasians—thanks to the influx of immigrants from Latin America. In some cities, like Los Angeles, collaboration between African-American and Latino leaders is on the rise when it is mutually beneficial.

But as Latinos grab the attention of marketers and gain political clout, many African-Americans feel that their influence is waning, and that the decline is disproportionate and unfair.

Tension has spilled into the workplace. In New Orleans, city officials have raised concerns that employers are hiring Latino immigrants for low wages to do the hurricane cleanup instead of tapping the native-born, mainly black, workforce. Last October, New Orleans Mayor Ray Nagin asked local business leaders: "How do I ensure that New Orleans is not overrun by Mexican workers?"

Workers from all backgrounds—whites, blacks, Asians and others—use networks within their ethnic groups to find employment. Hispanic workers often bring in other family members or people from their neighborhoods or home regions to join them on a job. In sectors like construction, this can be an aid to employers who can tap their workers to help them find a fresh supply of laborers.

The flip side is that employers can become vulnerable to lawsuits if it's determined that they have been shutting out qualified applicants based on their race.

In the Zenith National Insurance case, Charles Dennis, who applied for a mailroom job he spotted in a newspaper's classified section in 2001, says his interview with a Hispanic manager "went great." He first became suspicious that something wasn't right when, in a follow-up call, the company told him the $10-an-hour position was put on hold.

Then, a few weeks later, Mr. Dennis—who had worked in another large insurer's mailroom—got a call from an employment agency telling him they had "the perfect job" for him, he recalls. It turned out to be the same position. He says the agency then called back and told him that Zenith "just didn't want to go with me."

Mr. Dennis took his case to the EEOC, which began to investigate. It found that Mr. Dennis and several other black applicants with relevant experience were passed over in favor of a Latino candidate, whose previous work amounted to mainly "swabbing decks on aircraft carriers" in the Navy, according to Ms. Park, the EEOC attorney.

In the case of Farmer John Meats, the EEOC said that it found that the employer had an all-Hispanic hiring staff and recruited new hires by word of mouth.

One of the Latinos hired to work in Farmer John Meats instead of the black candidates had been a gardener, according to Ms. Park. Both discrimination lawsuits were brought against the employers under Title VII of the Civil Rights Act of 1964. The message for employers is that "all individuals deserve to compete for jobs on a level playing field," she says.

5

TENNESSEE JUDGE TELLS IMMIGRANT MOTHERS: LEARN ENGLISH OR ELSE

■ ■ ■

Ellen Barry

LEBANON, Tenn. A judge hearing child-abuse and neglect cases in Tennessee has given an unusual instruction to some immigrant mothers who have come before him: Learn English or else.

Most recently, it was an 18-year-old woman from Oaxaca, Mexico, who had been reported to the Department of Children's Services for failing to immunize her toddler and show up for appointments. At a hearing last month to monitor the mother's custody of the child, Wilson County Judge Barry Tatum instructed the woman to learn English and to use birth control, the *Lebanon Democrat* newspaper reported.

Last October, Tatum gave a similar order to a Mexican woman who had been cited for neglect of her 11-year-old daughter, said a lawyer who is representing the woman in her appeal. Setting a court date six months away, the judge told the woman she should be able to speak English at a fourth-grade level by that meeting. If she failed, he warned, he would begin the process of termination of parental rights.

"The court specially informs the mother that if she does not make the effort to learn English, she is running the risk of losing any connection—legally, morally and physically—with her daughter forever," reads a court order from the hearing, according to Jerry Gonzalez, the Nashville attorney who represents the woman.

Tatum's orders have become the subject of debate in this Tennessee community, which has seen an influx of non-English speakers over the past decade. Civil-rights advocates, including the American Civil Liberties Union, have called his orders discriminatory and unconstitutional. But many of Tatum's neighbors cheered the principle behind his act, saying new immigrants should be encouraged to assimilate more fully into American life.

Juvenile court proceedings are often more informal than adult cases, and it's not unusual for judges to give lifestyle advice to parents who come before them in neglect or abuse cases. And, when written down and signed by the judge, those instructions take on the force of a court order.

Such orders should pertain to behavior that contributes to abuse and neglect, said Susan Brooks, an expert on family law at Vanderbilt University Law School. Brooks said she was not familiar with Tatum's orders, but typically the inability to speak English would not fall into that category. The state Supreme Court regards the right to raise one's own children as fundamental, she added.

"That's treading on sacred ground," she said.

Tatum did not respond to interview requests from the Los Angeles Times, but he has explained that he gave the orders in hopes that the parents would make a greater effort to assimilate into American society, opening more opportunities to their children. He has given similar orders to non-English-speaking parents in as many as five cases.

He said he has never removed a child from a parent because the parent did not speak English.

Because records from juvenile court are sealed, further details of the cases were not available.

In Lebanon, a city 20 miles east of Nashville with a population of just more than 20,000, it was once rare to hear a foreign accent, much less a foreign language. Now Lebanon has become home to more than 1,200 foreign-born agricultural and manufacturing workers, including about 400 whose primary language is Mixteco, a language indigenous to Mexico.

Though the judge's order may have been a mistake, "the general sentiment is if people are going to be in this country, we all have a moral obligation to learn to speak the language," said Bob Bright, 61, who runs an insurance agency in Lebanon.

"I know if I was in Mexico I would make an effort to learn Hispanic."

In the October case, Tatum made a clear link between the mother's English abilities and her parental rights, said Gonzalez, the mother's attorney.

In the case, an 11-year-old girl had been placed with a foster family after allegations of neglect, Gonzalez said. The mother, who spoke only Mixteco, asked the court to arrange counseling, and the judge denied that request, instead giving the women a deadline for basic mastery of English.

6

THE SEGREGATED CLASSROOMS OF A PROUDLY DIVERSE SCHOOL

■ ■ ■

Jeffrey Gettleman

MAPLEWOOD, N.J., April 1 Columbia High School seems to have it all—great sports teams, great academics, famous alumni and an impressive campus with Gothic buildings. But no one boasts about one aspect of this blue-ribbon school, that its classrooms are largely segregated.

Though the school is majority black, white students make up the bulk of the advanced classes, while black students far outnumber whites in lower-level classes, statistics show.

"It's kind of sad," said Ugochi Opara, a senior who is president of the student council. "You can tell right away, just by looking into a classroom, what level it is."

This is a reality at many high schools coast to coast and one of the side effects of aggressive leveling, the increasingly popular practice of dividing students into ability groups.

But at Columbia High, the students nearly revolted. Two weeks ago, a black organization on campus planned a walkout to protest the leveling system. Word soon spread to the principal, who pleaded with the students not to go. The student leaders decided to hold an assembly instead, in which they lashed out at the racial gap.

The student uproar is now forcing district officials to take a hard look at the leveling system and decide how to strike a balance between their two main goals—celebrating diversity and pushing academic achievement.

Educators say that leveling allows smarter students to be challenged while giving struggling ones the special instruction they need. But many students, especially those in the lower levels, which often carry a stigma, say such stratification makes the rocky adolescent years only harder. And at Columbia High, there is no dispute that it is precisely the leveling system that has led to racial segregation.

Anthony Paolini, a senior at Columbia, is one of the few white students in a lower-level math class. The fact that most of his classmates are black does not bother him, he said. But the low expectations do.

"It makes you feel like you're in a hole," he said.

The school, about 15 minutes from downtown Newark, draws from the cosmopolitan towns of Maplewood and South Orange. Some students live in million-dollar homes. Others rely on government lunches. Of 2,024 students, 58 percent are black, 35 percent white, 4 percent Hispanic and 3 percent Asian. The public school sends more than 90 percent of graduates to college, has a dropout rate of less than half a percent and won a national Blue Ribbon award from the federal government for its academic excellence during the 1992–93 school year. Notable alumni include the actor Zach Braff and the singer Lauryn Hill, and the fact that the two stars, one white, one black, graduated in the same class is seen as a symbol of the diversity Columbia strives to project.

But racial tension is becoming more of an issue. In recent years, the number of black students in the school district has eclipsed the number of white students even though Maplewood and South Orange still are majority white. In the past year, the district has been sued twice for discrimination: once by two former black students who said they were mistreated by teachers after a food-fight in the cafeteria, and also by a group of teachers, mostly black, who accused the principal, who is white, of racial bias.

The superintendent of the district, Peter P. Horoschak, acknowledged that there were, in a sense, two Columbias. The de facto segregation is most visible at the extremes. Statistics for this year show that while a Level 5 math class, the highest, had 79 percent white students, a Level 2 math class, the lowest, had 88 percent black students. Levels 3 and 4 tend to be more mixed, though a school board member, Mila M. Jasey, said, "Some white parents tell me that they know their kid belongs in a Level 3 class but they don't want them to be the only white kid in the class."

Though parents and students are granted some input, students are supposed to be placed in levels primarily based on grades and test scores. Many black students complain that they are unfairly relegated to the lower levels and unable to move up.

Quentin Williams, the 17-year-old leader of the Martin Luther King Association at the school, calls it "contemporary segregation." He said that his organization, one of the largest on campus, had tried to meet with the administration over the issue several times but "got the runaround."

So in mid-March his group planned to walk out of school. They even had the backing of several parents, who volunteered to help. As the date approached, Quentin, a senior, said he felt "a lot of pressure coming in from a lot of different angles."

Student leaders eventually decided that holding an assembly would give them a better opportunity to publicly confront administrators, especially the principal, Renee Pollack. At the assembly, which was mandatory for all students, she stood in front of the student body and apologized for saying anything that might have been construed as insensitive.

Ms. Pollack said later that complaints about her were being spread by teachers on her own staff.

"They were trying to manipulate the kids in order to get at me," said Ms. Pollack, who has been the principal for three years and is up for tenure this month.

The flashpoint of the assembly came when Nathan Winkler, a skinny, intense senior who says he wants to be governor some day, grabbed the microphone and announced that he had no sympathy for people in lower levels because all it took was hard work to move up.

His short outburst was like a cleaver, splitting the student body in two. Many blacks booed him. Many whites cheered. He was then accused of using the term "you people" in his speech—though he did not, according to a videotape of the assembly. After the assembly, he said, he was stalked in the hallways.

He now admits that he spoke out of fear.

"I felt extremely isolated during that assembly," he said. "For the first time I was aware of being part of the minority. White kids are outnumbered at Columbia. I knew that, but I hadn't really felt it before."

Student leaders and administrators are now discussing ways to narrow the so-called achievement gap, like granting students more say in which level they are in; better identifying which level students belong in; expanding a summer school program for students who want to take upper-level classes. Administrators say they had been working on all this before the walkout threat.

"But the students forced the issue," Ms. Pollack acknowledged.

Ms. Pollack also pointed out that this year, more students of color from Columbia have been accepted into Ivy League universities than white students, with two Hispanic, three black and two white students gaining early admission.

The debate over leveling here boils down to fairness. Is it fair just to ensure equal access to upper-level classes? Or does fairness go farther than that and require administrators to truly level the playing field so that the racial make-up of upper classes better resembles the racial makeup of the school?

Stewart Hendricks, a senior whose father is from Guyana and whose mother is Swiss, said that some teachers do seem to have lower expectations for black students but that he did not let them get him down.

"The purpose of high school is to prepare you for the real world," he said. "And in the real world, you can't listen to other people's expectations, because in the real world, people are just waiting for you to fail."

Because of his mixed racial heritage, he said, "I guess you can say I'm in the middle of all this."

And in a way, that is why he sympathizes with the principal.

"She's got an entire black population that wants to get rid of the leveling system and an entire white population who would leave this town if they did that," he said. "What's she supposed to do?"

THE ECONOMICS OF RACE, CLASS AND GENDER

1

U.S. POVERTY RATE WAS UP LAST YEAR

■ ■ ■

David Leonhardt

WASHINGTON, Aug. 30 Even as the economy grew, incomes stagnated last year and the poverty rate rose, the Census Bureau reported Tuesday. It was the first time on record that household incomes failed to increase for five straight years.

The portion of Americans without health insurance remained roughly steady at 16 percent, the bureau said. A smaller percentage of people were covered by their employers, but two big government programs, Medicaid and military insurance, grew.

The census's annual report card on the nation's economic well-being showed that a four-year-old expansion had still not done much to benefit many households. Median pretax income, $44,389, was at its lowest point since 1997, after inflation.

Though the reasons are not wholly clear, economists say technology and global trade appear to be holding down pay for many workers. The rising cost of health care benefits has also eaten into pay increases.

After the report's release, Bush administration officials said that the job market had continued to improve since the end of 2004 and that they hoped incomes were now rising and poverty was falling. The poverty rate "is the last, lonely trailing indicator of the business cycle," said Elizabeth Anderson, chief of staff in the economics and statistics administration of the Commerce Department.

The census numbers also do not reflect the tax cuts passed in President Bush's first term, which have lifted the take-home pay of most families.

But the biggest tax cuts went to high-income families already getting raises, Democrats said Tuesday. The report, they added, showed that the cuts had failed to stimulate the economy as the White House had promised.

"The growth in the economy is not going to families," said Senator Jack Reed, Democrat of Rhode Island. "It's in stark contrast to what happened during the Clinton administration."

The main theme of the census report seemed to be the lingering weakness in compensation and benefits, even as the ranks of the unemployed have dwindled. Fewer people are getting health insurance from their employers or from policies of family members, while raises have generally trailed inflation.

Last year, households kept income from falling by working more hours than they did in 2003, the data showed. The median pay of full-time male workers declined more than 2 percent in 2004, to $40,800; for women, the median dropped 1 percent, to $31,200. When some people switch to full-time work from part-time, they can keep household incomes from dropping even when the pay of individual workers is declining.

"It looks like the gains from the recovery haven't really filtered down," said Phillip L. Swagel, a resident scholar at the American Enterprise Institute, a conservative research group in Washington. "The gains have gone to owners of capital and not to workers."

There has always been a lag between the end of a recession and the resumption of raises, Mr. Swagel added, but the length of this lag has been confounding.

In addition, the poverty rate rose last year for working-age people, those ages 18 to 64. The portion of people age 65 and older in poverty fell, while child poverty was essentially flat.

Over all, the poverty rate increased to 12.7 percent, from 12.5 percent in 2003. Poverty levels have changed only modestly in the last three decades, rising in the 1980's and falling in the 1990's, after having dropped sharply in the 1960's. They reached a low of 11.1 percent in 1973, from more than 22 percent in 1960.

In the same three decades that poverty has remained fairly steady, median incomes have grown significantly, lifting living standards for most families. After adjusting for inflation, the income of the median household, the one making more than half of all others and less than half of the rest, earns almost one-third more now than it did in the late 1960's.

But income inequality has also risen in that time and was near all-time highs last year, the bureau reported. The census numbers do not include gains from stock holdings, which would further increase inequality.

In New York, the poverty rate rose last year to 20.3 percent, from 19 percent, making it the only city of more than one million people with a significant change. The reason for the increase was not obvious.

Among populous counties, the Bronx had the fourth-highest poverty rate in the nation, trailing three counties on the Texas-Mexico border.

Many economists say the government's statistics undercount poverty in New York and other major cities because the numbers are not adjusted for cost of living. A family of two parents and two children is considered poor if it makes less than $19,157 a year, regardless of whether it lives in a city where $500,000 buys a small apartment or a mansion.

Households in New Hampshire made more last year ($57,400 at the median) than in any other state, while those in West Virginia made the least ($32,600). Fairfax County in Virginia ($88,100) and Somerset County in New Jersey ($84,900) were the counties with the highest earnings, the census said.

The decline in employer-provided health benefits came after four years of rapidly rising health costs. Some of the increases stemmed from inefficiencies in the health care system; others were a result of new treatments that improved health and prolonged life but were often expensive.

Either way, the bill for health care has risen, and more companies are deciding not to pay it for some workers. The percentage of people getting health insurance from an employer fell to 59.8 percent last year, from 63.6 percent in 2000. The percentage receiving it from the government rose to 27.2 percent, from 24.7 percent.

The trend is likely to continue unless the job market becomes as tight as it was in the late 1990's and companies decide they must offer health insurance to retain workers, said Paul Fronstin, director of the health research program at the Employee Benefit Research Group, a nonpartisan organization in Washington.

The numbers released Tuesday showed a slight decline in median income, but the bureau called the drop, $93, statistically insignificant. Incomes were also roughly flat among whites, blacks, Hispanics, and Asian-Americans.

The Midwest, which has been hurt by the weak manufacturing sector, was the only region where the median income fell and poverty rose. Elsewhere, they were unchanged.

Since 1967, incomes have failed to rise for four straight years on two other occasions: starting in the late 1970's and in the early 1990's. The Census Bureau does not report household income for years before 1967, but other data show that incomes were generally rising in the 40's, 50's and 60's.

2

WEALTH GAP BETWEEN RACES WIDENS

■ ■ ■

Genaro C. Armas

WHITE FAMILIES' NET WORTH MORE THAN 11 TIMES LATINOS', 14 TIMES BLACKS'

WASHINGTON The enormous wealth gap between white families and blacks and Hispanics grew larger after the most recent recession, a private analysis of government data finds.

White households had a median net worth of greater than $88,000 in 2002, 11 times more than Hispanics and more than 14 times that of blacks, the Pew Hispanic Center said in a study being released Monday.

Blacks were slowest to emerge from the economic downturn that started in 2000 and ended in late 2001, the report found.

Net worth accounts for the values of items such as a home and car, checking and savings accounts, and stocks, minus debts such as mortgage, car loans and credit card bills.

Greater wealth means a greater ability to weather a job loss, emergency home repairs, illness and other unexpected costs, as well as being able to save for retirement or a child's college tuition.

According to the group's analysis of Census Bureau data, nearly one-third of black families and 26 percent of Hispanic families were in debt or had no net assets, compared with 11 percent of white families.

"Wealth is a measure of cumulative advantage or disadvantage," said Roderick Harrison, a researcher at the Joint Center for Political and Economic Studies, a Washington think tank that focuses on black issues. "The fact that black and Hispanic wealth is a fraction of white wealth also reflects a history of discrimination."

After accounting for inflation, net worth for white households increased 17 percent between 1996 and 2002 and rose for Hispanic homes by 14 percent to about $7,900. It decreased for blacks by 16 percent, to roughly $6,000.

Regardless of race and ethnicity, the median net worth for all U.S. households was $59,700 in 2002, a 12 percent gain from 1996.

Only white homes recouped all their losses between 2001 and 2002. Both Hispanics and blacks lost nearly 27 percent of net worth between 1999 and 2001; the next year Latinos had gained almost all back (26 percent) though blacks were up only about 5 percent.

Disparities in Dollars

The median net worth in dollars of white, black and Hispanic households between 1996 and 2002, adjusted for inflation, and the percent change between those years, according to an analysis of Census Bureau data by the Pew Hispanic Center. Figures for whites and blacks refer to those not of Hispanic ethnicity:

Category	1996	2002	Pct.
Hispanic	$6,961	$7,932	14.0
Black	$7,135	$5,988	−16.1
White	$75,482	$86,651	17.4
All households	$53,160	$59,706	12.2

Associated Press

Roberto Suro, director of the Pew Hispanic Center, said the accumulation of wealth allows low-income families to rise into the middle class and "have some kind of assets beyond next week's paychecks."

"Having more assets enabled whites to ride out the jobless recovery better," he said.

Harrison says Hispanics were more insulated from the downturn than blacks, so they took less of a hit. For example, Hispanics made employment gains in lower-paid, lower-skilled areas such as the service and construction sectors.

Blacks were hit hard by job losses in the manufacturing industry and in professional fields, where they were victims of "last hired, first fired" policies, he said.

Only relatively recently were large numbers of blacks and Hispanics able to make investments and accumulate wealth. They were slower to enter the stock market during the 1990s rush and then had less of a cushion when the market began its decline in 2000.

Another factor affecting disparities is that whites are far more likely to own their homes; homeownership is among the most common ways to build wealth.

Census figures released in August showed the national median household income remained basically flat between 2002 and 2003 at $43,318. Median incomes for whites ($47,800) and blacks ($29,600) also were stagnant, while the median income for Hispanics fell about 2 percent to $33,000.

3

CLASS IN AMERICA—2006

■ ■ ■

Gregory Mantsios

People in the United States don't like to talk about class. Or so it would seem. We don't speak about class privileges, or class oppression, or the class nature of society. These terms are not part of our everyday vocabulary, and in most circles they are associated with the language of the rhetorical fringe. Unlike people in most other parts of the world, we shrink from using words that classify along economic lines or that point to class distinctions: phrases like "working class," "upper class," and "ruling class" are rarely uttered by Americans.

For the most part, avoidance of class-laden vocabulary crosses class boundaries. There are few among the poor who speak of themselves as lower class; instead, they refer to their race, ethnic group, or geographic location. Workers are more likely to identify with their employer, industry, or occupational group than with other workers, or with the working class.[1]

Neither are those at the other end of the economic spectrum likely to use the word "class." In her study of thirty-eight wealthy and socially prominent women, Susan Ostrander asked participants if they considered

The author wished to thank Mark Major for his assistance in updating this article. From Gregory Mantsios, *Class in America: Myths and Realities*. Copyright © Gregory Mantsios, 2006. Reprinted by permission of the author.

themselves members of the upper class. One participant responded, "I hate to use the word 'class'. We are responsible, fortunate people, old families, the people who have something."

Another said, "I hate [the term] upper class. It is so non-upper class to use it. I just call it 'all of us,' those who are wellborn."[2]

It is not that Americans, rich or poor, aren't keenly aware of class differences—those quoted above obviously are; it is that class is not in the domain of public discourse. Class is not discussed or debated in public because class identity has been stripped from popular culture. The institutions that shape mass culture and define the parameters of public debate have avoided class issues. In politics, in primary and secondary education, and in the mass media, formulating issues in terms of class is unacceptable, perhaps even un-American. See my paper, "Media Magic: Making Class Invisible."

There are, however, two notable exceptions to this phenomenon. First, it is acceptable in the United States to talk about "the middle class." Interestingly enough, such references appear to be acceptable precisely because they mute class differences. References to the middle class by politicians, for example, are designed to encompass and attract the broadest possible constituency. Not only do references to the middle class gloss over differences, but these references also avoid any suggestion of conflict or injustice.

This leads us to the second exception to the class-avoidance phenomenon. We are, on occasion, presented with glimpses of the upper class and the lower class (the language used is "the wealthy" and "the poor"). In the media, these presentations are designed to satisfy some real or imagined voyeuristic need of "the ordinary person." As curiosities, the ground-level view of street life and the inside look at the rich and the famous serve as unique models, one to avoid and one to aspire to. In either case, the two models are presented without causal relation to each other: one is not rich because the other is poor.

Similarly, when social commentators or liberal politicians draw attention to the plight of the poor, they do so in a manner that obscures the class structure and denies any sense of exploitation. Wealth and poverty are viewed as one of several natural and inevitable states of being: differences are only differences. One may even say differences are the American way, a reflection of American social diversity.

We are left with one of two possibilities: either talking about class and recognizing class distinctions are not relevant to U.S. society, or we mistakenly hold a set of beliefs that obscure the reality of class differences and their impact on people's lives.

Let us look at four common, albeit contradictory, beliefs about the United States.

Myth 1: The United States is fundamentally a classless society. Class distinctions are largely irrelevant today, and whatever differences do exist in economic standing, they are—for the most part—insignificant. Rich or poor, we are all equal in the eyes of the law, and such basic needs as health care and education are provided to all regardless of economic standing.

Myth 2: We are, essentially, a middle-class nation. Despite some variations in economic status, most Americans have achieved relative affluence in what is widely recognized as a consumer society.

Myth 3: We are all getting richer. The American public as a whole is steadily moving up the economic ladder, and each generation propels itself to greater economic well-being. Despite some fluctuations, the U.S. position in the global economy has brought previously unknown prosperity to most, if not all, Americans.

Myth 4: Everyone has an equal chance to succeed. Success in the United States requires no more than hard work, sacrifice, and perseverance: "In America, anyone can become a millionaire; it's just a matter of being in the right place at the right time."

In trying to assess the legitimacy of these beliefs, we want to ask several important questions. Are there significant class differences among Americans? If these differences do exist, are they getting bigger or smaller, and do these differences have a significant impact on the way we live? Finally, does everyone in the United States really have an equal opportunity to succeed?

THE ECONOMIC SPECTRUM

Let's begin by looking at difference. An examination of available data reveals that variations in economic well-being are, in fact, immense. Consider the following:

- The wealthiest 1 percent of the American population holds 34 percent of the total national wealth. That is, they own over one-third of all the consumer durables (such as houses, cars, and stereos) and financial assets (such as stocks, bonds, property, and savings accounts). The richest 20 percent of Americans hold nearly 85 percent of the total household wealth in the country.[3]
- Approximately 183,000 Americans, or approximately three-quarters of 1 percent of the adult population, earn more than $1 million **annually**.[4] There are nearly 400 billionaires in the U.S today, more than three dozen of them worth more than $10 billion each. It would take the average American (earning $35,672 and spending absolutely nothing at all) a total of 28,033 years (or approximately 400 lifetimes) to earn just $1 billion.

Affluence and prosperity are clearly alive and well in certain segments of the U.S. population. However, this abundance is in contrast to the poverty and despair that is also prevalent in the United States. At the other end of the spectrum:

- Approximately 13 percent of the American population—that is, nearly one of every eight people in this country—live below the official poverty line (calculated in 2004 at $9,645 for an individual and $19,307 for a family of four).[5] An estimated 3.5 million people—of whom nearly 1.4 million are children—experience homelessness in any given year.[6]
- Approximately one out of every five children (4.4 million) in the United States under the age of six lives in poverty.[7]

The contrast between rich and poor is sharp, and with nearly one-third of the American population living at one extreme or the other, it is difficult to argue that we live in a classless society. Big-payoff reality shows, celebrity salaries, and multimillion dollar lotteries notwithstanding, evidence suggests that the level of inequality in the United States is getting higher. Census data show the gap between the rich and the poor to be the widest since the government began collecting information in 1947[8] and that this gap is continuing to grow. In 2004 alone, the average real income of 99 percent of the U.S. population grew by little more than 1 percent, while the real income of the richest 1 percent saw their income rise by 12 percent in the same year.[9]

Nor is such a gap between rich and poor representative of the rest of the industrialized world. In fact, the United States has by far the most unequal distribution of household income.[10] The income gap between rich and poor in the United States (measured as the percentage of total income held by the wealthiest 20 percent of the population versus the poorest 20 percent) is approximately 12 to 1, one of the highest ratios in the industrialized world. The ratio in Japan and Germany, by contrast, is 4 to 1.[11]

Reality 1: There are enormous differences in the economic standing of American citizens. A sizable proportion of the U.S. population occupies opposite ends of the economic spectrum. In the middle range of the economic spectrum:

- Sixty percent of the American population holds less than 6 percent of the nation's wealth.[12]
- While the real income of the top 1 percent of U.S. families skyrocketed by more than 180 percent between 1979 and 2000, the income of the middle fifth of the population grew only slightly (12.4 percent over that same 21-year period) and its share of income (15 percent of the total

compared to 48 percent of the total for the wealthiest fifth) actually declined during this period.[13]

- Regressive changes in governmental tax policies and the weakening of labor unions over the last quarter century have led to a significant rise in the level of inequality between the rich and the middle class. Between 1979 and 2000, the gap in household income between the top fifth and middle fifth of the population rose by 31 percent.[14] During the economic boom of the 1990s, the top fifth of the nation's population saw their share of net worth increase (from 59 to 63 percent) while four out of five Americans saw their share of net worth decline.[15] One prominent economist described economic growth in the United States as a "spectator sport for the majority of American families."[16] Economic decline, on the other hand, is much more "inclusive," with layoffs impacting hardest on middle- and lower-income families—those with fewer resources to fall back on.

The level of inequality is sometimes difficult to comprehend fully by looking at dollar figures and percentages. To help his students visualize the distribution of income, the well-known economist Paul Samuelson asked them to picture an income pyramid made of children's blocks, with each layer of blocks representing $1,000. If we were to construct Samuelson's pyramid today, the peak of the pyramid would be much higher than the Eiffel Tower, yet almost all of us would be within six feet of the ground.[17] In other words, the distribution of income is heavily skewed; a small minority of families take the lion's share of national income, and the remaining income is distributed among the vast majority of middle-income and low-income families. Keep in mind that Samuelson's pyramid represents the distribution of income, not wealth. The distribution of wealth is skewed even further.

Reality 2: The middle class in the United States holds a very small share of the nation's wealth and that share is declining steadily. The gap between rich and poor and between rich and the middle class is larger than it has ever been.

American Life-Styles

At last count, nearly 37 million Americans across the nation lived in unrelenting poverty.[18] Yet, as political scientist Michael Harrington once commented, "America has the best dressed poverty the world has ever known."[19] Clothing disguises much of the poverty in the United States, and this may explain, in part, its middle-class image. With increased mass marketing of "designer" clothing and with shifts in the nation's economy from blue-collar (and often better-paying) manufacturing jobs to white-collar and pink-collar jobs in the service sector, it is becoming increasingly difficult to distinguish class differences based on appearance.[20] The dress-down environment prevalent in the high-tech industry (what one author refers to as the "no-collars movement") has reduced superficial distinctions even further.[21]

Beneath the surface, there is another reality. Let's look at some "typical" and not-so-typical life-styles.

American Profile

Name:	Harold S. Browning
Father:	manufacturer, industrialist
Mother:	prominent social figure in the community
Principal child-rearer:	governess
Primary education:	an exclusive private school on Manhattan's Upper East Side
	Note: a small, well-respected primary school where teachers and administrators have a reputation for nurturing student creativity and for providing the finest educational preparation
	Ambition: "to become President"
Supplemental tutoring:	tutors in French and mathematics
Summer camp:	sleep-away camp in northern Connecticut
	Note: camp provides instruction in the creative arts, athletics, and the natural sciences
Secondary education:	a prestigious preparatory school in Westchester County
	Note: classmates included the sons of ambassadors, doctors, attorneys, television personalities, and well-known business leaders
	Supplemental education: private SAT tutor
	After-school activities: private riding lessons
	Ambition: "to take over my father's business"
	High-school graduation gift: BMW

Family activities:	theater, recitals, museums, summer vacations in Europe, occasional winter trips to the Caribbean *Note:* as members of and donors to the local art museum, the Brownings and their children attend private receptions and exhibit openings at the invitation of the museum director
Higher education:	an Ivy League liberal arts college in Massachusetts *Major:* economics and political science *After-class activities:* debating club, college newspaper, swim team *Ambition:* "to become a leader in business"
First full-time job (age 23):	assistant manager of operations, Browning Tool and Die, Inc. (family enterprise)
Subsequent employment:	*3 years*—executive assistant to the president, Browning Tool and Die *Responsibilities included:* purchasing (materials and equipment), personnel, and distribution networks *4 years*—advertising manager, Lackheed Manufacturing (home appliances) *3 years*—director of marketing and sales, Comerex, Inc. (business machines)
Present employment (age 38):	executive vice president, SmithBond and Co. (digital instruments) *Typical daily activities:* review financial reports and computer printouts, dictate memoranda, lunch with clients, initiate conference calls, meet with assistants, plan business trips, meet with associates

Transportation to and from work:
chauffeured company limousine
Annual salary: $324,000
Ambition: "to become chief
executive officer of the firm, or
one like it, within the next five
to ten years"

Present residence: eighteenth-floor condominium
on Manhattan's Upper West Side,
eleven rooms, including five
spacious bedrooms and terrace
overlooking river
Interior: professionally decorated
and accented with elegant
furnishings, valuable antiques,
and expensive artwork
Note: building management
provides doorman and elevator
attendant; family employs au
pair for children and maid for
other domestic chores

Second residence: farm in northwestern Connecticut,
used for weekend retreats
and for horse breeding
(investment/hobby)
Note: to maintain the farm and
cater to the family when they are
there, the Brownings employ a
part-time maid, groundskeeper,
and horse breeder

Harold Browning was born into a world of nurses, maids, and governesses. His world today is one of airplanes and limousines, five-star restaurants, and luxurious living accommodations. The life and lifestyle of Harold Browning is in sharp contrast to that of Bob Farrell.

American Profile

Name:	Bob Farrell
Father:	machinist
Mother:	retail clerk
Principal child-rearer:	mother and sitter

Primary education:	a medium-size public school in Queens, New York, characterized by large class size, outmoded physical facilities, and an educational philosophy emphasizing basic skills and student discipline *Ambition:* "to become President"
Supplemental tutoring:	none
Summer camp:	YMCA day camp *Note:* emphasis on team sports, arts and crafts
Secondary education:	large regional high school in Queens *Note:* classmates included the sons and daughters of carpenters, postal clerks, teachers, nurses, shopkeepers, mechanics, bus drivers, police officers, " salespersons *Supplemental education:* SAT prep course offered by national chain *After-school activities:* basketball and handball in school park *Ambition:* "to make it through college" *High-school graduation gift:* $500 savings bond
Family activities:	family gatherings around television set, softball, an occasional trip to the movie theater, summer Sundays at the public beach
Higher education:	a two-year community college with a technical orientation *Major:* electrical technology *After-school activities:* employed as a part-time bagger in local supermarket *Ambition:* "to become an electrical engineer"
First full-time job (age 19):	service-station attendant *Note:* continued to take college classes in the evening

Subsequent employment:	mail clerk at large insurance firm; manager trainee, large retail chain
Present employment (age 38):	assistant sales manager, building supply firm
	Typical daily activities: demonstrate products, write up product orders, handle customer complaints, check inventory
	Transportation to and from work: city subway
Annual salary:	$45,261
	Ambition: "to open up my own business"
	Additional income: $6,100 in commissions from evening and weekend work as salesman in local men's clothing store
Present residence:	the Farrells own their own home in a working-class neighborhood in Queens, New York

Bob Farrell and Harold Browning live very differently: the life-style of one is privileged; that of the other is not so privileged. The differences are class differences, and these differences have a profound impact on the way they live. They are differences between playing a game of handball in the park and taking riding lessons at a private stable; watching a movie on television and going to the theater; and taking the subway to work and being driven in a limousine. More important, the difference in class determines where they live, who their friends are, how well they are educated, what they do for a living, and what they come to expect from life.

Yet, as dissimilar as their life-styles are, Harold Browning and Bob Farrell have some things in common; they live in the same city, they work long hours, and they are highly motivated. More important, they are both white males.

Let's look at someone else who works long and hard and is highly motivated. This person, however, is black and female.

American Profile	
Name:	Cheryl Mitchell
Father:	janitor
Mother:	waitress
Principal child-rearer:	grandmother

Primary education:	large public school in Ocean Hill-Brownsville, Brooklyn, New York *Note:* rote teaching of basic skills and emphasis on conveying the importance of good attendance, good manners, and good work habits; school patrolled by security guards *Ambition:* "to be a teacher"
Supplemental tutoring:	none
Summer camp:	none
Secondary education:	large public school in Ocean Hill-Brownsville *Note:* classmates included sons and daughters of hairdressers, groundskeepers, painters, dressmakers, dishwashers, domestics *Supplemental education:* none *After-school activities:* domestic chores, part-time employment as babysitter and housekeeper *Ambition:* "to be a social worker" *High-school graduation gift:* corsage
Family activities:	church-sponsored socials
Higher education:	one semester of local community college *Note:* dropped out of school for financial reasons
First full-time job (age 17):	counter clerk, local bakery
Subsequent employment:	file clerk with temporary-service agency, supermarket checker
Present employment (age 38):	nurse's aide at a municipal hospital *Typical daily activities:* make up hospital beds, clean out bedpans, weigh patients and assist them to the bathroom, take temperature readings, pass out and collect food trays, feed patients who need help, bathe patients, and change dressings *Annual salary:* $15,820 *Ambition:* "to get out of the ghetto"

Present residence:	three-room apartment in the South Bronx, needs painting, has poor ventilation, is in a high-crime area
	Note: Cheryl Mitchell lives with her four-year-old son and her elderly mother

When we look at the lives of Cheryl Mitchell, Bob Farrell, and Harold Browning, we see life-styles that are very different. We are not looking, however, at economic extremes. Cheryl Mitchell's income as a nurse's aide puts her above the government's official poverty line.[22] Below her on the income pyramid are 37 million poverty-stricken Americans. Far from being poor, Bob Farrell has an annual income as an assistant sales manager that puts him well above the median income level—that is, more than 50 percent of the U.S. population earns less money than Bob Farrell.[23] And while Harold Browning's income puts him in a high-income bracket, he stands only a fraction of the way up Samuelson's income pyramid. Well above him are the 183,000 individuals whose annual salary exceeds $1 million. Yet Harold Browning spends more money on his horses than Cheryl Mitchell earns in a year.

Reality 3: Even ignoring the extreme poles of the economic spectrum, we find enormous class differences in the life-styles among the haves, the have-nots, and the have-littles.

Class affects more than life-style and material well-being. It has a significant impact on our physical and mental well-being as well.

Researchers have found an inverse relationship between social class and health. Lower-class standing is correlated to higher rates of infant mortality, eye and ear disease, arthritis, physical disability, diabetes, nutritional deficiency, respiratory disease, mental illness, and heart disease.[24] In all areas of health, poor people do not share the same life chances as those in the social class above them. Furthermore, lower-class standing is correlated with a lower quality of treatment for illness and disease. The results of poor health and poor treatment are borne out in the life expectancy rates within each class. Researchers have found that the higher your class standing, the higher your life expectancy. Conversely, they have also found that within each age group, the lower one's class standing, the higher the death rate; in some age groups, the figures are as much as two and three times as high.[25]

Reality 4: From cradle to grave, class standing has a significant impact on our chances for survival.

The lower one's class standing, the more difficult it is to secure appropriate housing, the more time is spent on the routine tasks of everyday life, the greater is the percentage of income that goes to pay for food and other basic necessities, and the greater is the likelihood of crime victimization.[26] Class can accurately predict chances for both survival and success.

CLASS AND EDUCATIONAL ATTAINMENT

School performance (grades and test scores) and educational attainment (level of schooling completed) also correlate strongly with economic class. Furthermore, despite some efforts to make testing fairer and schooling more accessible, current data suggest that the level of inequity is staying the same or getting worse.

In his study for the Carnegie Council on Children nearly thirty years ago, Richard De Lone examined the test scores of over half a million students who took the College Board exams (SATs). His findings were consistent with earlier studies that showed a relationship between class and scores on standardized tests; his conclusion: "the higher the student's social status, the higher the probability that he or she will get higher grades."[27] Almost thirty years after the release of the Carnegie report, College Board surveys reveal data that are no different: test scores still correlate strongly with family income.

Average Combined Scores by Income (400 to 1600 scale)[28]

Family Income	Median Score
More than $100,000	1119
$80,000 to $100,000	1063
$70,000 to $80,000	1039
$60,000 to $70,000	1026
$50,000 to $60,000	1014
$40,000 to $50,000	996
$30,000 to $40,000	967
$20,000 to $30,000	937
$10,000 to $20,000	906
less than $10,000	884

These figures are based on the test results of 987,584 SAT takers in 2005.

A little more than thirty years ago, researcher William Sewell showed a positive correlation between class and overall educational achievement. In comparing the top quartile (25 percent) of his sample to the bottom quartile, he found that students from upper-class families were twice as likely to obtain training beyond high school and four times as likely to attain a postgraduate degree. Sewell concluded: "Socioeconomic background . . . operates independently of academic ability at every stage in the process of educational attainment."[29]

Today, the pattern persists. There are, however, two significant changes. On the one hand, the odds of getting into college have improved for the bottom quartile of the population, although they still remain relatively low compared to the top. On the other hand, the chances of completing a college degree have deteriorated markedly for the bottom quartile. Researchers estimate the chances of completing a four-year college degree (by age 24) to be nineteen times as great for the top 25 percent of the population as it is for the bottom 25 percent.[30]

Reality 5: Class standing has a significant impact on chances for educational achievement.

Class standing, and consequently life chances, are largely determined at birth. Although examples of individuals who have gone from rags to riches abound in the mass media, statistics on class mobility show these leaps to be extremely rare. In fact, dramatic advances in class standing are relatively infrequent. One study showed that fewer than one in five men surpass the economic status of their fathers.[31] For those whose annual income is in six figures, economic success is due in large part to the wealth and privileges bestowed on them at birth. Over 66 percent of the consumer units with incomes of $100,000 or more have inherited assets. Of these units, over 86 percent reported that inheritances constituted a substantial portion of their total assets.[32]

Economist Harold Wachtel likens inheritance to a series of Monopoly games in which the winner of the first game refuses to relinquish his or her cash and commercial property for the second game. "After all," argues the winner, "I accumulated my wealth and income by my own wits." With such an arrangement, it is not difficult to predict the outcome of subsequent games.[33]

Reality 6: All Americans do not have an equal opportunity to succeed. Inheritance laws ensure a greater likelihood of success for the offspring of the wealthy.

SPHERES OF POWER AND OPPRESSION

When we look at society and try to determine what it is that keeps most people down—what holds them back from realizing their potential as healthy, creative, productive individuals—we find institutional forces that are largely beyond individual control. Class domination is one of these forces. People do not choose to be poor or working class; instead, they are limited and confined by the opportunities afforded or denied them by a social and economic system. The class structure in the United States is a function of its economic system: capitalism, a system that is based on private rather than public ownership and control of commercial enterprises. Under capitalism, these enterprises are governed by the need to produce a profit for the owners, rather than to fulfill societal needs. Class divisions arise from the differences between those who own and control corporate enterprise and those who do not.

Racial and gender domination are other forces that hold people down. Although there are significant differences in the way capitalism, racism, and sexism affect our lives, there are also a multitude of parallels. And although class, race, and gender act independently of each other, they are at the same time very much interrelated.

On the one hand, issues of race and gender cut across class lines. Women experience the effects of sexism whether they are well-paid professionals or poorly paid clerks. As women, they are not only subjected to catcalls and stereotyping, but face discrimination and are denied opportunities and privileges that men have. Similarly, a wealthy black man faces racial oppression, is subjected to racial slurs, and is denied opportunities because of his color. Regardless of their class standing, women and members of minority races are constantly dealing with institutional forces that are holding them down precisely because of their gender, the color of their skin, or both.

On the other hand, the experiences of women and minorities are differentiated along class lines. Although they are in subordinate positions vis-à-vis white men, the particular issues that confront women and people of color may be quite different depending on their position in the class structure.

Power is incremental, and class privileges can accrue to individual women and to individual members of a racial minority. While power is incremental, oppression is cumulative, and those who are poor, black, and female are often subject to all of the forces of class, race, and gender discrimination simultaneously. This cumulative situation is what is meant by the double and triple jeopardy of women and minorities.

Furthermore, oppression in one sphere is related to the likelihood of oppression in another. If you are black and female, for example, you are much more likely to be poor or working class than you would be as a white male. Census figures show that the incidence of poverty varies greatly by race and gender.

Chances of Being Poor in America[34]

White male/ female	White female head*	Hispanic male/ female	Hispanic female head*	Black male/ female	Black female head*
1 in 10	1 in 5	1 in 5	1 in 3	1 in 4	1 in 3

*Persons in families with female householder, no husband present.

In other words, being female and being nonwhite are attributes in our society that increase the chances of poverty and of lower-class standing.

Reality 7: Racism and sexism significantly compound the effects of class in society.

None of this makes for a very pretty picture of our country. Despite what we like to think about ourselves as a nation, the truth is that opportunity for success and life itself are highly circumscribed by our race, our gender, and the class we are born into. As individuals, we feel hurt and anger when someone is treating us unfairly; yet as a society we tolerate unconscionable injustice. A more just society will require a radical redistribution of wealth and power. We can start by reversing the current trends that further polarize us as a people and adapt policies and practices that narrow the gaps in income, wealth, and privilege.

NOTES

1. See Jay MacLead, *Ain't No Makin' It: Aspirations and Attainment in a Lower-Income Neighborhood* (Boulder, CO: Westview Press, 1995); Benjamin DeMott, *The Imperial Middle* (New York: Morrow, 1990); Ira Katznelson, *City Trenches: Urban Politics and Patterning of Class in the United States* (New York: Pantheon Books, 1981); Charles W. Tucker, "A Comparative Analysis of Subjective Social Class: 1945–1963," *Social Forces*, no. 46, June 1968, pp. 508–514; Robert Nisbet, "The Decline and Fall of Social Class," *Pacific Sociological Review*, vol. 2, Spring 1959, pp. 11–17; and Oscar Glantz, "Class Consciousness and Political Solidarity," *American Sociological Review*, vol. 23, August 1958, pp. 375–382.

2. Susan Ostander, "Upper-Class Women: Class Consciousness as Conduct and Meaning," in G. William Domhoff, *Power Structure Research* (Beverly Hills, CA: Sage Publications, 1980), pp. 78–79. Also see Stephen Birmingham, *America's Secret Aristocracy* (Boston: Little Brown, 1987).

3. Lawrence Mishel, Jared Bernstein, and Sylvia Allegretto, *The State of Working America: 2004–2005* (Ithaca: ILR Press, Cornell University Press, 2005), p. 282.

4. The number of individuals filing tax returns showing a gross adjusted income of $1 million or more in 2003 was 182,932 (Tax Stats at a Glance, Internal Revenue Service, U.S. Treasury Department, available at http://www.irs.gov/taxstats/article/0,,id = 102886,00.html).

5. Carmen DeNavas-Walt, Bernadette D. Proctor, and Cheryl Hill Lee, U.S. Census Bureau, Current Population Reports, P60–229, *Income, Poverty, and Health Insurance in the United States: 2004* (Washington, DC: U.S. Government Printing Office, 2005), pp. 9, 45.

6. National Coalition for the Homeless "How many people experience homelessness?" NCH Fact Sheet #2 (June 2006), citing a 2004 National Law Center on Homelessness and Poverty study. Available at http://www.nationalhomeless.org/publications/facts/How_Many.pdf

7. Mishel et al., op. cit., pp. 318–319.

8. Lawrence Mishel, Jared Bernstein, and Heather Boushey, *The State of Working America: 2002–2003* (Ithaca: ILR Press, Cornell University Press, 2003), p. 53.

9. Paul Krugman, "Left Behind Economics" *New York Times*, July 14, 2006.

10. Based on a comparison of 19 industrialized states: Mishel et al., *2004–2005*, pp. 399–401.

11. Mishel et al., ibid, p. 64.

12. Derived from Mishel et al., *2002–2003*, p. 281.

13. Mishel et al., *2004–2005*, ibid, pp. 62–63.

14. Mishel et al. *2002–2003* ibid, p. 70.

15. Mishel et al., ibid, p. 280.

16. Alan Blinder, quoted by Paul Krugman, in "Disparity and Despair," *U.S. News and World Report*, March 23, 1992, p. 54.

17. Paul Samuelson, *Economics*, 10th ed. (New York: McGraw-Hill, 1976), p. 84.

18. DeNavas-Walt et al., op. cit., p. 9.

19. Michael Harrington, *The Other America* (New York: Macmillan, 1962), pp. 12–13.

20. Stuart Ewen and Elizabeth Ewen, *Channels of Desire: Mass Images and the Shaping of American Consciousness* (New York: McGraw-Hill, 1982).

21. Andrew Ross, *No-Collar: The Humane Work Place and Its Hidden Costs* (New York: Basic Books, 2002).

22. Based on a poverty threshold for a three-person household in 2004 of $15,205. DeNavas et al., op. cit., p. 45.

23. The median income in 2004 was $40,798 for men, $31,223 for women, and $44,389 for households. DeNavas-Walt et al., op. cit., pp. 3–5.

24. E. Pamuk, D. Makuc, K. Heck, C. Reuben, and K. Lochner, *Socioeconomic Status and Health Chartbook, Health, United States, 1998* (Hyattsville, MD: National Center for Health Statistics, 1998), pp. 145–159; Vincente Navarro "Class, Race, and Health Care in the United States," in Bersh Berberoglu, *Critical Perspectives in Sociology*, 2nd ed. (Dubuque, IA: Kendall/Hunt, 1993), pp. 148–156; Melvin Krasner, *Poverty and Health in New York City* (New York: United Hospital Fund of New York, 1989). See also U.S. Dept. of Health and Human Services, *Health Status of Minorities and Low Income Groups*, 1985; and Dan Hughes, Kay Johnson, Sara Rosenbaum, Elizabeth Butler, and Janet Simons, *The Health of America's Children* (The Children's Defense Fund, 1988).

25. E. Pamuk et al., op. cit.; Kenneth Neubeck and Davita Glassberg, *Sociology; A Critical Approach* (New York: McGraw-Hill, 1996), pp. 436–438; Aaron Antonovsky, "Social Class, Life Expectancy, and Overall Mortality," in *The Impact of Social Class* (New York: Thomas Crowell, 1972), pp. 467–491. See also Harriet Duleep, "Measuring the Effect of Income on Adult Mortality Using Longitudinal Administrative Record Data," *Journal of Human Resources*, vol. 21, no. 2, Spring 1986. See also Paul Farmer, *Pathologies of Power: Health, Human Rights, and the New War on the Poor*, (Berkeley: University of California Press, 2005).

26. E. Pamuk et al., op. cit., fig. 20; Dennis W. Roncek, "Dangerous Places: Crime and Residential Environment," *Social Forces*, vol. 60, no. 1, September 1981, pp. 74–96.

27. Richard De Lone, *Small Futures* (New York: Harcourt Brace Jovanovich, 1978), pp. 14–19.

28. Derived from "2005 College-Bound Seniors, Total Group Profile," *College Board*, p. 7, available at http://www.collegeboard.com/prod_downloads/about/news_info/cbsenior/yr2005/2005-college-bound-seniors.pdf.

29. William H. Sewell, "Inequality of Opportunity for Higher Education," *American Sociological Review*, vol. 36, no. 5, 1971, pp. 793–809.

30. The Mortenson Report on Public Policy Analysis of Opportunity for Postsecondary Education, "Postsecondary Education Opportunity" (Iowa City, IA: September 1993, no. 16).

31. De Lone, op. cit., pp. 14–19.

32. Howard Tuchman, *Economics of the Rich* (New York: Random House, 1973), p. 15. For more information on inheritance see, Sam Bowles and Herbert Gintis, "The Inheritance of Inequality," *The Journal of Economic Perspectives*, vol. 16, no. 3 (summer, 2002) pp. 2–30 and Tom Hertz, *Understanding Mobility in America*, Center for American Progress, http://www.americanprogress.org/site/pp.asp?c = biJRJ8OVF&b = 1579981.

33. Howard Wachtel, *Labor and the Economy* (Orlando, FL: Academic Press, 1984), pp. 161–162.

34. Derived from DeNavas et al., op. cit., pp. 46–51.

4

WOMEN'S PAY: WHY THE GAP REMAINS A CHASM

■ ■ ■

Aaron Bernstein

During the heyday of the women's movement more than 30 years ago, "59¢ on the dollar" was an oft-heard rallying cry, referring to how little women earned compared with men. Those concerns seem outdated today, when it's easy to find female doctors, lawyers, pop stars, even Presidential advisers. The progress toward equality in the workplace also shows up in government data on wages, which pegs women's average pay at 77% of men's compensation today.

But there's new evidence that women's advances may not be quite so robust after all. When you look at how much the typical woman actually earns over much of her career, the true figure is more like 44% of what the average man makes. That's the conclusion of a new study by Stephen J. Rose, an economist at Macro International Inc., a consulting firm, and Heidi I. Hartmann, President of the Institute for Women's Policy Research in Washington.

Why the big discrepancy? The Bureau of Labor Statistics (BLS) numbers, published every year, are accurate as far as they go. But they only measure the earnings of those who work full-time for an entire year. Only one-quarter of women, though, achieve this level of participation consistently throughout their working lives. So Rose and Hartmann looked at the pay of all men and women over 15 years, including those who worked part-time and dipped in and out of the labor force to care for children or elderly parents. This long-term perspective still shows an arc of progress: The 44%, based on average earnings between 1983 and 1998, jumped from 29% in the prior 15 years. But the more comprehensive view gives a less rosy picture of women's position in the work world.

Outright discrimination against women probably accounts for only about 10 percentage points of the pay gap, according to numerous studies. The bulk of the problem, then, lies with the conflicting needs and norms of society and employers. A majority of men and women still work in largely sex-segregated occupations, Rose and Hartmann's study shows, leaving many women stuck in lower-paying jobs such as cashiers and maids.

Family responsibilities, too, typically still fall more heavily on women, and neither society nor employers have found good ways to mesh those with job demands. Rose and Hartmann's data show that women can get equal treatment today—but mostly when they behave like traditional men and leave the primary family responsibilities at home. For the majority who can't or won't do that, the work world remains much less accommodating. Of course, many women choose to take time off or to work part-time to be with their children rather than stay on the job. Yet that choice itself is constrained by the widespread lack of day care and flexible job options, Hartmann argues. "The 44% gap we found shows that there are still tremendous differences in how the labor market treats men and women," she says.

Hartmann and Rose came to their results by examining long-term earnings trends. The 77% figure comes from the BLS's 2002 earnings survey and looks at how much full-time, year-round workers make in a given year. By contrast, Rose and Hartmann used a University of Michigan survey that has tracked a sample of randomly chosen people and their children since 1968. They looked at how much each person made between 1983 and 1998 in every year from age 26 to 59 (to exclude students and retirees).

One surprise was just how many women work most of their adult lives. Fully 96% of these prime-age women worked at least one of those 15 years, and they clocked an average of 12 years on the job. In other words, few women these days drop out altogether once they have kids.

But those few years out of the labor market carry a stiff penalty. More than half of all women spent at least a year out of the labor force, the study found, and they earned an average of $21,363 a year over the years they worked, after inflation adjustments, vs. nearly $30,000 for women who stuck with it for all 15 years. Indeed, anyone who drops out risks derailing their career and permanently slashing their pay. Just one year off cuts a woman's total earnings over 15 years by 32%, while two years slice it by 46% and three by 56%, according to Hartmann and Rose. The work world penalizes men nearly as much; their average pay drops by 25% if they take off a year. Fewer than 8% of men did so, however. "Our economic system is still based on a family division of labor, and women pay the price," says Rose.

Women also take a big hit for going part-time. On average, they work a lot less than men: 1,498 hours a year, vs. 2,219 worked by the typical man. The fewer hours women work account for about half of the total pay gap between the sexes, Rose and Hartmann concluded. Some women have turned to self-employment as a way to fit work and family together. But they often must accept lower pay in the process. Brita Bergland, a Windsor (Vt.) resident, found it difficult to manage her sales job at a printing company while she also cared for her aging mother and her daughter. So she struck out on her own six years ago and has managed the work-life balance much better ever since. The cost: about a $15,000 cut in annual earnings, down from the $55,000 to $60,000 she made as an employee. "These are the choices women make because society doesn't help them to support children and parents," says Bergland, who's now 50.

And while many women have made great strides in some highly visible professions such as law and medicine, historical patterns of sex segregation remain strong across much of the economy. Overall, just 15% of women work in jobs typically held by men, such as engineer, stockbroker, and judge, while fewer than 8% of men hold female-dominated jobs such as nurse, teacher, or sales clerk. These findings were reiterated in a detailed BLS analysis released on June 2 that uses the 2000 Census to look at the jobs men and women hold.

Such a sex-segregated economy leaves women with some startling disadvantages. Overall, they earn less than men with the same education at all levels. Incredibly, male dropouts pulled down an average of $36,000 a year between 1983 and 1998, after inflation adjustments, while women with a bachelor's degree made $35,000. Women with a graduate degree averaged $42,000, but men got nearly $77,000.

The good news is that the pay gap continues to narrow no matter how it's measured. That's likely to continue; female college graduation rates surpass those of men, and they're catching up in grad school, too, so they're likely to gain from an economy that rewards skill. Women also should benefit from the ongoing shift to services, where they're more likely to work, and lose less than men from the decline of factory jobs.

Still, speedier progress probably won't happen without more employers making work sites family-friendly and revamping jobs to accommodate women and men as they seek to balance work and family demands. "The workplace needs to change to match the workforce," says Ellen Bravo, national director of 9to5, National Association of Working Women. Until that happens, a woman's labor will continue to be worth a fraction of a man's.

5

THE WAGE GAP AND ITS COSTS

■ ■ ■

WHAT IS THE WAGE GAP?

The wage gap is the difference between the wages of women and men. Full-time working women still get paid—on average—only 77 cents for each dollar full-time working men get paid.

Differences in Earnings Between Women and Men, 1960–2002

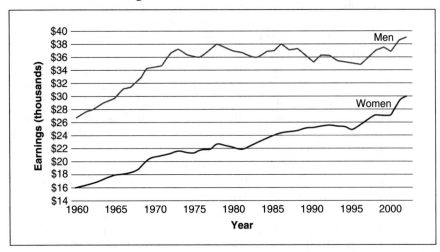

And this is a conservative estimate. The Institute for Women's Policy Research found that women workers in their primary earning ages between 26 and 59 years old make only 38% of what men earn if part-time work and years out of the work force due to family care are taken into account.

Two decades ago, full-time women workers earned 59 cents for every dollar earned by men. The common explanation was that the gender wage gap existed because of a "merit gap." Women, this theory went, were not as educated as men, hadn't worked as long, or were working in stopgap jobs until they got married, while men were family breadwinners. With increases in women's education and employment, the wage gap did begin to narrow, although part of the narrowing was accounted for by declines in male wages.

But, in 1994, despite a booming economy, the wage gap widened. Worse, over the next several years women continued to lose ground. This flew in the face of the merit gap theory. More than forty million American working women were educated, experienced, and holding full-time jobs comparable to men's. Like men, these women had families dependent on their earnings.

Why, instead of catching up, were hard-working women suddenly falling further behind? Over the course of the decade, many women's earnings rose. Yet, on average, women's earnings did not go up as much as men's did. Women's real wages grew 94 percent—while men's real wages had grown 160 percent.

If women's earnings could not catch up to men's in a time of nearly unreal prosperity, at a time when women's qualifications had caught up, what was holding them back? The answer is simple: discrimination.

WHO IS AFFECTED BY THE WAGE GAP?

While most women suffer from the wage gap, it does not affect all women equally. According to 2004 Median Annual Earning U.S. Census data, African American women earn only 68 cents for every dollar a man earns, while Hispanic women earn only 57 cents to the male dollar.

Wage Gap by Race

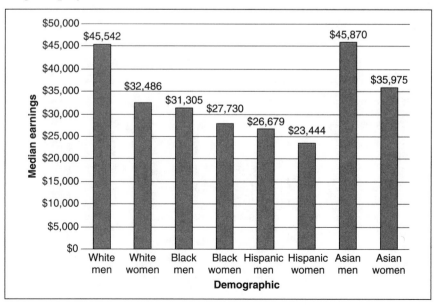

Wage Gap by Age

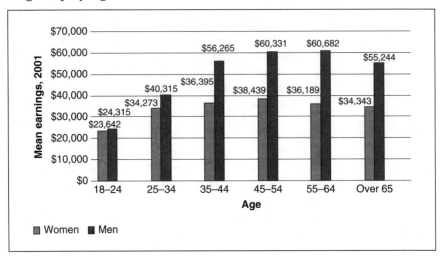

But young women do not escape the wage gap either. If you graduated from college in 2000, your pay started much farther behind men's
than the pay of women who graduated a decade earlier. In 1991, the
wage gap between young women and men with college degrees was
only 9 percent, or a few thousand dollars difference. But in 2000, the
wage gap for young women and men with these same credentials was
31 percent.

Wage Gap by Education

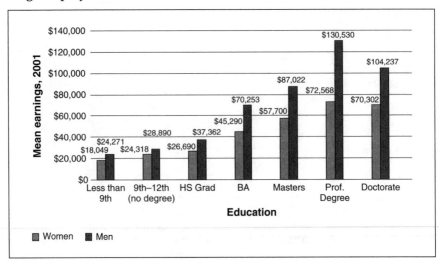

WHAT ARE THE COSTS OF THE WAGE GAP?

Because of the wage gap, more women than men fear—and experience— poverty, or teeter right on the edge. They are missing almost a quarter of their rightful earnings—money that few women can afford to miss.

Eleven million older American women (and only four million older men) make do with less than $8,300 a year, the federal definition of poverty. Nearly three times as many women as men live at subsistence level in their old age.

The wage gap isn't some meaningless abstraction. It adds up. It takes a personal toll. Discrimination is costing women (and their loved ones) the paychecks, pensions, and security that they need and deserve.

- A high school graduate loses $700,000. A young woman graduates from high school this year and goes straight to work at $20,000 a year. Over her lifetime, she will make $700,000 less than the young man graduating with her.
- A college graduate loses $1.2 million. A young woman graduates from college into a $30,000 starting salary. Over her lifetime, she will make $1.2 million less than the young man getting his diploma in line right behind her.
- A professional school graduate loses $2 million. A young woman gets a degree in business, medicine, or law and graduates into a $70,000 starting salary (along with staggering student loan debts). Over her lifetime, she will make $2 million less than the young man at her side.

What would you, your daughter, your mother, your niece, your grand-mother, or your sister do with another $700,000, or $1,200,000, or $2,000,000 over your lifetime?

High School Graduate Woman

College Graduate Woman

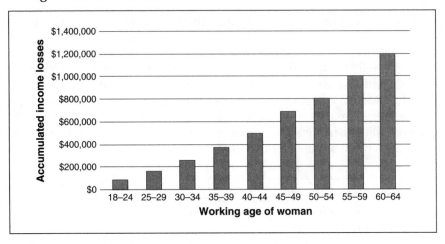

WHY IS THERE A WAGE GAP?

The wage gap is the result of a variety of forms of sex discrimination in the workplace, including discrimination in hiring, promotion and pay, sexual harassment, occupational segregation, bias against mothers, and other ways in which women workers and women's work are undervalued.

Hiring, Promotion, Pay

First comes what most people think of as sex discrimination: the simple and straightforward refusal to hire, promote, or fairly pay women who are just as qualified as men.

Sexual Harassment

Few people realize that sexual harassment also constitutes wage discrimination. After long and repeated sexual harassment, women leave or lose their jobs, potential raises, promotions, opportunities, emotional stability, ability to work, and sometimes their lives.

Occupational Segregation

In 2000, two-thirds of all U.S. working women were still crowded into twenty-one of the 500 occupational categories. And, then women's work is consistently paid less than men's work. Are janitors really worth more than nurses' aides, parking lot attendants more than child care workers, construction laborers more than bookkeepers and cashiers? According to American payrolls, they are.

Taxing Motherhood

Many people believe that the wage gap exists because women choose to care for children. But do they really choose to be paid less for doing the same work they did before giving birth? Forget the mommy track: too many women find themselves shunted unwillingly onto the mommy sidetrack. Frustrated women talk about how, once they came back from maternity leave, colleagues began to treat them as unreliable and unpromotable—almost willfully overlooking any evidence of productivity.

Undervaluing Women Workers

Everyday, women workers' suggestions are dismissed—only to be discussed seriously when made by a man. Or when employers turn to old boy networks rather than public postings to recruit new talent. Or when interviews or screening tests prize male strengths or deeper voices, even though women's strengths and communication styles could accomplish the job just as well.

6

"SAVAGE INEQUALITIES" REVISITED

■ ■ ■

Bob Feldman

RICHER, WHITER SCHOOL DISTRICTS ARE STILL GETTING MORE PUBLIC FUNDS, WHILE THE FEDERAL GOVERNMENT LOOKS THE OTHER WAY

In the late 1980s, I taught health and social studies in a New York City public school. My students came largely from African-American and Caribbean families, and the school was located in a high-poverty district. Because funding was so tight, we had no textbooks for a required eighth-grade health class, no classroom maps for seventh- and eighth-grade history classes, and no photocopying machines that teachers or students could use for free. There was also no school newspaper or yearbook, and the school band had fewer than twenty instruments.

The conditions in this school illustrated a crisis of funding inequality in the U.S. public school system. In his 1991 book *Savage Inequalities*, Jonathan Kozol, a long-time critic of unequal education, famously exposed this crisis. He noted, for instance, that schools in the rich suburbs of New York City spent more than $11,000 per pupil in 1987, while those in the city itself spent only $5,500. The story was the same throughout the country: per-capita spending for poor students and students of color in urban areas was a fraction of that in richer, whiter suburbs just miles away.

Over ten years after *Savage Inequalities* was first published, how close has the U.S. public school system come to providing equitable funding for

Reprinted by permission of *Dollars & Sense*, a progressive economics magazine. www.dollarsandsense.org

all students—funding that is at least equal between districts, or better yet, higher in poorer areas that have greater needs?

Not very far, according to a new report by the Washington, D.C.-based Education Trust. Entitled "The Funding Gap: Low-Income and Minority Students Receive Fewer Dollars," the report examines state and local expenditures in 15,000 school districts during 1999–2000. Since federal funds account for only 7% of public school resources, this study of state and local spending zeroes in on the source of funding inequality.

According to the Education Trust study, the poorest 25% of school districts in each state receive an average of $966 less in state and local funds per pupil than the richest 25%. This gap has narrowed by $173 since 1997, but it does not reflect uniform progress: in nine of 47 states examined, the gap widened by at least $100. In states like New York and Illinois, spending differences remain staggering, totaling $2,152 and $2,060 per student, respectively. These figures, like all those in the study, are adjusted to account for the greater expense of educating students in poor districts and areas with a high cost of living. (See Chart 1.)

Funding inequality puts students of color at a special disadvantage. In two-thirds of states in the Education Trust study, the quarter of school districts with the highest percentage of students of color received at least $100 less in state and local funding than the quarter of districts with the lowest percentage of students of color. New York topped the charts for racial inequality: the quarter of districts with the highest percentage of students of color received $2,034 less in state and local funds per student than the quarter of districts enrolling the smallest percentage. (See Chart 2.)

Between 1997 and 2000, 30 of the 47 states studied did move toward providing equal or greater funding for students in poorer districts—and some states made significant progress. Why did this happen? According to Michael Rebell, executive director of the Campaign for Fiscal Equity, lawsuits have produced some changes. New Jersey, for instance, began channeling funds to its poorest districts after a court challenge; as of 2000, the state government provided roughly three times as much per-capita funding to the poorest quarter of districts as it did to the richest quarter. While the state government's targeted funds are counterbalanced by wildly unequal local resources, students in the poorest quarter of districts now receive a net of $324 more per capita than those in the richest quarter. States like Oregon have achieved similar results not by targeting poorer districts, but by assuming a greater share of responsibility for school funding state-wide. Strategies like New Jersey's and Oregon's help explain the narrowing funding gap, and could be models for other states.

CHART 1
Poor Students Get Less: States with Largest Per-Student Funding Gaps, and U.S. Average

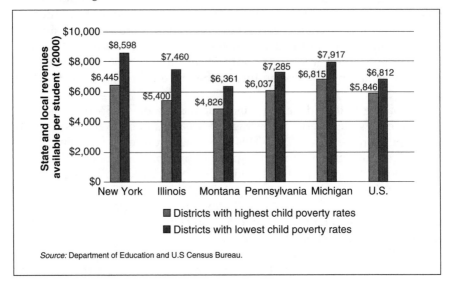

Source: Department of Education and U.S Census Bureau.

CHART 2
Students of Color Get Less: States with Largest Per-Student Funding Gaps, and U.S. Average

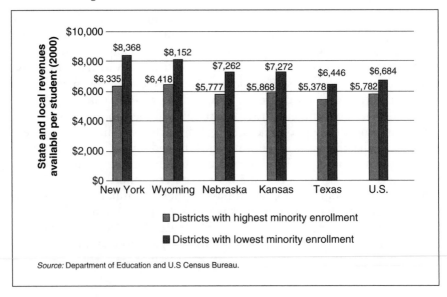

Source: Department of Education and U.S Census Bureau.

Rebell notes, however, that state-level remedies are fundamentally limited: among states, they are "complex and uneven," and nationally, they leave millions of students unaffected. A more powerful solution might be for the federal government to fund the public school system directly, as governments do in Canada, Japan, and most social democratic countries of Western Europe. Today, the U.S. government does channel money to poor districts through Title I, the largest single federal investment in education. But Title I funds are not intended to equalize funding within states: the federal government leaves that responsibility to state and local authorities, who plainly do not comply.

The needs of students would be justly served by federally guaranteed funding, but current state and federal policies guarantee something very different. As Jonathan Kozol explained a decade ago, "The present system guarantees that those who can buy a $1 million home in an affluent suburb will also be able to provide their children with superior schools." The U.S. public school system is still rigged in favor of students from richer, whiter districts; and as Rebell remarks, the United States remains "the only major developed country in the world that exhibits this shameful pattern of educational inequity."

Bob Feldman is *a* Dollars & Sense *intern.*

RESOURCES

Jonathan Kozal, Savage Inequalities: *Children in American's Schools* (Crown Publishers, 1991).

Educational Leadership, December 1, 1993 interview with Jonathan Kozol. (www. ACCESSednetwork.org).

"The Funding Gap: Low-Income and Minority Students Receive Fewer Dollars," The Educational Trust, Inc., (www.edtrust.org).

7

CAUSE OF DEATH:
INEQUALITY

■ ■ ■

Alejandro Reuss

INEQUALITY KILLS

You won't see inequality on a medical chart or a coroner's report under "cause of death." You won't see it listed among the top killers in the United States each year. All too often, however, it is social inequality that lurks behind a more immediate cause of death, be it heart disease or diabetes, accidental injury or homicide. Few of the top causes of death are "equal opportunity killers." Instead, they tend to strike poor people more than rich people, the less educated more than the highly educated, people lower on the occupational ladder more than those higher up, or people of color more than white people.

Statistics on mortality and life expectancy do not provide a perfect map of social inequality. For example, in 2002, the life expectancy for women in the United States was about five years longer than the life expectancy for men, despite the many ways in which women are subordinated to men. Take most indicators of socioeconomic status, however, and most causes of death, and it's a strong bet that you'll find illness and injury (or "morbidity") and mortality increasing as status decreases.

Among people between the ages of 25 and 64, those with less than a high school diploma (or equivalent) had an age-adjusted mortality rate more than three times that of people with at least some college, as of 2003. Those without a high school diploma had more than triple the death rate from chronic noncommunicable diseases (e.g., heart disease), more than $3^{1}/_{2}$ times the death rate from injury, and nearly six times the death rate

Reprinted by permission of *Dollars & Sense*, a progressive economics magazine. www.dollarsandsense.org

from HIV/AIDS, compared to those with at least some college. People with incomes below the poverty line were nearly twice as likely to have had an asthma attack in the previous year (among those previously diagnosed with asthma) as people with incomes at least twice the poverty line. Poor people were over $2^1/_2$ times as likely to suffer from a chronic condition that limited their activity and over three times as likely to characterize their own health as "fair" or "poor" (rather than "good" or "very good"), compared to those with incomes over double the poverty line. African Americans have higher death rates than whites from cancer ($^1/_4$ higher), heart disease ($^1/_3$ higher), stroke ($^1/_2$ higher), diabetes (twice as high), homicide (more than 5 times as high), and AIDS (more than 8 times as high). The infant mortality rate for African Americans was, in 2002–2003, over twice as high as for whites. In all, the lower you are in a social hierarchy, the worse your health and the shorter your life are likely to be.

THE WORSE OFF IN THE UNITED STATES ARE NOT WELL OFF BY WORLD STANDARDS

You often hear it said that even poor people in rich countries like the United States are rich compared to ordinary people in poor countries. While that may be true when it comes to consumer goods like televisions or telephones, which are widely available even to poor people in the United States, it's completely wrong when it comes to health.

In a 1996 study published in the *New England Journal of Medicine*, University of Michigan researchers found that African-American females living to age 15 in Harlem had a 65% chance of surviving to age 65. That is less than the probability at birth of surviving to age 65 for women in India, according to 2000–2005 data. Meanwhile, Harlem's African-American males reaching age 15 had only a 37% chance of surviving to age 65. That is less than the probability at birth of surviving to age 65 for men in Haiti. Among both African-American men and women, diseases of the circulatory system and cancers were the leading causes of death.

It takes more income to achieve a given life expectancy in a rich country like the United States than it does to achieve the same life expectancy in a less affluent country. So the higher money income of a low-income person in the United States, compared to a middle-income person in a poor country, does not necessarily translate into a longer life span. The average income per person in African-American households ($15,200), for example, is about three times the per capita income of Peru. As of 2002, however, the life expectancy for African-American men in the United States was about 69 years, less than as the average life expectancy in Peru. The infant mortality rate for African Americans, 13.5 per 1000 live births, is between that of Uruguay and Bulgaria, both of which have per capita incomes around $8,000.

HEALTH INEQUALITIES IN THE UNITED STATES ARE
NOT JUST ABOUT ACCESS TO HEALTH CARE

Nearly one sixth of the U.S. population below age 65 lacks health insurance of any kind, private or Medicaid. Among those with incomes below $1\frac{1}{2}$ times the poverty line, over 30% lack health coverage of any kind, compared to 10% for those with incomes more than twice the poverty line. African Americans under age 65 were about $1\frac{1}{2}$ times as likely as whites to lack health insurance; Latinos, nearly three times as likely. Among those aged 55 to 64, uninsured people were about $\frac{2}{3}$ as likely as insured people to have seen a primary-care doctor in the last year, and less than half as likely to have seen a specialist, as of 2002–2003. Among women over 40, about 55% of those with incomes below the poverty line had gotten a mammogram in the last two years, compared to 75% of those with incomes over twice the poverty line, as of 2003. Obviously, disparities in access to health care are a major health problem.

But so are environmental hazards; communicable diseases; homicide and accidental death; and smoking, lack of exercise, and other risk factors. These dangers all tend to affect lower-income people more than higher-income, less-educated people more than more-educated, and people of color more than whites. African-American children between the ages of 3 and 10 were nearly twice as likely to have had an asthma attack in the last year as white children, among those previously diagnosed with asthma. The frequency of attacks is linked to air pollution. Among people between ages 25 and 64, those without a high school diploma had over five times the death rate from communicable diseases, compared to those with at least some college. African-American men were, as of 2003, more than seven times as likely to fall victim to homicide as white men; African-American women, more than four times as likely as white women. People without a high school diploma (or equivalent) were nearly three times as likely to smoke as those with at least a bachelor's degree, as of 2003. People with incomes below the poverty line were nearly twice as likely to get no exercise as people with incomes over double the poverty line.

Michael Marmot, a pioneer in the study of social inequality and health, notes that so-called diseases of affluence—disorders, like heart disease or diabetes, associated with high-calorie and high-fat diets, lack of physical activity, etc. increasingly typical in rich societies—are most prevalent among the *least* affluent people in these societies. While recognizing the role of such "behavioral" risk factors as smoking in producing poor health, he argues, "It is not sufficient . . . to ask what contribution smoking makes to generating the social gradient in ill health, but we must ask, why is there a social gradient in smoking?" What appear to be individual "lifestyle" decisions often reflect a broader social epidemiology.

GREATER INCOME INEQUALITY GOES HAND IN HAND WITH POORER HEALTH

Numerous studies suggest that the more unequal the income distribution in a country, state, or city, the lower the life expectancies for people at all income levels. A 1996 study published in the *American Journal of Public Health*, for example, shows that U.S. metropolitan areas with low per capita incomes and low levels of income inequality have lower mortality rates than areas with high median incomes and high levels of income inequality. Meanwhile, for a given per capita income range, mortality rates always decline as inequality declines.

R.G. Wilkinson, perhaps the researcher most responsible for relating health outcomes to overall levels of inequality (rather than individual income levels), argues that greater income inequality causes worse health outcomes independent of its effects on poverty. Wilkinson and his associates suggest several explanations for this relationship. First, the bigger the income gap between rich and poor, the less inclined the well-off are to pay taxes for public services they either do not use or use in low proportion to the taxes they pay. Lower spending on public hospitals, schools, and other basic services does not affect wealthy people's life expectancies very much, but it affects poor people's life expectancies a great deal. Second, the bigger the income gap between rich and poor, the lower the overall level of social cohesion. High levels of social cohesion are associated with good health outcomes for several reasons. For example, people in highly cohesive societies are more likely to be active in their communities, reducing social isolation, a known health risk factor.

Numerous researchers have criticized Wilkinson's conclusions, arguing that the real reason income inequality tends to be associated with worse health outcomes is that it is associated with higher rates of poverty. But even if they are right and income inequality causes worse health simply by bringing about greater poverty, that hardly makes for a defense of inequality. Poverty and inequality are like partners in crime. "Whether public policy focuses primarily on the elimination of poverty or on reduction in income disparity," argue Wilkinson critics Kevin Fiscella and Peter Franks, "neither goal is likely to be achieved in the absence of the other."

DIFFERENCES IN STATUS MAY BE JUST AS IMPORTANT AS INCOME LEVELS

Even after accounting for differences in income, education, and other factors, the life expectancy for African Americans is less than that for whites, U.S. researchers are beginning to explore the relationship between high blood pressure among African Americans and the racism of the surrounding society. African Americans tend to suffer from high blood pressure, a risk factor for circulatory disease, more often than whites. Moreover, studies have found that, when confronted with racism, African Americans suffer larger and longer-lasting increases in blood pressure than when faced with other stressful situations. Broader surveys relating blood pressure in African Americans to perceived instances of racial discrimination have yielded complex results, depending on social class, gender, and other factors.

Stresses cascade down social hierarchies and accumulate among the least empowered. Even researchers focusing on social inequality and health, however, have been surprised by the large effects on mortality. Over 30 years ago, Michael Marmot and his associates undertook a landmark study, known as Whitehall I, of health among British civil servants. Since the civil servants shared many characteristics regardless of job classification—an office work environment, a high degree of job security, etc.—the researchers expected to find only modest health differences among them. To their surprise, the study revealed a sharp increase in mortality with each step down the job hierarchy—even from the highest grade to the second highest. Over ten years, employees in the lowest grade were three times as likely to die as those in the highest grade. One factor was that people in lower grades showed a higher incidence of many "lifestyle" risk factors, like smoking, poor diet, and lack of exercise. Even when the researchers controlled for such factors, however, more than half the mortality gap remained.

Marmot noted that people in the lower job grades were less likely to describe themselves as having "control over their working lives" or being "satisfied with their work situation," compared to those higher up. While people in higher job grades were more likely to report "having to work at a fast pace," lower-level civil servants were more likely to report feelings of hostility, the main stress-related risk factor for heart disease. Marmot concluded that "psycho-social" factors—the psychological costs of being lower in the hierarchy—played an important role in the unexplained mortality gap. Many of us have probably said to ourselves, after a trying day on the job, "They're killing me." Turns out it's not just a figure of speech. Inequality kills—and it starts at the bottom.

RESOURCES

Health, United States, 2005, with Chartbook on Trends in the Health of Americans, National Center for Health Statistics www.cdc.gov/nchs.

Health, United States, 1998, with Socioeconomic Status and Health Chartbook, National Center for Health Statistics www.cdc.gov/nchs.

Human Development Report 2005, UN Development Programme hdr.undp.org.

Human Development Report 2000, UN Development Programme hdr.undp.org.

World Development Indicators 2000, World Bank.

Lisa Berkman, "Social Inequalities and Health: Five Key Points for Policy-Makers to Know," February 5, 2001, Kennedy School of Government, Harvard University.

Ichiro Kawachi, Bruce P. Kennedy, and Richard G. Wilkinson, eds., *The Society and Population Health Reader, Volume I: Income Inequality and Health*, 1999.

Michael Marmot, "Social Differences in Mortality: The Whitehall Studies," in Alan D. Lopez, Graziella Caselli, and Tapani Valkonen, eds., *Adult Mortality in Developed Countries: From Description to Explanation*, 1995.

Michael Marmot, "The Social Pattern of Health and Disease," in David Blane, Eric Brunner, and Richard Wilkinson, eds., *Health and Social Organization: Towards a Health Policy for the Twenty-First Century*, 1996.

Arline T. Gronimus et al., "Excess Mortality Among Blacks and Whites in the United States, *The New England Journal of Medicine*, 335(21), November 21, 1996.

Nancy Krieger, Ph.D., and Stephen Sidney, M.D., "Racial Discrimination and Blood Pressure: The CARDIA Study of Young Black and White Adults," *American Journal of Public Health*, 86(10), October 1996.

8

A PARK PRETTY FOR THE RICH YET RUN-DOWN FOR THE POOR

Prospect Park Overseers Direct Money to Make East Side More Like the West

■ ■ ■

Michael Brick

Here is a place of measured contemplation. Sunbathers doze into afternoon dazes, children romp and hounds do too, soundlessly in the distance. Gossamer pink petal pathways follow low-rolling hillsides past ball fields and into the knotty woods.

And here is a trail of stones broken or gone, a weather-beaten and flood-prone zone where plastic wrappers consort with cigarette cartons. Sagging, broken benches line the way, and sirens honk from a street nearby. Cyclists and horsemen venture apace.

These places appear on a New York City road atlas as one, but Brooklyn knows better. Though this rocket ship-shaped patch in the center of the borough is labeled Prospect Park, in the physical world there are two Prospect Parks.

The reasons for this twinning are complex, but the result is plain and defiant of euphemism. The rich people on the west side have a pretty Prospect Park, and the poor people on the east side have a run-down Prospect Park.

The park's overseers make no effort to dispute this contrast; rather, they cite it as a priority for work in the coming years.

Uniformity could hardly be expected of a thing so vast. It spans 526 acres, including a 60-acre manmade lake and 250 acres of woodlands. Walking the perimeter provides more than four miles of exercise.

Still, to walk the park's width now, from northwest to southeast, is to witness decay with each footfall.

Begin in Park Slope, where blooming trees fill sidewalk boxes, awnings proclaim parkside addresses and doormen greet taxicabs. This is the 78th Police Precinct, scene of 67 robberies and 30 felonious assaults this year. Almost all of the people here, the latest census showed, are American-born, 85 percent of them are white and about half of them own their homes. Their most common level of schooling has earned them a bachelor's degree, and more than half of them make more than $60,000 a year.

They enter the park at Long Meadow, its western edge unfolding into a verdant tableland. On warm afternoons, they come with children or in bikinis. Wheeled things go by. A white butterfly floats toward whatever it is that butterflies enjoy.

"It's a great place to come and read a book or take a nap," says Mariel Greenlee, 23, of Park Slope. "I mostly stay close to this side."

So do the mothers on the grass, whose infant companions can find a world of entertainment within the span of a blanket.

"This is, kind of, our spot," says Elizabeth Redwine, 34, of Prospect Heights. "No one cares if you breast-feed here. There's not a lot of creepy people."

Down the path, past a patch of water reserved for dogs that swim, through a short wooded passage, lies another meadow. Its stone pathways are split by asphalt. Bare patches in the grass become tiny accidental lakes after a rain. Policemen linger on horseback, and there are call boxes for when they do not. Their mounts leave trampled manure next to where others have left tin foil, a plastic cup, newspapers and broken bottles. Past this place known as the Nethermead are the broader banks of the lake, and on its shores a second, different Prospect Park begins.

Here, fully half of the main roadway floods in the days after a hard rain. The grass is patchy, unmowed in places and not worth mowing in others. Dandelions, rocks, weeds, and clover mark the terrain. Downed branches, some nine feet in length, go uncollected. The benches here are lopsided and weather-weary, their green paint all but gone to splinters.

In a gazebo by the water, a wrinkled woman burdened with plastic bags channels a rhythm-and-blues singer, caterwauling across a shaky treble clef: "If you're playing me, keep it on the low, because my heart can't take it anymore."

Her voice drifts to a circle of felled logs, assembled for sitting as an alternative to the pitiable benches. Two men drink beers from paper bags, and one of them, John Satin, 38, says he prefers this side of the park because he finds the lake peaceful.

"There's no recreational park on this side, for whatever reason," Mr. Satin said. "On this side, you don't have much at all."

You do have drum circles on the weekends, and men playing dominoes on garbage cans, improvised entertainments. You have Michael Leonce, 65, who arrays his possessions in a semicircle around an unturned shopping cart and pounds out a calypso sound on a keyboard. Behind him, the men slam down their dominoes, signaling to their partners with sharp slaps that resound across the path. They play on a dirt patch 50 feet from Parkside Avenue, amid cigarette butts and rusted beer caps.

"The other side, they treat them good, they clean it four or five times a week," said Boog Josoph, 27, between turns on the domino board. "This side, you have to wait a week."

Many of the people here are immigrants from the Caribbean. They live in the 71st Precinct, where there have been 143 robberies and 127 felonious assaults this year. Nearly half of them were born outside the United States, 86 percent are black and 13 percent own their homes. Those among them with the most common amount of education have earned a high school diploma or equivalency degree, and more than half of them are paid less than $30,000 a year.

From Prospect Park's earliest days, its destiny was tied to geography, as documented by Clay Lancaster, the park's onetime curator, in a handbook published in 1967. Mr. Lancaster wrote that the designer Calvert Vaux, a partner of Frederick Law Olmsted, advocated buying land to the west because the east side could not be landscaped attractively.

By the time Mr. Lancaster was researching his handbook in the 1960s, he could use only grim words to describe Concert Grove, near the park's southeastern side: "catastrophe," "wrecking," "desecration" and "obliterating." Lest his own point be lost, Mr. Lancaster added, "what one would expect to find serving as a snack bar on a busy freeway."

HUMAN SEXUALITY

1

THE SOCIAL CONSTRUCTION OF SEXUALITY

■ ■ ■

Ruth Hubbard

There is no "natural" human sexuality. This is not to say that our sexual feelings are "unnatural" but that whatever feelings and activities our society interprets as sexual are channeled from birth into socially acceptable forms of expression.

Western thinking about sexuality is based on the Christian equation of sexuality with sin, which must be redeemed through making babies. To fulfill the Christian mandate, sexuality must be intended for procreation, and thus all forms of sexual expression and enjoyment other than heterosexuality are invalidated. Actually, for most Christians nowadays just plain heterosexuality will do, irrespective of whether it is intended to generate offspring.

These ideas about sexuality set up a major contradiction in what we tell children about sex and procreation. We teach them that sex and sexuality are about becoming mommies and daddies and warn them not to explore sex by themselves or with playmates of either sex until they are old enough to have babies. Then, when they reach adolescence and the entire culture pressures them into heterosexual activity, whether they themselves feel ready for it or not, the more "enlightened" among us tell them how to be sexually (meaning heterosexually) active without having babies. Surprise: It doesn't work very well. Teenagers do not act "responsibly"—teenage pregnancies and abortions are on the rise and teenage fathers do not acknowledge and support their partners and babies. Somewhere we forget that we have been telling lies. Sexuality and procreation are not linked in societies like ours. On the contrary, we expect youngsters to be heterosexually active from their teens on but to put off having children until they are economically independent and married, and even then to have only two or, at most, three children.

Other contradictions: This society, on the whole, accepts Freud's assumption that children are sexual beings from birth and that society channels their polymorphously perverse childhood sexuality into the accepted forms. Yet we expect our children to be asexual. We raise girls and boys together more than is done in many societies while insisting that they must not explore their own or each other's sexual parts or feelings.

What if we acknowledged the separation of sexuality from procreation and encouraged our children to express themselves sexually if they were so inclined? What if we, further, encouraged them to explore their own bodies as well as those of friends of the same and the other sex when they felt like it? They might then be able to feel at home with their sexuality, have some sense of their own and other people's sexual needs, and know how to talk about sexuality and procreation with their friends and sexual partners before their ability to procreate becomes an issue for them. In this age of AIDS and other serious sexually transmitted infections, such a course of action seems like essential preventive hygiene. Without the embarrassment of unexplored and unacknowledged sexual needs, contraceptive needs would be much easier to confront when they arise. So, of course, would same-sex love relationships.

Such a more open and accepting approach to sexuality would make life easier for children and adolescents of either sex, but it would be especially advantageous for girls. When a boy discovers his penis as an organ of pleasure, it is the same organ he is taught about as his organ of procreation. A girl exploring her pleasurable sensations finds her clitoris, but when she is taught about making babies, she hears about the functions of the vagina in sex and birthing. Usually, the clitoris goes unmentioned, and she doesn't even learn its name until much later. Therefore for boys there is an obvious link between procreation and their own pleasurable, erotic explorations; for most girls, there isn't.

INDIVIDUAL SEXUAL SCRIPTS

Each of us writes our own sexual script out of the range of our experiences. None of this script is inborn or biologically given. We construct it out of our diverse life situations, limited by what we are taught or what we can imagine to be permissible and correct. There is no unique female sexual experience, no male sexual experience, no unique heterosexual, lesbian, or gay male experience. We take the experiences of different people and sort and lump them according to socially significant categories. When I hear generalizations about *the* sexual experience of some particular group, exceptions immediately come to mind. Except that I refuse to call them exceptions: They are part of the range of our sexual experiences. Of course, the similar circumstances in which members of a particular group find themselves will give rise to group similarities. But we tend to exaggerate them when we go looking for similarities within groups or differences between them.

This exaggeration is easy to see when we look at the dichotomy between "the heterosexual" and "the homosexual." The concept of "the homosexual," along with many other human typologies, originated toward the end of the nineteenth century. Certain kinds of behavior stopped being attributed to particular persons and came to define them. A person who had sexual relations with someone of the same sex became a certain kind of person, a "homosexual"; a person who had sexual relations with people of the other sex, a different kind, a "heterosexual."

This way of categorizing people obscured the hitherto accepted fact that many people do not have sexual relations exclusively with persons of one or the other sex. (None of us has sex with a kind of person; we have sex with a person.) This categorization created the stereotypes that were popularized by the sex reformers, such as Havelock Ellis and Edward Carpenter, who biologized the "difference." "The homosexual" became a person who is different by nature and therefore should not be made responsible for his or her so-called deviance. This definition served the purpose of the reformers (although the laws have been slow to change), but it turned same-sex love into a medical problem to be treated by doctors rather than punished by judges—an improvement, perhaps, but not acceptance or liberation. . . .

TOWARD A NONDETERMINISTIC MODEL OF SEXUALITY

. . . Some gay men and lesbians feel that they were born "different" and have always been homosexual. They recall feeling strongly attracted to members of their own sex when they were children and adolescents. But many women who live with men and think of themselves as heterosexual also had strong affective and erotic ties to girls and women while they were growing up. If they were now in loving relationships with women, they might look back on their earlier loves as proof that they were always lesbians. But if they are now involved with men, they may be tempted to devalue their former feelings as "puppy love" or "crushes."

Even within the preferred sex, most of us feel a greater affinity for certain "types" than for others. Not any man or woman will do. No one has seriously suggested that something in our innate makeup makes us light up in the presence of only certain women or men. We would think it absurd to look to hormone levels or any other simplistic biological cause for our preference for a specific "type" within a sex. In fact, scientists rarely bother to ask what in our psychosocial experience shapes these kinds of tastes and preferences. We assume it must have something to do with our relationship to our parents or with other experiences, but we do not probe deeply unless people prefer the "wrong" sex. Then, suddenly, scientists begin to look for specific causes.

Because of our recent history and political experiences, feminists tend to reject simplistic, causal models of how our sexuality develops. Many women who have thought of themselves as heterosexual for much of their life and who have been married and have had children have fallen in love with a woman (or women) when they have had the opportunity to rethink, refeel, and restructure their lives.

The society in which we live channels, guides, and limits our imagination in sexual as well as other matters. Why some of us give ourselves permission to love people of our own sex whereas others cannot even imagine doing so is an interesting question. But I do not think it will be answered by measuring our hormone levels or by trying to unearth our earliest affectional ties. As women begin to speak freely about our sexual experiences, we are getting a varied range of information with which we can reexamine, reevaluate, and change ourselves. Lately, increasing numbers of women have begun to acknowledge their "bisexuality"—the fact that they can love women and men in succession or simultaneously. People fall in love with individuals, not with a sex. Gender need not be a significant factor in our choice, although for some of us it may be.

2

AM I THIN ENOUGH YET?

■ ■ ■

Sharlene Hesse-Biber

"Ever since I was ten years old, I was just a very vain person. I always want-ed to be the thinnest, the prettiest. 'Cause I thought, if I look like this, then I'm going to have so many boyfriends, and guys are going to be so in love with me, and I'll be taken care of for the rest of my life. I'll never have to work, you know?"

—DELIA, COLLEGE SENIOR

WHAT'S WRONG WITH THIS PICTURE?

Pretty, vivacious, and petite, Delia was a picture of fashionable perfection when she first walked into my office. Her tight blue jeans and fringed Western shirt showed off her thin, 5-ft frame; her black cowboy boots and silver earrings completed a presentation that said, "Look at me!"

The perfect picture had a serious price. Delia had come to talk about her "problem." She is bulimic. In secret, she regularly binges on large amounts of food, then forces herself to vomit. It has become a powerful habit, one that she is afraid to break because it so efficiently maintains her thin body. For Delia, as for so many others, being thin is everything.

"I mean, how many bumper stickers have you seen that say 'No Fat Chicks,' you know? Guys don't like fat girls. Guys like little girls. I guess because it makes them feel bigger and, you know, they want somebody who looks pretty. Pretty to me is you have to be thin and you have to have like good facial features. It's both. My final affirmation of myself is how many guys look at me when I go into a bar. How many guys pick up on me. What my boyfriend thinks about me."

DELIA'S STORY

Delia is the eldest child, and only girl, in a wealthy Southern family. Her father is a successful dentist and her mother has never worked outside the home. They fought a lot when she was young—her father was an alcoholic—and they eventually divorced. According to Delia, both parents doted on her.

"I've never been deprived of anything in my entire life. I was spoiled, I guess, because I've never felt any pressure from my parents to do anything. My Dad would say, 'Whatever you want to do, if you want to go to Europe, if you want to go to law school, if you don't want to do anything . . . whatever you want to do, just be happy.' No pressure."

He was unconcerned about her weight, she said, but emphasized how important it was to be pretty. Delia quickly noticed this message everywhere, especially in the media.

"I am so affected by *Glamour* magazine and *Vogue* and all that, because that's a line of work I want to get into. I'm looking at all these beautiful women. They're thin. I want to be just as beautiful. I want to be just as thin. Because that is what guys like."

When I asked what her mother wanted for her, she recited, "To be nice and pretty and sweet and thin and popular and smart and successful and have everything that I could ever want and just to be happy." "Sweet and pretty and thin" meant that from the age of ten she was enrolled in a health club, and learned to count calories. Her mom, who at 45 is "beautiful, gorgeous, thin," gave her instructions on how to eat.

"'Only eat small amounts. Eat a thousand calories a day; don't overeat.' My mom was never critical like, 'You're fat.' But one time, I went on a camping trip and I gained four pounds and she said, 'You've got to lose weight.' I mean, she watched what I ate. Like if I was going to get a piece of cake she would be, 'Don't eat that.'"

At age 13 she started her secret bingeing and vomiting. "When I first threw up I thought, well, it's so easy," she told me. "I can eat and not get the calories and not gain weight. And I was modeling at the time, and I wanted to look like the girls in the magazines."

Delia's preoccupation with thinness intensified when she entered high school. She wanted to be a cheerleader, and she was tiny enough to make it. "When I was sixteen I just got into this image thing, like tiny, thin . . . I started working out more. I was Joe Healthy Thin Exercise Queen and I'd just fight eating because I was working out all the time, you know? And so I'm going to aerobics two or three times a day sometimes, eating only salad and a bagel, and like, no fat. I just got caught up in this circle."

College in New England brought a new set of social pressures. She couldn't go running every day because of the cold. She hated the school gym, stopped working out, and gained four pounds her freshman year. Her greatest stress at college had nothing to do with academics. "The most stressful thing for me is whether I'm going to eat that day, and what am I going to eat," she told me, "more than getting good grades."

After freshman year Delia became a cheerleader again. "Going in, I know I weighed like 93 or 94 pounds, which to me was this enormous hang-up, because I'd never weighed more than 90 pounds in my entire life. And I was really freaked out. I knew people were going to be looking at me in the crowd and I'm like, I've got to lose this weight. So I would just not eat, work out all the time. I loved being on the squad, but my partner was a real jerk. He would never work out, and when we would do lifts he'd always be, 'Delia, go run. Go run, you're too heavy.' I hadn't been eating that day. I had already run seven or eight miles and he told me to run again. And I was surrounded by girls who were all so concerned about their weight, and it was just really this horrible situation."

College life also confirmed another issue for Delia, a cultural message from her earliest childhood. She did *not* want to be a breadwinner. She put it this way, "When I was eight I wanted to be President of the United States. As I grew older and got to college I was like, wow, it's hard for women. I mean, I don't care what people say. If they say the society's liberated, they're wrong. It's still really hard for women. It's like they look through a glass window [*sic*]. They're vice presidents, but they aren't the president. And I just figured, God, how much easier would it be for me to get married to somebody I know is going to make a lot of money and just be taken care of . . . I want somebody else to be the millionaire." . . .

Economic and career achievement is a primary definition of success for men. (Of course, men can also exhibit some self-destructive behaviors in pursuit of this success, such as workaholism or substance abuse.) Delia's upbringing and environment defined success for her in a different way. She was not interested in having a job that earned $150,000 a year, but in marrying the guy who did. She learned to use any tool she could to stay thin, to look good, and to have a shot at her goal.

No wonder she was reluctant to give up her behavior. She was terrified of losing the important benefits of her membership in the Cult of Thinness. She knew she was hurting psychologically and physically, but, in the final analysis, being counted among "the chosen" justified the pain.

"God forbid anybody else gets stuck in this trap. But I'm already there, and I don't really see myself getting out, because I'm just so obsessed with how I look. I get personal satisfaction from looking thin, and receiving attention from guys."

I told Delia about women who have suggested other ways of coping with weight issues. There are even those who advocate fat liberation, or who suggest that fat is beautiful. She was emphatic about these solutions.

"Bullshit. They live in la-la land . . . I can hold onto my boyfriend because he doesn't need to look anywhere else. The bottom line is that appearance counts. And you can sit here and go, 'I feel good about myself twenty pounds heavier,' but who is the guy going to date?"

A WOMAN'S SENSE OF WORTH

Delia's devotion to the rituals of beauty work involved a great deal of time and energy. She weighed herself three times a day. She paid attention to what she put in her mouth; when she had too much, she knew she must get rid of it. She had to act and look a certain way, buy the right clothes, the right makeup. She also watched out for other women who might jeopardize her chances as they vied for the rewards of the system.

A woman's sense of worth in our culture is still greatly determined by her ability to attract a man. Social status is largely a function of income and occupation. Women's access to these resources is generally indirect, through marriage.[1] Even a woman with a successful and lucrative career may fear that her success comes at the expense of her femininity. . . .

Cultural messages on the rewards of thinness and the punishments of obesity are everywhere. Most women accept society's standards of beauty as "the way things are," even though these standards may undermine self-image, self-esteem, or physical well-being. Weight concerns or even obsessions are so common among women and girls that they escape notice. Dieting is not considered abnormal behavior, even among women who are not overweight. But only a thin line separates "normal" dieting from an eating disorder.[2] . . .

PROFITING FROM WOMEN'S BODIES

Because women feel their bodies fail the beauty test, American industry benefits enormously, continually nurturing feminine insecurities. Ruling patriarchal interests, like corporate culture, the traditional family, the government, and the media also benefit. If women are so busy trying to control their bodies through dieting, excessive exercise, and self-improvement activities, they lose control over other important aspects of selfhood that might challenge the status quo.[3] In the words of one critic, "A secretary who bench-presses 150 pounds is still stuck in a dead-end job; a housewife who runs the marathon is still financially dependent on her husband."[4]

In creating women's concept of the ideal body image, the cultural mirror is more influential than the mirror reflecting peer group attitudes. Research has shown that women overestimate how thin a body their male and female peers desire. In a recent study using body silhouettes, college students of both sexes were asked to indicate an ideal female figure, the one that they believed most attractive to the same-sex peer and other-sex peer.

Not only did the women select a thinner silhouette than the men,[5] but when asked to choose a *personal* ideal, rather than a peer ideal, the women selected an even skinnier model.

ADVERTISEMENTS AND BEAUTY ADVICE: BUY, TRY, COMPLY

Capitalism and patriarchy most often use the media to project the culturally desirable body to women. These images are everywhere—on TV, in the movies, on bill-boards, in print. Women's magazines, with their glossy pages of advertising, advertorials, and beauty advice, hold up an especially devious mirror. They offer "help" to women, while presenting a standard nearly impossible to attain. As one college student named Nancy noted in our interviews,

> The advertisement showed me exactly what I should be, not what I was. I wasn't tall, I wasn't blonde, I wasn't skinny. I didn't have thin thighs, I didn't have a flat stomach. I am short, have brown curly hair, short legs. They did offer me solutions like dying my hair or a workout or the use of this cream to take away cellulite. . . .

Not everyone is taken in, of course. One student I interviewed dismissed the images she saw in the advertising pages of magazines as "constructed people."

> I just stopped buying women's magazines. They are all telling you how to dress, how to look, what to wear, the type of clothes. And I think they are just ridiculous. . . . You can take the most gorgeous model and make her look terrible. Just like you can take a person who is not that way and make them look beautiful. You can use airbrushing and many other techniques. These are not really people. They are constructed people.

Computer-enhanced photography has advanced far beyond the techniques that merely airbrushed blemishes, added highlights to hair, and lengthened the legs with a camera angle. The September 1994 issue of *Mirabella* featured as a cover model "an extraordinary image of great American beauty." According to the magazine, the photographer "hints that she's something of a split personality . . . it wasn't easy getting her together. Maybe her identity has something to do with the microchip floating through space, next to that gorgeous face . . . true American beauty is a combination of elements from all over the world." In other words, the photo is a computerized composite. It is interesting that *Mirabella's* "melting pot" American beauty has white skin and predominantly Caucasian features, with just a hint of other ethnicities.

There are a number of industries that help to promote image, weight, and body obsession, especially among women. If we examine the American food and weight loss industries, we'll understand how their corporate practices and advertising campaigns perpetuate the American woman's dissatisfaction with her looks.

THE AMERICAN FOOD INDUSTRY:
FATTEN UP AND SLIM DOWN

... It is not uncommon for the average American to have a diet cola in one hand and high-fat fries and a burger in the other. Food and weight loss are inescapably a key part of the culture of the 1990's. The media bombard us with images of every imaginable type of food—snack foods, fast foods, gourmet foods, health foods, and junk foods. Most of these messages target children, who are very impressionable, and women, who make the purchasing decisions for themselves and their families. At the same time women are subjected to an onslaught of articles, books, videos, tapes, and TV talk shows devoted to dieting and the maintenance of sleek and supple figures. The conflicting images of pleasurable consumption and an ever leaner body type give us a food consciousness loaded with tension and ambivalence.

Social psychologist Brett Silverstein explains that the food industry, like all industries under capitalism, is always striving to maximize profit, growth, concentration, and control. It does so at the expense of the food consumer. "[It] promotes snacking so that consumers will have more than three opportunities a day to consume food, replaces free water with purchased soft drinks, presents desserts as the ultimate reward, and bombards women and children with artificially glamorized images of highly processed foods."[6]

Diet foods are an especially profitable segment of the business. . . .

In 1983, the food industry came up with a brilliant marketing concept, and introduced 91 new "lite" fat-reduced or calorie-reduced foods.[7] The success of lite products has been phenomenal. The consumer equated "lightness" with health. The food industry seemed to equate it with their own expenses—lite foods have lower production costs than "regular" lines, but they are often priced higher. . . .

THE DIET AND WEIGHT-LOSS INDUSTRY:
WE'LL SHOW YOU THE WAY

... Increasingly, American women are told that they can have the right body if only they consume more and more products. They can change the color of their eyes with tinted contacts, they can have a tanned skin by using self-tanning lotion. They can buy cellulite control cream, spot firming cream, even contouring shower and bath firming gel to get rid of the "dimpled" look. One diet capsule on the market is supposed to be the "fat cure." It is called Anorex-eck, evoking the sometimes fatal eating disorder known as anorexia. It promises to "eliminate the cause of fat formation . . . so quickly and so effectively you will know from the very start why it has taken more than 15 years of research . . . to finally bring you . . . an ultimate cure for fat!"[8] . . .

There are currently more than 17,000 different diet plans, products, and programs from which to choose.[9] Typically, these plans are geared to the female market. They are loaded with promises of quick weight loss and delicious low-calorie meals. . . .

Many of these programs produce food products that they encourage the dieter to buy. The Jenny Craig member receives a set of pre-packaged meals that cost about $10 per day. (It allows for some outside food as well.) Some diet companies are concerned with the problem of gaining weight back and have developed "maintenance" products. Maintenance programs are often expensive and their long-term outcomes are unproven. What *can* be proven are bigger profits and longer dependence on their programs.

THE DIS-EASED BODY: MEDICALIZING WOMEN'S BODY ISSUES

The therapeutic and medical communities tend to categorize women's eating and weight problems as a disease.[10] In this view, behavior like self-starvation or compulsive eating is often called an addiction. An addiction model of behavior assumes that the cause and the cure of the problem lies within the individual. Such an emphasis fails to examine the larger mirrors that society holds up to the individual.[11]

. . . While a disease model lessens the burden of guilt and shame and may free people to work on change, it also has political significance. According to feminist theorist Bette S. Tallen, "The reality of oppression is replaced with the metaphor of addiction." It places the problem's cause within a biological realm, away from outside social forces.[12] Issues such as poverty, lack of education and opportunity, racial and gender inequality remain unexamined. More important, a disease-oriented model of addiction, involving treatment by the health care system, results in profits for the medical-industrial complex. Addiction, Tallen notes, suggests a solution that is personal—"Get treatment!"—rather than political—"Smash patriarchy!" It replaces the feminist view, that the personal is political, with the attitude of "therapism," that the "political is personal."[13] One of Bette Tallen's students told her that she had learned a lot from reading *Women Who Love Too Much* after her divorce from a man who had beaten her. Tallen suggested that "perhaps the best book to read would not be about women who love too much but about men who hit too much."[14]

The idea that overweight is a disease, and overeating represents an addiction, reinforces the dis-ease that American women feel about their bodies. The capitalist and patriarchal mirror held before them supports and maintains their obsession and insecurity. . . .

Women continue to follow the standards of the ideal thin body because of how they are rewarded by being in the right body. Thinness gives women access to a number of important resources: feelings of power, self-confidence, even femininity; male attention or protection; and the social and economic benefits that can follow. . . .

NOTES

1. Pauline B. Bart, "Emotional and Social Status of the Older Woman," in *No Longer Young: The Older Woman in America. Proceedings of the 26th Annual Conference on Aging*, ed. Pauline Bart et al. (Ann Arbor: University of Michigan Institute of Gerontology, 1975), pp. 3–21; Daniel Bar-Tal and Leonard Saxe, "Physical Attractiveness and Its Relationship to Sex-Role Stereotyping," *Sex Roles* 2 (1976): 123–133; Peter Blumstein and Pepper W. Schwartz, *American Couples: Money, Work and Sex* (New York: Willian Morrow, 1983); Glen H. Elder, "Appearance and Education in Marriage Mobility," *American Sociological Review* 34 (1969): 519–533; Susan Sontag, "The Double Standard of Aging," *Saturday Review* (September, 1972), pp. 29–38.
2. J. Polivy and C. P. Herman, "Dieting and Binging: A Causal Analysis," *American Psychologist* 40 (1985):193–201.
3. Ilana Attie and J. Brooks-Gunn, "Weight Concerns as Chronic Stressors in Women," in *Gender and Stress*, eds. Rosalind K. Barnett, Lois Biener, and Grace Baruch (New York: Free Press, 1987), pp. 218–252.
4. Katha Pollitt, "The Politically Correct Body," *Mother Jones* (May 1982): 67. I don't want to disparage the positive benefits of exercising and the positive self-image that can come from feeling good about one's body. This positive image can spill over into other areas of one's life, enhancing, for example, one's self-esteem, or job prospects.
5. See Lawrence D. Cohn and Nancy E. Adler, "Female and Male Perceptions of Ideal Body Shapes: Distorted Views Among Caucasian College Students," *Psychology of Women Quarterly* 16 (1992): 69–79; A. Fallon and P. Rozin, "Sex Differences in Perceptions of Desirable Body Shape," *Journal of Abnormal Psychology* 94 (1985): 102–105.
6. Brett Silverstein, *Fed Up!* (Boston: South End Press, 1984), pp. 4, 47, 110. Individuals may be affected in many different ways, from paying too much (in 1978, concentration within the industry led to the overcharging of consumers by $12 to $14 billion [p. 47]) to the ingestion of unhealthy substances.
7. Warren J. Belasco, "'Lite' Economics: Less Food, More Profit," *Radical History Review* 28–30 (1984): 254–278; Hillel Schwartz, *Never Satisfied* (New York: Free Press, 1986), p. 241.
8. Advertised in *Parade* magazine (December 30, 1984).
9. Deralee Scanlon, *Diets That Work* (Chicago: Contemporary Books, 1991), p. 1.

10. See Stanton Peele, *Diseasing of America: Addiction Treatment Out of Control* (Lexington, MA: D.C. Heath and Co., 1989).
11. There are a few recovery books that point to the larger issues of the addiction model. Anne Wilson Schaef's book, *When Society Becomes an Addict*, looks at the wider institutions of society that perpetuate addiction. She notes that society operates on a scarcity model. This is the "Addictive System." This model assumes that there is never enough of anything to go around and we need to get what we can. Schaef sees society as made up of three systems: A White Male System (the Addictive System), A Reactive Female System (one where women respond passively to men by being subject to their will), and the Emerging Female System (a system where women lead with caring and sensitivity). Society needs to move in the direction of the Emerging Female System in order to end addiction. Another important book is Stanton Peele's *Love and Addiction*. Another book by Stanton Peele, *The Diseasing of America: How the Addiction Industry Captured Our Soul* (Lexington, MA: Lexington Books, 1989), stresses the importance of social change in societal institutions and advocates changing the given distribution of resources and power within the society as a way to overcome the problem of addiction. See Anne Wilson Schaef, *When Society Becomes an Addict* (New York: Harper & Row, 1987), and Stanton Peele, *Love and Addiction* (New York: New American Library, 1975).
12. Bette S. Tallen, "Twelve Step Programs: A Lesbian Feminist Critique," *NWSA Journal* 2 (1990): 396.
13. Tallen, "Twelve Step Programs: A Lesbian Feminist Critique," 404–405.
14. Tallen, "Twelve Step Programs: A Lesbian Feminist Critique," 405.

3

MASCULINITY AS HOMOPHOBIA

Fear, Shame, and Silence in the Construction of Gender Identity

■ ■ ■

Michael S. Kimmel

We think of manhood as eternal, a timeless essence that resides deep in the heart of every man. We think of manhood as a thing, a quality that one either has or doesn't have. We think of manhood as innate, residing in the particular biological composition of the human male, the result of androgens or the possession of a penis. We think of manhood as a transcendent tangible property that each man must manifest in the world, the reward presented with great ceremony to a young novice by his elders for having successfully competed an arduous initiation ritual . . . .

In this chapter, I view masculinity as a constantly changing collection of meanings that we construct through our relationships with ourselves, with each other, and with our world. Manhood is neither static nor timeless; it is historical. Manhood is not the manifestation of an inner essence; it is socially constructed. Manhood does not bubble up to consciousness from our biological makeup; it is created in culture. Manhood means different things at different times to different people. We come to know what it means to be a man in our culture by setting our definitions in opposition to a set of "others"—racial minorities, sexual minorities, and, above all, women . . . .

From *Theorizing Masculinities*, Harry Brod and Michael Kaufman, eds., pp. 119–141. Copyright © 1994. Reprinted by permission of Sage Publications, Inc. I am grateful to Tim Beneke, Harry Brod, Michael Kaufman, Iona Mara-Drita, and Lillian Rubin for comments on earlier versions of the chapter.

CLASSICAL SOCIAL THEORY AS A HIDDEN
MEDITATION OF MANHOOD

Begin this inquiry by looking at four passages from that set of texts commonly called classical social and political theory. You will, no doubt, recognize them, but I invite you to recall the way they were discussed in your undergraduate or graduate courses in theory:

> The bourgeoisie cannot exist without constantly revolutionizing the instruments of production, and thereby the relations of production, and with them the whole relations of society. Conservation of the old modes of production in unaltered form, was, on the contrary, the first condition of existence for all earlier industrial classes. Constant revolutionizing of production, uninterrupted disturbance of all social conditions, everlasting uncertainty and agitation distinguish the bourgeois epoch from all earlier ones. All fixed, fast-frozen relations, with their train of ancient and venerable prejudices and opinions are swept away, all new-formed ones become antiquated before they can ossify. All that is solid melts into air, all that is holy is profaned, and man is at last compelled to face with sober senses, his real conditions of life, and his relation with his kind. (Marx & Engels, 1848/1964)

> An American will build a house in which to pass his old age and sell it before the roof is on; he will plant a garden and rent it just as the trees are coming into bearing; he will clear a field and leave others to reap the harvest; he will take up a profession and leave it, settle in one place and soon go off elsewhere with his changing desires . . . . At first sight there is something astonishing in this spectacle of so many lucky men restless in the midst of abundance. But it is a spectacle as old as the world; all that is new is to see a whole people performing in it. (Tocqueville, 1835/1967)

> Where the fulfillment of the calling cannot directly be related to the highest spiritual and cultural values, or when, on the other hand, it need not be felt simply as economic compulsion, the individual generally abandons the attempt to justify it at all. In the field of its highest development, in the United States, the pursuit of wealth, stripped of its religious and ethical meaning, tends to become associated with purely mundane passions, which often actually give it the character of sport. (Weber, 1905/1966)

> We are warned by a proverb against serving two masters at the same time. The poor ego has things even worse: it serves three severe masters and does what it can to bring their claims and demands into harmony with one another. These claims are always divergent and often seem incompatible. No wonder that the ego so often fails in its task. Its three tyrannical masters are the external world, the super ego and the id . . . . It feels hemmed in on three sides, threatened by three kinds of danger, to which, if it is hard pressed, it reacts by generating anxiety . . . . Thus the ego, driven by the id, confined by the super ego, repulsed by reality, struggles to master its economic task of bringing about harmony among the forces and influences working in and upon it; and we can

understand how it is that so often we cannot suppress a cry: "Life is not easy!" (Freud, "The Dissection of the Psychical Personality," 1933/1966)

If your social science training was anything like mine, these were offered as descriptions of the bourgeoisie under capitalism, of individuals in democratic societies, of the fate of the Protestant work ethic under the ever rationalizing spirit of capitalism, or of the arduous task of the autonomous ego in psychological development. Did anyone ever mention that in all four cases the theorists were describing men? Not just "man" as in generic mankind, but a particular type of masculinity, a definition of manhood that derives its identity from participation in the marketplace, from interaction with other men in that marketplace—in short, a model of masculinity for whom identity is based on homosocial competition? Three years before Tocqueville found Americans "restless in the midst of abundance," Senator Henry Clay had called the United States "a nation of self-made men."

What does it mean to be "self-made"? What are the consequences of self-making for the individual man, for other men, for women? It is this notion of manhood—rooted in the sphere of production, the public arena, a masculinity grounded not in land ownership or in artisanal republican virtue but in successful participation in marketplace competition—this has been the defining notion of American manhood. Masculinity must be proved, and no sooner is it proved that it is again questioned and must be proved again—constant, relentless, unachievable, and ultimately the quest for proof becomes so meaningless than it takes on the characteristic, as Weber said, of a sport. He who has the most toys when he dies wins . . . .

MASCULINITY AS HISTORY AND THE HISTORY OF MASCULINITY

The idea of masculinity expressed in the previous extracts in the product of historical shifts in the grounds on which men rooted their sense of themselves as men. To argue that cultural definitions of gender identity are historically specific goes only so far; we have to specify exactly what those models were. In my historical inquiry into the development of these models of manhood[1] I chart the fate of two models for manhood at the turn of the 19th century and the emergence of a third in the first few decades of that century.

In the late 18th and early 19th centuries, two models of manhood prevailed. The *Genteel Patriarch* derived his identity from landownership. Supervising his estate, he was refined, elegant, and given to casual sensuousness. He was a doting and devoted father, who spent much of his time supervising the estate and with his family. Think of George Washington or Thomas Jefferson as examples. By contrast, the *Heroic Artisan* embodied the physical strength and republican virtue that Jefferson observed in the yeoman farmer, independent urban craftsman, or shopkeeper. Also a devoted father, the Heroic Artisan taught his son his craft, bringing him through ritual apprenticeship to status as master craftsman. Economically autonomous, the Heroic Artisan also cherished his democratic community, delighting in the participatory democracy of the town meeting. Think of Paul Revere at his pewter shop, shirtsleeves rolled up, a leather apron—a man who took pride in his work.

Heroic Artisans and Genteel Patriarchs lived in casual accord, in part because their gender ideals were complementary (both supported participatory democracy and individual autonomy, although patriarchs tended to support more powerful state machineries and also supported slavery) and because they rarely saw one another: Artisans were decidedly urban and the Genteel Patriarchs ruled their rural estates. By the 1830s, though, this casual symbiosis was shattered by the emergence of a new vision of masculinity, *Marketplace Manhood*.

Marketplace Man derived his identity entirely from his success in the capitalist marketplace, as he accumulated wealth, power, status. He was the urban entrepreneur, the businessman. Restless, agitated, and anxious, Marketplace Man was an absentee landlord at home and an absent father with his children, devoting himself to his work in an increasingly homosocial environment—a male-only world in which he pits himself against other men. His efforts at self-making transform the political and economic spheres, casting aside the Genteel Patriarch as an anachronistic feminized dandy— sweet, but ineffective and outmoded, and transforming the Heroic Artisan into a dispossessed proletarian, a wage slave.

As Tocqueville would have seen it, the coexistence of the Genteel Patriarch and the Heroic Artisan embodied the fusion of liberty and equality. Genteel Patriarchy was the manhood of the traditional aristocracy, the class that embodied the virtue of liberty. The Heroic Artisan embodied democratic community, the solidarity of the urban shopkeeper or craftsman. Liberty and democracy, the patriarch and the artisan, could, and did, coexist. But Marketplace Man is capitalist man, and he makes both freedom and equality problematic, eliminating the freedom of the aristocracy and proletarianizing the equality of the artisan. In one sense, American history has been an effort to restore, retrieve, or reconstitute the virtues of Genteel Patriarchy and Heroic Artisanate as they were being transformed in the capitalist marketplace.

Marketplace Manhood was a manhood that required proof, and that required the acquisition of tangible goods as evidence of success. It reconstituted itself by the exclusion of "others"—women, nonwhite men, nonnative-born men, homosexual men—and by terrified flight into a pristine mythic homosocial Eden where men could, at last, be real men among other men. The story of the ways in which Marketplace Man becomes American Everyman is a tragic tale, a tale of striving to live up to impossible ideals of success leading to chronic terrors of emasculation, emotional emptiness, and a gendered rage that leave a wide swath of destruction in its wake.

MASCULINITIES AS POWER RELATIONS

Marketplace Masculinity describes the normative definition of American masculinity. It describes his characteristics—aggression, competition, anxiety—and the arena in which those characteristics are deployed—the public sphere, the marketplace. If the marketplace is the arena in which manhood is tested and proved, it is a gendered arena, in which tensions between women and men and tensions among different groups of men are weighted with meaning. These tensions suggest that cultural definitions of gender are played out in a contested terrain and are themselves power relations.

All masculinities are not created equal; or rather, we are all *created* equal, but any hypothetical equality evaporates quickly because our definitions of masculinity are not equally valued in our society. One definition of manhood continues to remain the standard against which other forms of manhood are measured and evaluated. Within the dominant culture, the masculinity that defines white, middle class, early middle-aged, heterosexual men is the masculinity that sets the standards for other men, against which other men are measured and, more often than not, found wanting. Sociologist Erving Goffman (1963) wrote that in America, there is only "one complete, unblushing male":

> a young, married, white, urban, northern heterosexual, Protestant father of college education, fully employed, of good complexion, weight and height, and a recent record in sports. Every American male tends to look out upon the world from this perspective. . . . Any male who fails to qualify in any one of these ways is likely to view himself . . . as unworthy, incomplete, and inferior. (p. 128)

This is the definition that we will call "hegemonic" masculinity, the image of masculinity of those men who hold power, which has become the standard in psychological evaluations, sociological research, and self-help and advice literature for teaching young men to become "real men" (Connell, 1987). The hegemonic definition of manhood is a man *in* power, a man *with* power, and a man *of* power. We equate manhood with being strong, successful, capable, reliable, in control. The very definitions of manhood we have developed in our culture maintain the power that some men have over other men and that men have over women.

Our culture's definition of masculinity is thus several stories at once. It is about the individual man's quest to accumulate those cultural symbols that denote manhood, signs that he has in fact achieved it. It is about those standards being used against women to prevent their inclusion in public life and their consignment to a devalued private sphere. It is about the differential access that different types of men have to those cultural resources that confer manhood and about how each of these groups then develop their own modifications to preserve and claim their manhood.

It is about the power of these definitions themselves to serve to maintain the real-life power that men have over women and that some men have over other men.

This definition of manhood has been summarized cleverly by psychologist Robert Brannon (1976) into four succinct phrases:

1. "No Sissy Stuff!" One may never do anything that even remotely suggests femininity. Masculinity is the relentless repudiation of the feminine.
2. "Be a Big Wheel." Masculinity is measured by power, success, wealth, and status. As the current saying goes, "He who has the most toys when he dies wins."
3. "Be a Sturdy Oak." Masculinity depends on remaining calm and reliable in a crisis, holding emotions in check. In fact, proving you're a man depends on never showing your emotions at all. Boys don't cry.
4. "Give 'em Hell." Exude an aura of manly daring and aggression. Go for it. Take risks.

These rules contain the elements of the definition against which virtually all American men are measured. Failure to embody these rules, to affirm the power of the rules and one's achievement of them is a source of men's confusion and pain. Such a model is, of course, unrealizable for any man. But we keep trying, valiantly and vainly, to measure up. American masculinity is a relentless test.[2] The chief test is contained in the first rule. Whatever the variations by race, class, age, ethnicity, or sexual orientation, being a man means "not being like women." This notion of anti-femininity lies at the heart of contemporary and historical conceptions of manhood, so that masculinity is defined more by what one is not rather than who one is.

MASCULINITY AS THE FLIGHT FROM THE FEMININE

Historically and developmentally, masculinity has been defined as the flight from women, the repudiation of femininity . . . .

The drive to repudiate the mother as the indication of the acquisition of masculine gender identity has three consequences for the young boy. First, he pushes away his real mother, and with her the traits of nurturance, compassion, and tenderness she may have embodied. Second, he suppresses those traits in himself, because they will reveal his incomplete separation from mother. His life becomes a lifelong project to demonstrate that he possesses none of his mother's traits. Masculine identity is born in the renunciation of the feminine, not in the direct affirmation of the masculine, which leaves masculine gender identity tenuous and fragile.

Third, as if to demonstrate the accomplishment of these first two tasks, the boy also learns to devalue all women in his society, as the living embodiments of those traits in himself he has learned to despise. Whether or not he was aware of it, Freud also described the origins of sexism—the systematic devaluation of women—in the desperate efforts of the boy to separate from mother. We may *want* "a girl just like the girl that married dear old Dad," as the popular song had it, but we certainly don't want to *be like* her.

This chronic uncertainty about gender identity helps us understand several obsessive behaviors. Take, for example, the continuing problem of the school-yard bully. Parents remind us that the bully is the *least* secure about his manhood, and so he is constantly trying to prove it. But he "proves" it by choosing opponents he is absolutely certain he can defeat; thus the standard taunt to a bully is to "pick on someone your own size." He can't, though, and after defeating a smaller and weaker opponent, which he was sure would prove his manhood, he is left with the empty gnawing feeling that he has not proved it after all, and he must find another opponent, again one smaller and weaker, that he can again defeat to prove it to himself.[3] . . .

When does it end? Never. To admit weakness, to admit frailty or fragility, is to be seen as a wimp, a sissy, not a real man. But seen by whom?

MASCULINITY AS A HOMOSOCIAL ENACTMENT

Other men: We are under the constant careful scrutiny of other men. Other men watch us, rank us, grant our acceptance into the realm of manhood. Manhood is demonstrated for other men's approval. It is other men who evaluate the performance. Literary critic David Leverenz (1991) argues that "ideologies of manhood have functioned primarily in relation to the gaze of male peers and male authority" (p. 769). Think of how men boast to one another of their accomplishments—from their latest sexual conquest to the size of the fish they caught—and how we constantly parade the markers of manhood—wealth, power, status, sexy women—in front of other men, desperate for their approval.

That men prove their manhood in the eyes of other men is both a consequence of sexism and one of its chief props. "Women have, in men's minds, such a low place on the social ladder of this country that it's useless to define yourself in terms of a woman," noted playwright David Mamet. "What men need is men's approval." Women become a kind of currency that men use to improve their ranking on the masculine social scale. (Even those moments of heroic conquest of women carry, I believe, a current of homosocial evaluation.) Masculinity is a *homosocial* enactment. We test ourselves, perform heroic feats, take enormous risks, all because we want other men to grant us our manhood. . . .

MASCULINITY AS HOMOPHOBIA

... That nightmare from which we never seem to awaken is that those other men will see that sense of inadequacy, they will see that in our own eyes we are not who we are pretending to be. What we call masculinity is often a hedge against being revealed as a fraud, an exaggerated set of activities that keep others from seeing through us, and a frenzied effort to keep at bay those fears within ourselves. Our real fear "is not fear of women but of being ashamed or humiliated in front of other men, or being dominated by stronger men" (Leverenz, 1986, p. 451).

This, then, is the great secret of American manhood: *We are afraid of other men.* Homophobia is a central organizing principle of our cultural definition of manhood. Homophobia is more than the irrational fear of gay men, more than the fear that we might be perceived as gay. "The word 'faggot' has nothing to do with homosexual experience or even with fears of homosexuals," writes David Leverenz (1986). "It comes out of the depths of manhood: a label of ultimate contempt for anyone who seems sissy, untough, uncool" (p. 455). Homophobia is the fear that other men will unmask us, emasculate us, reveal to us and the world that we do not measure up, that we are not real men. We are afraid to let other men see that fear. Fear makes us ashamed, because the recognition of fear in ourselves is proof to ourselves that we are not as manly as we pretend, that we are, like the young man in a poem by Yeats, "one that ruffles in a manly pose for all his timid heart." Our fear is the fear of humiliation. We are ashamed to be afraid.

Shame leads to silence—the silences that keep other people believing that we actually approve of the things that are done to women, to minorities, to gays and lesbians in our culture. The frightened silence as we scurry past a woman being hassled by men on the street. That furtive silence when men make sexist or racist jokes in a bar. That clammy-handed silence when guys in the office make gay-bashing jokes. Our fears are the sources of our silences, and men's silence is what keeps the system running. This might help to explain why women often complain that their male friends or partners are often so understanding when they are alone and yet laugh at sexist jokes or even make those jokes themselves when they are out with a group.

The fear of being seen as a sissy dominates the cultural definitions of manhood. It starts so early. "Boys among boys are ashamed to be unmanly," wrote one educator in 1871 (cited in Rotundo, 1993, p. 264). I have a standing bet with a friend that I can walk onto any playground in America where 6-year-old boys are happily playing and by asking one question, I can provoke a fight. That question is simple: "Who's a sissy around here?" Once posed, the challenge is made. One of two things is likely to happen. One boy will accuse another of being a sissy, to which that boy will respond that he is not a sissy, that the first boy is. They may have to fight it out to see who's lying. Or a whole group of boys will surround one boy and all shout "He is!" That boy will either burst into tears and run home crying, disgraced, or he will have to take on several boys at once, to prove that he's not a sissy. (And what will his father or older brothers tell him if he chooses to run home crying?) It will be some time before he regains any sense of self-respect.

Violence is often the single most evident marker of manhood. Rather it is the willingness to fight, the desire to fight. The origin of our expression that one has a chip on one's shoulder lies in the practice of an adolescent boy in the country or small town at the turn of the century, who would literally walk around with a chip of wood balanced on his shoulder—a signal of his readiness to fight with anyone who would take the initiative of knocking the chip off (see Gorer, 1964, p. 38; Mead, 1965).

As adolescents, we learn that our peers are a kind of gender police, constantly threatening to unmask us as feminine, as sissies. One of the favorite tricks when I was an adolescent was to ask a boy to look at his fingernails. If he held his palm toward his face and curled his fingers back to see them, he passed the test. He'd look at his nails "like a man." But if he held the back of his hand away from his face, and looked at his fingernails with arm outstretched, he was immediately ridiculed as sissy.

As young men we are constantly riding those gender boundaries, checking the fences we have constructed on the perimeter, making sure that nothing even remotely feminine might show through. The possibilities of being unmasked are everywhere. Even the most seemingly insignificant thing can pose a threat or activate that haunting terror. On the day the students in my course "Sociology of Men and Masculinities" were scheduled to discuss homophobia and male-male friendships, one student provided a touching illustration. Noting that it was a beautiful day, the first day of spring after a brutal northeast winter, he decided to wear shorts to class. "I had this really nice pair of new Madras shorts," he commented. "But then I thought to myself, these shorts have lavender and pink in them. Today's class topic is homophobia. Maybe today is not the best day to wear these shorts."

Our efforts to maintain a manly front cover everything we do. What we wear. How we talk. How we walk. What we eat. Every mannerism, every movement contains a coded gender language. Think, for example, of how you would answer the question: How do you "know" if a man is homosexual? When I ask this question in classes or workshops, respondents invariably provide a pretty standard list of stereotypically effeminate behaviors. He walks a certain way, talks a certain way, acts a certain way. He's very emotional; he shows his feelings. One woman commented that she "knows" a man is gay if he really cares about her; another said she knows he's gay if he shows no interest in her, if he leaves her alone.

Now alter the question and imagine what heterosexual men do to make sure no one could possibly get the "wrong idea" about them. Responses typically refer to the original stereotypes, this time as a set of negative rules about behavior. Never dress that way. Never talk or walk that way. Never show your feelings or get emotional. Always be prepared to demonstrate sexual interest in women that you meet, so it is impossible for any woman to get the wrong idea about you. In this sense, homophobia, the fear of being perceived as gay, as not a real man, keeps men exaggerating all the traditional rules of masculinity, including sexual predation with women. Homophobia and sexism go hand in hand. . . .

HOMOPHOBIA AS A CAUSE OF SEXISM, HETEROSEXISM, AND RACISM

Homophobia is intimately interwoven with both sexism and racism. The fear—sometimes conscious, sometimes not—that others might perceive us as homosexual propels men to enact all manner of exaggerated masculine behaviors and attitudes to make sure that no one could possibly get the wrong idea about us. One of the centerpieces of that exaggerated masculinity is putting women down, both by excluding them from the public sphere and by the quotidian put-downs in speech and behaviors that organize the daily life of the American man. Women and gay men become the "other" against which heterosexual men project their identities, against whom they stack the decks so as to compete in a situation in which they will always win, so that by suppressing them, men can stake a claim for their own manhood. Women threaten emasculation by representing the home, workplace, and familial responsibility, the negation of fun. Gay men have historically played the role of the consummate sissy in the American popular mind because homosexuality is seen as an inversion of normal gender development. There have been other "others." Through American history, various groups have represented the sissy, the non-men against whom American men played out their definitions of manhood, often with vicious results. In fact, these changing groups provide an interesting lesson in American historical development.

At the turn of the 19th century, it was Europeans and children who provided the contrast for American men. The "true American was vigorous, manly, and direct, not effete and corrupt like the supposed Europeans," writes Rupert Wilkinson (1986). "He was plain rather than ornamented, rugged rather than luxury seeking, a liberty loving common man or natural gentleman rather than an aristocratic oppressor or servile minion" (p. 96). The "real man" of the early 19th century was neither noble nor serf. By the middle of the century, black slaves had replaced the effete nobleman. Slaves were seen as dependent, helpless men, incapable of defending their women and children, and therefore less than manly. Native Americans were cast as foolish and naive children, so they could be infantalized as the "Red Children of the Great White Father" and therefore excluded from full manhood.

By the end of the century, new European immigrants were also added to the list of the unreal men, especially the Irish and Italians, who were seen as too passionate and emotionally volatile to remain controlled sturdy oaks, and Jews, who were seen as too bookishly effete and too physically puny to truly measure up. In the mid-20th century, it was also Asians—first the Japanese during the Second World War, and more recently, the Vietnamese during the Vietnam War—who have served as unmanly templates against which American men have hurled their gendered rage. Asian men were seen as small, soft, and effeminate—hardly men at all.

Such a list of "hyphenated" Americans—Italian-, Jewish-, Irish-, African-, Native-, Asian-, gay—composes the majority of American men. So manhood is only possible for a distinct minority, and the definition has been constructed to prevent the others from achieving it. Interestingly, this emasculation of one's enemies has a flip side—and one that is equally gendered. These very groups that have historically been cast as less than manly were also, often simultaneously, cast as hypermasculine, as sexually aggressive, violent rapacious beasts, against whom "civilized" men must take a decisive stand and thereby rescue civilization. Thus black men were depicted as rampaging sexual beasts, women as carnivorously carnal, gay men as sexually insatiable, southern European men as sexually predatory and voracious, and Asian men as vicious and cruel torturers who were immorally disinterested in life itself, willing to sacrifice their entire people for their whims. But whether one saw these groups as effeminate sissies or as brutal savages, the terms with which they were perceived were gendered. These groups become the "others," the screens against which traditional conceptions of manhood were developed. . . .

POWER AND POWERLESSNESS IN THE LIVES OF MEN

I have argued that homophobia, men's fear of other men, is the animating condition of the dominant definition of masculinity in America, that the reigning definition of masculinity is a defensive effort to prevent being emasculated. In our efforts to suppress or overcome those fears, the dominant culture exacts a tremendous price from those deemed less than fully manly: women, gay men, nonnative-born men, men of color. This perspective may help clarify a paradox in men's lives, a paradox in which men have virtually all the power and yet do not feel powerful (see Kaufman, 1993).

Manhood is equated with power—over women, over other men. Everywhere we look, we see the institutional expression of that power—in state and national legislatures, on the boards of directors of every major U.S. corporation or law firm, and in every school and hospital administration. . . .

When confronted with the analysis that men have all the power, many men react incredulously. "What do you mean, men have all the power?" they ask. "What are you talking about? My wife bosses me around. My kids boss me around. My boss bosses me around. I have no power at all! I'm completely powerless!"

Men's feelings are not the feelings of the powerful, but of those who see themselves as powerless. These are the feelings that come inevitably from the discontinuity between the social and the psychological, between the aggregate analysis that reveals how men are in power as a group and the psychological fact that they do not feel powerful as individuals. They are the feelings of men who were raised to believe themselves entitled to feel that power, but do not feel it. No wonder many men are frustrated and angry . . . .

Why, then, do American men feel so powerless? Part of the answer is because we've constructed the rules of manhood so that only the tiniest fraction of men come to believe that they are the biggest of wheels, the sturdiest of oaks, the most virulent repudiators of femininity, the most daring and aggressive. We've managed to disempower the overwhelming majority of American men by other means—such as discriminating on the basis of race, class, ethnicity, age, or sexual preference . . .

Others still rehearse the politics of exclusion, as if by clearing away the playing field of secure gender identity of any that we deem less than manly—women, gay men, nonnative-born men, men of color—middle-class, straight, white men can re-ground their sense of themselves without those haunting fears and that deep shame that they are unmanly and will be exposed by other men. This is the manhood of racism, of sexism, of homophobia. It is the manhood that is so chronically insecure that it trembles at the idea of lifting the ban on gays in the military, that is so threatened by women in the workplace that women become the targets of sexual harassment, that is so deeply frightened of equality that it must ensure that the playing field of male competition remains stacked against all newcomers to the game.

Exclusion and escape have been the dominant methods American men have used to keep their fears of humiliation at bay. The fear of emasculation by other men, of being humiliated, of being seen as a sissy, is the leitmotif in my reading of the history of American manhood. Masculinity has become a relentless test by which we prove to other men, to women, and ultimately to ourselves, that we have successfully mastered the part. The restlessness that men feel today is nothing new in American history; we have been anxious and restless for almost two centuries. Neither exclusion nor escape has ever brought us the relief we've sought, and there is no reason to think that either will solve our problems now. Peace of mind, relief from gender struggle, will come only from a politics of inclusion, not exclusion, from standing up for equality and justice, and not by running away.

NOTES

1. Much of this work is elaborated in *Manhood: The American Quest* (in press).
2. Although I am here discussing only American masculinity, I am aware that others have located this chronic instability and efforts to prove manhood in the particular cultural and economic arrangements of Western society. Calvin, after all, inveighed against the disgrace "for men to become effeminate," and countless other theorists have described the mechanics of manly proof. (see, for example, Seidler, 1994.)
3. Such observations also led journalist Heywood Broun to argue that most of the attacks against feminism came from men who were shorter than 5 ft. 7 in. "The man who, whatever his physical size, feels secure in his own masculinity and in his own relation to life is rarely resentful of the opposite sex" (cited in Symes, 1930, p. 139).

REFERENCES

Brannon, R. (1976). The male sex role—and what it's done for us lately. In R. Brannon & D. David (Eds.), *The forty-nine percent majority* (pp. 1–40). Reading, MA: Addison-Wesley.

Connell, R. W. (1987). *Gender and power*. Stanford, CA: Stanford University Press.

Freud, S. (1933/1966). *New introductory lectures on psychoanalysis* (L. Strachey, Ed.). New York: Norton.

Goffman, E. (1963). *Stigma*. Englewood Cliffs, NJ: Prentice Hall.

Gorer, G. (1964). *The American people: A study in national character*. New York: Norton.

Kaufman, M. (1993). *Cracking the armour: Power and pain in the lives of men*. Toronto: Viking Canada.

Leverenz, D. (1986). Manhood, humiliation and public life: Some stories. *Southwest Review, 71*, Fall.

Leverenz, D. (1991). The last real man in America: From Natty Bumppo to Batman. *American Literary Review, 3*.

Marx, K., & F. Engels. (1848/1964). The communist manifesto. In R. Tucker (Ed.), *The Marx-Engels reader*. New York: Norton.

Mead, M. (1965). *And keep your powder dry*. New York: William Morrow.

Rotundo, E. A. (1993). *American manhood: Transformations in masculinity from the revolution to the modern era*. New York: Basic Books.

Seidler, V. J. (1994). *Unreasonable men: Masculinity and social theory*. New York: Routledge.

Symes, L. (1930). The new masculinism. *Harper's Monthly, 161*, January.

Tocqueville, A. de. (1835/1967). *Democracy in America*. New York: Anchor.

Weber, M. (1905/1966). *The Protestant ethic and the spirit of capitalism*. New York: Charles Scribner's.

Wilkinson, R. (1986). *American tough: The tough-guy tradition and American character*. New York: Harper & Row.

4

LESBIAN SUES SCHOOL DISTRICT OVER HARASSMENT

■ ■ ■

Judy Peet

All she ever wanted, Nancy Wadington said, was an education.

Instead, the Holmdel teenager said she got a daily lesson in humiliation from classmates who called her names, threw bottles at her, urinated in her backpack and pushed her down a flight of stairs.

Wadington, 18, is a lesbian. She was when she started Holmdel High School in 2001 and when she left after nearly three years of what her mother called "a living nightmare."

Yesterday, Lambda Legal, a national gay rights organization, filed suit on behalf of Wadington, charging that Holmdel school officials knew about the abuse and ignored it.

The lawsuit is the first in New Jersey asking for a jury to determine monetary damages for anti-gay harassment in the schools, which is illegal under the state's civil rights laws.

"It is an atrocity that school officials would ignore laws in New Jersey, which are touted as being the most comprehensive nondiscrimination laws on the books," Alphonso David, a Lambda staff attorney, said at a news conference announcing the suit.

Holmdel officials said they were unaware of Wadington's allegations and first learned of them from court papers yesterday.

"If it's true, of course it's distressing," said school board attorney Martin Barger, who has represented the Monmouth County district since 1978. "But it wasn't ignored at the highest level because we never heard of it."

Superintendent Maureen Flaherty said the school code of conduct explicitly bans harassment based on various factors, including sexual orientation, and requires principals to report all harassment.

She said she never heard of Wadington. The principal during the time Wadington was a student has since left the district.

Though the lawsuit may be the first seeking a jury trial in a case involving alleged gay-bashing in New Jersey schools, there is precedent.

In 1998, a Wisconsin school district paid $1 million to a student who suffered similarly after a federal appeals court ruled that schools are liable for ignoring anti-gay harassment.

Last year, the New Jersey Division on Civil Rights ordered the Toms River Regional School District to pay $50,000 to a boy who was slapped, punched and taunted by classmates who thought he was gay. The district was also fined $10,000 and ordered to upgrade its policies.

Wadington's suit said the abuse began in 2001 when she was in ninth grade. Wadington was not the only gay or lesbian student at Holmdel High, but was the only one "outed" by one of her classmates, said David, who did not allow his client to answer questions.

David said the classmates—whom he identified as a small cluster of males and females—called Wadington names and threw food and bottles at her in the cafeteria. She and her mother complained several times, but "school officials took no effective measures in response."

In the spring of ninth grade, Wadington's backpack was stolen. It was found in one of the boys' bathrooms, covered with urine. Soon after that, her locker was broken into and her books and belongings scattered around the school hallway, spat on and damaged, according to the lawsuit.

Wadington complained and was again told nothing could be done. "Instead school administrators charged Nancy for the books that had been destroyed," the complaint stated.

When she was in 10th grade, the abuse became physical, culminating when students, who were not identified, pushed her down a flight of stairs, according to the lawsuit.

Her mother, Barbara, continued to beg for help from school authorities, but without success, David said. He did not comment on whether the family attempted to contact the school board or superintendent.

By her junior year, Wadington was so upset that a counselor at the local YMCA intervened with school administrators, according to court papers. The school placed Wadington on home instruction for the rest of the year.

The school also classified her as "emotionally disturbed" and transferred her for her senior year to Collier High School, a private school for special education students.

The suit seeks compensatory damages for physical and emotional pain and suffering. It also seeks an order forcing Holmdel to implement better anti-discrimination policies.

5

BOY PUNISHED
FOR TALKING ABOUT
GAY MOM

■ ■ ■

LAFAYETTE, Louisiana (AP) A 7-year-old boy was scolded and forced to write "I will never use the word 'gay' in school again" after he told a classmate about his lesbian mother, the American Civil Liberties Union alleged Monday.

Second-grader Marcus McLaurin was waiting for recess November 11 at Ernest Gaullet Elementary School when a classmate asked about Marcus' mother and father, the ACLU said in a complaint.

Marcus responded he had two mothers because his mother is gay. When the other child asked for an explanation, Marcus told him: "Gay is when a girl likes another girl," according to the complaint.

A teacher who heard the remark scolded Marcus, telling him "gay" was a "bad word" and sending him to the principal's office. The following week, Marcus had to come to school early and repeatedly write: "I will never use the word 'gay' in school again."

A phone message left for Lafayette Parish schools superintendent James Easton was not immediately returned.

The ACLU is demanding the case be removed from Marcus' file and that the school apologize to the boy and his mother, Sharon Huff.

"I was concerned when the assistant principal called and told me my son had said a word so bad that he didn't want to repeat it over the phone," Huff said. "But that was nothing compared to the shock I felt when my little boy came home and told me that his teacher had told him his family is a dirty word."

6

SHOW ME
THE CLOUT

■ ■ ■

Sheila Gibbons

What must it be like to be a woman reporting on the economy and the
national gender pay gap, knowing you're a victim yourself? And knowing
that the longer you work, the less will be your compensation compared
with the guy at the next desk? And that down the road, your pay gap will
create a pension gap?

After reading the latest report about the shatter-proof glass ceiling in
communications companies—in the December report from the Annenberg
Public Policy Center of the University of Pennsylvania—I can only assume
that plenty of female employees out there are entertaining such bitter
thoughts.

Yes, we can continue to rejoice over individual successes of executives
such as Carol Leigh Hutton, who this month becomes the first female
publisher of the 172-year-old *Detroit Free Press*. But such stories are scarce.

According to the Annenberg report, women still constitute just
15 percent of executive leaders and just 12 percent of board members in
top communication companies. The numbers are virtually unchanged
from the previous year.

TOKENISM AT THE TOP

"With few exceptions," said former Federal Communications Commission
Commissioner Susan Ness at the report's release, "we have not moved
beyond tokenism in the number of women in top leadership positions

Reprinted by permission of Women's eNews.

or serving on the boards of communications companies. Men still hold the vast majority of positions. The glass ceiling is firmly in place."

The study examined board members and top executives at the 57 communications companies in the Fortune 500. The 57 comprised 25 telecom, 18 publishing and printing, 11 entertainment and 3 advertising companies.

For executive positions, this year's report showed that the presence of women varied from as high as 50 percent at the Scholastic Corporation to nonexistent at seven—or 12 percent—of the 57 companies. Those with no women in their top jobs included McGraw-Hill, Fox Entertainment and the advertising giants Omnicom and Grey Global Group. For boards, the range went from 31 percent at the New York Times Company to zero at Fox Entertainment, Grey Global Group and a host of entertainment and telecom companies. Ten of the 57–18 percent—had no women on their boards. No company had boards or executive teams with a majority of women.

To assess influence, the Annenberg study counted how many women had "clout" titles (senior vice president up through chief executive officer). Of 1,247 executives in these companies, a paltry 68 women—5 percent— had such titles.

PAY GAP WIDER THAN IN 1980

The paltry female presence in the executive ranks correlates with the stalling out of women's pay gains in the broader working world. A congressional study in November 2003 confirmed that U.S. working women earn 79.7 cents for every dollar paid to men. By this measure, women were doing a tiny fraction better nearly a quarter of a century ago: In 1980, women were earning slightly more, 80.4 cents to every dollar for men.

An analysis released in December by the National Association of Female Executives considered salary studies in a broad range of fields and confirmed a substantial pay gap for women in media. The organization reported that U.S. women in advertising made an average of $20,000 less than men in comparable jobs. Female print journalists made $9,000 less a year than their male colleagues while female television news directors made $4,000 less.

The gap widens as women log more years on the job and become more experienced, a sort of reverse reward system. Take magazines: Male managing editors out-earn female managing editors by less than $3,000, according to CareerJournal.com, but male senior editors earn an average of $66,472 while senior editors who are women pull down $55,602, a disparity of nearly $11,000, or 20 percent.

The trend line is just as dismal among journalists reporting for newsmagazines, radio, newspapers, television and wire services. The American Journalist survey released in April 2003 showed that female journalists' median salary in 2001 was $37,731, about 81 percent of men's median salary of $46,758, the same percentage as in 1991. Male and female journalists with less than 15 years of experience have comparable median salaries, but for those with 15 to 19 years' experience, the gender gap is $4,425. Among those with 20 or more years of experience, the gap is $7,314.

The annual study by the Indiana University of Journalism also finds that the number of female journalists isn't increasing overall; they are still only one-third of all full-time journalists working for the traditional mainstream media (the proportion they have been since 1982), even though since 1977 they have been the majority of students graduating from journalism schools.

The frustration these female professionals experience running into a compensation wall is extremely high. Many deal with it by leaving the business just when they could be making the biggest contribution to it.

For example, a 2002 survey of top U.S. newspaper editors by the American Press Institute and the Pew Center for Civic Journalism found that 45 percent of women (but only 33 percent of men) interviewed antici-pate leaving the newspapers where they now work, either for another newspaper job or something outside the industry altogether. Men also are more likely to anticipate moving up at their current newspaper (42 percent of men vs. 33 percent of women).

It's sheer folly for media companies to lurch along this way, given the plentiful data documenting the female pay gap and the brain drain it sets in motion. It's costly to lose a long-time employee, and employers who are pleased with a cheaper new hire are just kidding themselves. The smart media employers will protect their people assets and reward men and women equally.

Suggestions for Further Reading

See daily papers as well as weekly and monthly national magazines for continuing accounts of discrimination and harassment.